MARITAL HAPPINESS IS A CHOICE

Following the Path to an Enjoyable Relationship with Your Spouse

J.A. ALEXANDRE

CROSSBOOKS

CrossBooks™
A Division of LifeWay
1663 Liberty Drive
Bloomington, IN 47403
www.crossbooks.com
Phone: 1-866-879-0502

First published by CrossBooks 5/2/2013

ISBN: 978-1-4627-2701-8 (sc)
ISBN: 978-1-4627-2702-5 (e)

Library of Congress Control Number: 2013906507

Printed in the United States of America.

This book is printed on acid-free paper.

This book is a tribute to the love of my life, Myrlande Edith Alexandre with whom I have discovered the secrets and the true meaning of Marital Happiness for the past 27 years.

I also dedicate Marital Happiness Is a Choice to my sons and my pals, Jean Abede II and Jonathan Michel whose encouragement, support and love have been invaluable to me. I thank God for the joy they have brought my wife and me. I hope that they will follow the path of an enjoyable journey with their future spouses.

TABLE OF CONTENTS

Foreword xv
Acknowledgements xix
Introduction xxi

I. DECIDING ON THE JOURNEY, PART 1:
    WHOSE CHOICE IS IT ANYWAY? 1

    Solitude, Singleness, and Celibacy 5
    Loneliness 6
    Loneliness and Singleness 7
    Contributing Factors to Loneliness 8
        Developmental Issues 9
        Psychological Issues 12
        Rejection 12
        Family Dysfunction 14
        Fear of Marriage 16
        Religious or Spiritual Factors 17

II. DECIDING ON THE JOURNEY, PART II:
    CELIBACY AND THE BIBLE 20

    Christ's Teaching in Matthew 19 21
    Eunuchs 24
    Paul's Teaching in 1 Corinthians 7 28

III. BEGINNING THE JOURNEY WITH THE
      DESIGNER'S BLUEPRINT AND GOD'S
      PURPOSE AND PLAN 34

      Back to the Basics 35
      Use of the Fundamentals by Jesus and Paul 35
      The Creation of Man and Woman in God's Image 37
      Image of God and Marital Relationship 40
        Intellect 40
        Will...40
        Emotion 41
      The Image of God and the Nature of Man and Woman 43
        Male and Female Equality/Similarity.......................44
        Male and Female Differences 45
      Understanding God's Design 47
      Adam's Reaction to Eve's Creation..........................48

IV.   BEGINNING THE JOURNEY: THE
      DESIGNER'S BLUEPRINT AND THE
      NATURE OF MARRIAGE 51

      The Meaning of Leaving..52
        Physical Separation...53
        Emotional Detachment 53
      The Meaning of Cleaving 55
        Emotional Attachment...56
        Physical Attachment..57
        Spiritual Attachment 58
      Becoming One Flesh 58
        A Divine Act..59
        A Human Responsibility 60
        Emotional Interdependence....................................61
        Oneness..63
        Sexual Intimacy..65

V.   BEGINNING THE JOURNEY: CHOOSING
THE RIGHT PARTNER 68

Knowing Yourself 71
Knowing the Partner You Want to Choose 76
The AFDEM Theory...78
    The Acquaintance Stage 79
    The Friendship Stage...79
    The Dating Stage..81
    The Engagement Stage 82
Using the Process..83
    Praying for the Right Mate 83
    What We Have Not Yet Talked About.................84

VI.   ENJOYING THE JOURNEY: FOLLOWING
THE RIGHT PATH 87

Marital Happiness is God's Ideal and Purpose 91
Marital Happiness is a Personal and Continual Choice.......92
Marital Happiness is Sacrificial 95
Marital Happiness is Related to Emotional and
Spiritual Maturity 97
What Marital Happiness Does Not Mean..............101
I Will be Happy Only if my Spouse is Happy 103

VII. ENJOYING THE JOURNEY: APPLYING THE
MARRIAGE VOWS ALONG THE WAY 105

Ruth's Loyalty to Naomi: The Best Illustration of the
Marriage Covenant...114

VIII. ENJOYING THE JOURNEY: MEETING EACH
OTHER'S SEXUAL NEEDS IN MARRIAGE 120

The Biblical Teaching on Sex 122
   Physical/sexual attraction between a male and a female
   is normal..122
   Sex before and outside of marriage is sin 123
      Fornication 123
      Adultery...124
   Sexual Intimacy According the Bible 125
   The Purpose of Sex According to the Bible......................126
      Fruitfulness and multiplication 126
      Physical Union as Experience and Expression
      of Intimacy 126
      Fun and Pleasure between Husband and Wives 127
   Sexual Behavior Between Husbands and Wives.................128
The Christ's Teaching about Sexuality............................130
Paul's Teaching on Sexuality..131
   It is Good for a Man not to Touch a Woman 132
   Sex is a Mutual Obligation 132
   Giving Oneself for the Pleasure of the Partner...............135
   Abstinence in the Marriage must be Only by Mutual
   Consent 136

IX. ENJOYING THE JOURNEY:
     COMMUNICATING WITH ONE ANOTHER............138

What Communication Is 140
What Communication is Not..141
How do We Communicate? 141
   Verbal Language 141
   Tone...142
   Body Language 142

Patterns or Styles of Communication 143
　　No Communication.. 143
　　Aggressive Communication...144
　　Passive Communication or Avoidance....................................144
　　Immature Communication 146
　　Passive-Aggressive Communication 147
　　Delayed Communication..148
　　No Communication 150
　　Assertive Communication 150
The Message in these Patterns of Communication.............. 151
　　In Aggressive Communication 152
　　In Passive Communication 152
　　In Immature Communication 153
　　In Passive-Aggressive Communication....................................153
　　In Assertive Communication 153
The Key To Good Communication...154

X.　ENJOYING THE JOURNEY: RESOLVING
　　THE INEVITABLE CONFLICTS 158

Conflicts and Why They Exist..159
Why Couples Avoid Conflicts.. 161
　　Emotional Insecurity 162
　　Insincerity 163
　　Saving Face 163
　　Wrong Conflict Management 163
Principles of Conflict Resolution and Management............168
　　Acknowledge the Conflict and the Issue to be Addressed 168
　　Define the Problem 168
　　Stick to One Issue at a Time 169
　　Settle Matters Quickly..170
　　Constructive Confrontation...172
　　Practice Forgiveness 173

XI. ENINGING THE JOURNEY: ACCEPTING
AND FULFILLING YOUR ROLE AND
RESPONSIBILITY 174

The Essential Equality of Man and Woman in Marriage .. 175
The Similar Purpose for Man and Woman in Marriage 176
The Functional Difference between Man and Woman
in Marriage 177
The Basis for Man's Leadership in the Home
According to Scripture 179
    The Meaning of "Head" in Ephesians 5:23 180
    The Role and Responsibility of the Leader in the Home 182
The Meaning of Submission 183
The Interdependence of the Roles 186
    Roles of Men and Women in the Marriage According
    to 1 Peter 3:1-7 186
    The Role of the Wife 187
    The Role of the Husband 188
    The Role in General of All Christians 189

XII. ENJOYING THE JOURNEY: REKINDLING
THE FLAME OF YOUR LOVE 190

Forsaking Your First love 192
The Commendation 192
The Rebuke 194
Overcoming the Barriers to Rekindling the Flame of
Your Love 201
Failure to Pay Attention to the Needs that are not
Being Met 201
The Various Levels of Intimacy 202
    The Physical Level 202
    The Social Level 202

The Affective Level 202
The Spiritual Level 202
Lack of Creativity 203
Taking Each Other for Granted 204

XIII. ENJOYING THE JOURNEY: ADJUSTING TO
      THE STAGES OF MARRIAGE 206

Stage One: Illusion of Passion or Foundational Phase 207
Stage Two: Disillusion Versus Adjustment 210
Self-Awareness 210
Growing Together 212
Disappointment with Ourselves 213
Stage Three: Commitment Versus Resignation 213
Making Use of or Refusing Available Resources 216
Commitment to God Versus Commitment to a Conviction...217
*Commitment to Each Other Versus Commitment to the
Marriage* 218
Happiness Versus Consented Misery 218
Stage Four: Resolution Versus Dejection 219

XIV. ENJOYING THE JOURNEY: COPING WITH
      THE STRESSES OF LIFE 222

Personal and Marital Equilibrium 224
Styles of Coping 226
Freezing Panic 226
Procrastination 226
Prayer..226
Problem-Solving Strategies and Planning 227
Worrying /Complaining 227
Being Irritable..228

Things That Husbands and Wives Need to Avoid in Coping with Life Stress 228

Confusing Life Stress with Marital Stress............................228

Blaming Each Other/Being Critical of Each Other...............229

Ignoring/Neglecting Each Other's Needs..............................229

Displacing Negative Feelings..229

Getting the Wrong People Involved 230

Resentment and Passive—Aggressiveness 230

Disrespecting and/or Embarrassing Each Other....................230

Making Personal Decisions that will Likely Affect Both of You..230

Effective Methods of Coping..231

The Problem-Oriented Approach 231

Emotion or Person-Oriented Approach..................................234

Biblical Principles in Dealing with Life Storms and Pressures Taken from Acts 27..237

FOREWORD

MARITAL HAPPINESS IS A CHOICE does not mean you flip on a switch and marital happiness appears like light does when you flip on a light switch. It means rather that YOU CAN CHOOSE to have marital happiness, and you can then begin a lifelong process of working on it and improving it throughout your life. You cannot control your spouse, but with God's help, you can control yourself. This book will teach you a host of things you can do, including great communication methods that will make it more likely that your spouse will want to choose marital happiness as well.

Without a doubt, Dr. Alexandre has woven together the best, most thorough, and deepest book on marriage-building that I have ever read. Dr. Alexandre himself is a humble, warm, and loving genius who would never think such things of himself. I am an MD/psychiatrist, founder of a national chain of non-profit clinics, and author of over 90 books, including the best seller book: *Happiness Is a Choice* that sold more than seven million copies in more than 20 languages. I am also an ordained minister who taught counseling courses to seminary students for twelve years. I have taught many thousands of people around the world. But my most outstanding student ever was J. A. Alexandre.

While attending Dallas Theological Seminary, he took several of my courses, and received the highest scores of any of my students. He had a great heart and spirit, and a constant thirst to keep learning and growing. After graduating from this four year seminary with high grades, he went on to get a PsyD in clinical psychology. He has also received additional post-doctoral training from some of our top therapists at the Meier Clinic in Wheaton, Illinois, and has completed his residency at Cambridge Hospital/Harvard Medical School where he also lectured and offered seminars on Cross-cultural Mental Health. He has practiced psychology in hospitals, clinics, and public schools for the last 23 years in the Boston area. God made only one J. A. Alexandre, and now the world has only one MARITAL HAPPINESS IS A CHOICE.

I urge everyone who wants to understand just how wonderful marriage CAN BE to read and re-read this book. But I also urge psychiatrists, psychologists, therapists, pastors, missionaries and lay counselors to study it as well. I urge them because it not only covers a host of important aspects of marriage that include practical tips but also deep spiritual and emotional concepts—even unconscious personality dynamics and how we all, to one extent or another, deceive ourselves in many ways that are detrimental to our marriages.

Our own nation has been declining morally and culturally for several decades now. Teen suicide rates are up 300% higher than 50 years ago. Narcissism is becoming the norm rather than the exception. And research has proven that one of the top causes of our national moral, cultural, and emotional decline is the breakdown of marriages in America. Just this weekend, I delivered a two-hour speech and a one hour workshop on our national scene during this era to some of our nation's top political leaders and other people of influence. They wanted to better understand how to help our citizens have more peace, joy, and meaning in their lives and in their marriages. They wanted a deeper understanding of how to promote and preserve healthy marriages in America because our future depends on it. At lunch just a few hours ago I told a U.S. Senator and a Congressman about Dr. J. A. Alexandre and an excellent book on these topics that would be available very soon that would not only help them to better understand solid marriages, but also therapists, and MOST IMPORTANTLY, YOU—THE READERS of this book. It is written with easy-to-understand terminology. Dr. Alexandre took complex subjects like attachment, fear of intimacy, human sexuality, true spirituality, unconscious codependency, passive-aggressiveness, and even addictions, and then masterfully wove these deep and often difficult-to-understand concepts into an easy-to-comprehend work of art.

Paul Meier MD
Founder of the national chain of Meier Clinics
(1-888-7-CLINIC or www.meierclinics.org)

ACKNOWLEDGEMENTS

I thank my longtime friend, teacher and mentor, Dr. Paul Meier who encouraged me to write this book and graciously wrote the Foreword. My wife and I are grateful to God and to him for providing the funds to cover all the expenses leading to the completion of my Doctorate in Clinical Psychology.

Special thanks to my brother of thirty-nine years, Pastor Brave Laverdure, and his wife Marie, for opening their house to me when I needed a place away from home to complete the manuscript in Atlanta, Georgia.

I thank Samuel Jocelyn and his wife Johanne for sacrificing their time together to help in various aspects of completing this project including the book cover design.

I also want to thank all the couples who over the years have participated in various marital retreats and conferences and whose questions, input and encouragement have contributed to the writing of this book. May all of them continue to make the choice to experience the happiness that God has intended for their marriages.

I am indebted to Mrs Greta Price for taking the time to review and edit the entire manuscript and getting it ready for publication. Both she and her husband, Dr. Rodney Price have been some of the most precious friends the Lord has given my wife and me.

INTRODUCTION

D avid Hume, the eighteenth century Scottish philosopher, writes: "The great end of all human industry is the attainment of happiness. For this were arts invented, sciences cultivated, laws ordained, and societies modeled, by the most profound wisdom of patriots and legislators. Even the lonely savage, who lies exposed to the inclemency of the elements, and the fury of wild beast, forgets not, for a moment, this grand object of his being."[1] Many people would agree with Hume that the pursuit of happiness seems to be the primary motivation of all human endeavors, such as going to school, working, vacationing, belonging to a religion and even getting married. However, Hume's statement raises two fundamental questions that have troubled men for centuries: First, what is happiness? Second, how can it be attained? Attempts to answer those two questions have been the subject of many books and articles. Many seem to perceive happiness as a goal to pursue with all diligence, while others see it as a result or as a by-product of the pursuit of virtues. Still others see happiness as a by-product of pursuing Christ. The latter would also argue that happiness can be experienced through following certain principles and engaging in certain worthwhile activities. For instance, while marital happiness may be a worthy aspiration, it can be experienced in the process of practicing certain virtues and applying certain principles. As such, happiness, more specifically marital happiness, can be based on the choice of whether to practice those virtues or to apply those

---

[1] David Hume, "The Stoic Part 1," *Essays Moral, Political, and Literary Pt. 1* (1742), 205.

principles in their lives. These virtues and principles are in conjunction with God's Word.

In Scripture, there is a close relationship between happiness and blessing. Throughout the Bible, being happy and being blessed are closely related. Furthermore, being blessed or happy is also linked with spiritual and moral virtues with obedience to and fear of the Lord. After battling meaninglessness and the disappointment of material success and pleasure, the writer of Ecclesiastes concludes that true happiness is found in the fear of God and the keeping of His commandments according to Ecclesiastes 12:13 KJV. The same thought is expressed in Psalms 128:1, Proverbs 3:21 and Proverbs 29:18, all of which express that happiness comes from fearing the Lord, walking in His ways and keeping His words. Jesus summarizes these thoughts in John 15:10-11 where He explains that the fullness of joy (happiness) is experienced through keeping His commandments and abiding in Him and in His love.

Another theme that is prevalent in the Bible is the relationship between happiness and obedience. In Deuteronomy 10:12-13, the Lord outlined His requirements for the children of Israel. They included: (1) Fear the Lord your God; (2) Walk in His ways; (3) Love the Lord your God; (4) Serve Him and (5) Obey His commands. Then the Lord ends His instructions by saying, "This is for your own good." Therefore, obedience to God's laws and principles result in happiness in their lives. The Prophet Isaiah expressed a similar idea when he established the relationship between obedience and "eating the good of the land" (Isa 1:19).

As such, the practice of spiritual virtues through obedience to God's word is considered an important element for experiencing lasting happiness. This is the position I espouse in the book, *Marital Happiness is a Choice: Following the Path of An Enjoyable Relationship with Your Spouse.*

This book is written with a view to make people's marriages an enjoyable journey. Pastors and teachers, who are engaged in both marital and pre-marital counseling, will have a tool that they can use as a resource. This book intends to clarify the biblical and psychological principles that will guide people to discover that marital happiness is not only possible; it is a choice they can make at any time. This choice begins with a conscious, well-informed decision to find the right partner for the journey. The readers will unravel the mystery that marital happiness is not something to be pursued but an ongoing experience to enjoy as a result of following the right path. Couples who are struggling in their marriage will find that it is never too late to follow the right direction in their marriage. Those who are contemplating marriage will know ahead of time what road they must travel if they are to avoid the pain and the suffering of poor marriages and experience the joy of living with their soul mate. While not exhaustive, the book will attempt to be as comprehensive as possible whereby most marital questions and issues are discussed.

There are many books written on the issue of marriage and marital happiness. *Marital Happiness is a Choice* seeks to make a contribution to the field by offering a fresh perspective on the whole concept of marital happiness and how it can be achieved or experienced. I bring my training in the field of psychology and theology to facilitate an approach that integrates the two disciplines to address the various issues of marriage. In addition to my training, I have had the privilege over the years to teach classes on the subject of marriage and to conduct marital retreats on a regular basis. My experience in both marital and premarital counseling has equipped me to address issues that couples face in their marriages such as communication, conflict resolution, and intimacy between couples. This book will also give ideas and concepts that leaders, conference speakers and teachers may use in their presentations to couples and to students.

The following guidelines helped to form the purpose of writing this book. First, it must not be just another book on marriage. Second, it must be appealing to the reader. Third, it must be relevant enough to catch the interest of an audience who might be saturated with ideas about what makes marriage work. The readers of the manuscript submitted for evaluation have concluded that the book has accomplished such goals by the book addressing and dealing with most if not all issues related to marriage. They also found that it integrates both psychological and biblical principles related to married life. Finally, they all agreed that it is both insightful and practical. It is my hope that you will reach the same conclusions.

Over the years of interacting with couples, I discovered six factors that contribute to the pain and disappointments of marriage. The following factors will be addressed in *Marital Happiness is a Choice*:

1. A poor conception of marriage and its purpose.
2. Irresponsible and unproductive belief that our happiness depends totally on how we are treated in the marriage. There is a lack of personal responsibility for one's own happiness.
3. Wrong expectations of the marriage, wrong expectations of themselves, and wrong expectations of the mate.
4. Difficulties in managing their emotions in the marriage: A lot of people have never learned how to properly manage their emotions and to understand how their emotional outbursts affect their relationships. Emotions such as anger, sadness, fear and anxiety, if not managed well, can destroy a relationship.
5. Lack of creativity in rekindling and maintaining the flame of their marriages including their sexual love.
6. A lack of understanding of what people are going through in adjusting to various stages of their lives and their marriages and failure to cope effectively with the stress of those various stages.

Whether or not those factors constitute your marital experiences, this book will challenge your thinking and offer you some fresh insights into discovering and/or maintaining the joy of being married. It is my earnest hope and prayer that *Marital Happiness Is a Choice* will fulfill such purpose in your life. Then I will invite you to exclaim with me: "To God Alone Be the Glory!"

{ I }

DECIDING ON THE JOURNEY, PART 1: WHOSE CHOICE IS IT ANYWAY?

Loneliness is not healthy. Obviously, you did not hear this from me first. I just expanded on it a little bit; it's depressing, depleting, and hazardous to you emotionally, physically, and spiritually. In fact, as the 17th. Century English author John Milton said: "Loneliness was the first thing that God's eye named not good." Milton was certainly referring to the Creator's statement in Genesis: "The LORD God said, "It is not good for the man to be alone. I will make a helper suitable for him" (Genesis 2:18). If you read the previous statements God made about creation in Genesis 1, the expression "it was good" repeatedly followed God's assessment of his work. However, when you come to Genesis 2, you will find that loneliness was the only dark spot in the splendor of God's marvelous creation. No wonder the experience of loneliness is so painful whether it is outside, within, before, or after marriage. It is interesting to note that the text suggests that Adam experienced a certain degree of loneliness when he was naming the animals, that is, he did not find one that matched him. It seemed as though God made him realize his need for another human being who would be in many ways different from him and yet compatible or suitable for him.

Although Adam was in perfect harmony with God and perfectly secure in his relationship with him, Adam still needed Eve's company. It is evident that God created him intentionally with a void that would only be filled by an intimate counterpart, friend, partner, lover, and companion. Furthermore, Adam had everything he would ever want; he had the whole universe at his disposal. All the riches of the world would be for him alone. He literally was the richest man who ever lived prior to Solomon. Yet, neither the world's possessions, nor even his relationship with the Lord could fill the void, and nothing could make up for the lack of human companionship. Even though he had everything, God decided that Adam needed another human being. He needed Eve. God had created him that way. His need to give and receive affection would not be met by his material possessions, but by the love, the support, the attention, and the trust of a helpmate. Today, it is sad to note that career advancement, intellectual pursuits, and even "religious" or spiritual endeavors have taken precedent over the needs to cultivate and maintain healthy human relationships. It is no wonder that in spite of all the progress that has been made and the wealth that has been accumulated, many people are depressed and frustrated, and their suffering is often related to the endurance of the pain of loneliness that nothing can appease.

When the desire to love and be loved is suppressed, and when the longing for someone with whom to share life is frustrated, we tend to have feelings of general dissatisfaction with life as well as a lack of a sense of fulfillment. Usually, it is felt more intensely as we get older and as we start to take an honest inventory of our lives. Often we realize later on in life that our accomplishments and possessions cannot truly substitute for the need to hold someone's hands as we contemplate the end of our life's journey.

About twenty years ago, my phone rang at two o'clock one morning. First, I thought it was the fire alarm. Then after mistaking my wife's ear for the receiver and having a few bad thoughts about Alexander Graham Bell, I finally picked up the phone. On the other end was a childhood friend whom I had not seen for a long time. When I asked him how I could help him, he answered, "I called you because I am about to set my apartment on fire." I responded, "You should have called 911!" He then proceeded to tell me that he had spent about fifteen thousand dollars in entertaining equipment: stereos, big screen TV, VCR, and whatever other gadgets he could find to occupy himself in times of leisure. He had had several broken relationships and could not maintain any friendships. He thought entertainment could substitute for people in his life. His way of healing his wounds was to have enough gadgets to fill the void of loneliness. My response to him was simple. "You are lonely, and nothing in your house or in the store will ever meet your need for interaction with other human beings." After sharing a few words of encouragement and comfort with him, I went back to bed. I have to admit that I hugged my wife a little tighter after that and silently praised God for putting her in my life. As a psychology intern at that time, I did not have a tenth of this man's possessions, but I had someone I could hold, I could talk to, and with whom I could share ideas, laughter, and concerns. I did not need to experience his pain of loneliness.

In interviews conducted over the years with various groups of young adults, I found that a good percentage of them would openly admit to the pain of loneliness and their desire to meet the right person. A few have attempted to ignore or minimize it. There are still others who have tried to justify it by denying the hurt they feel. They would even go as far as comparing their own pain to that of being in a bad marriage. Many have tried to compensate for the void they feel while making all the efforts in the world to suppress its negative effects. It is not uncommon to meet people who attempt to denigrate the institution of marriage in order to appease the pain of not having been able to find the right person to marry or for having been too selfish to share their life with someone else.

Through various studies, men have discovered the truth of God's declaration about man's loneliness. It is indeed not good for man to be alone. According to Dr. Rick Neuter, senior editor of Psych Central, "Feeling a connection to others is a critical component of a person's mental and physical health." Many studies, including those published in a book entitled, *Loneliness: Human Nature and the Need for Social Connection* by social neuroscientist, John T. Cacioppo have shown that "rejection or isolation disrupts not only abilities, will power, and perseverance, but also key cellular processes deep within the human body." Other studies have established the link between emotional stresses and depressed immunity. They also found a high correlation between loneliness and depression with poorer health and wellbeing. As such, loneliness may cause susceptibility to a variety of health issues.

Yes, the truth of God's Word has prevailed again and again: "It is not good for man to be alone." When compared to the risks and hazards of loneliness, deciding to embark in the marital journey appears to be a legitimate and rewarding endeavor. It is an enjoyable journey that requires preparation before starting the trip. It does not happen by chance; it must be undertaken with a sense of purpose, prayer, soul-searching, diligence, and careful study. You do not have to apologize for a strong desire to find a mate with whom to share your life.

It has been observed that among those who are considering marriage, there is a tendency to take a passive approach to dating and to finding a spouse. In most cultures, women in particular are encouraged to wait passively with the hope that someone would come along and ask them out. While women should not be encouraged to go against their culture in this regard, men and women should not look at marriage as a chance opportunity. Instead, active and personal involvement should be encouraged in the process. There is no shame for either men or women to actively and prayerfully pursue meaningful relationships that may eventually lead to marriage. Often, the need or the desire to get married tends to be suppressed like the "elephant" in the room no one wants to talk about. We have made it shameful and embarrassing for people to openly express their desire to get married while there are others in the world who have no shame in flaunting their sinful lifestyle when it comes to relationships.

How often, even in small group prayer meetings, have you heard anyone ask for prayer to find the right spouse? How would you look at a young lady who would say, "Pray for me; I am looking for the right man to become my husband?" It's usually a parent who would offer such a request on behalf of a son or daughter, and almost always, that conversation ends with a finger across their lips.

Finding someone with whom to share your life till "death do you part" is the most crucial decision a person will ever make after salvation. It should not be taken passively, haphazardly, or carelessly. Marital happiness is a choice. It is a choice that begins as an active decision to embark on the journey. This will be elaborated on later in this book. Avoiding the pain of loneliness is worth the effort of overcoming whatever personal or cultural barriers there may be to pray, make oneself available, and be attentive to opportunities of developing meaningful relationships. As for now, the factors that may interfere at the beginning of the decision process will be considered.

Before delving too deeply into the subject, it is important to make a few distinctions between some concepts related to the decision to marry or not to marry. They are singleness, loneliness, solitude, aloneness, and celibacy. Those concepts should not be used interchangeably as though they mean the same thing. For instance, being single or being alone does not necessarily mean to be lonely.

Solitude, Singleness, and Celibacy

On one hand, solitude, as a temporal choice, can be a very good opportunity for personal reflection, growth, meditation, and inspiration. There can be various legitimate reasons for someone to choose to be alone. Solitude can be quite enriching and fulfilling when it is appropriate and used for meaningful purpose. On the other hand, singleness is the state of being unmarried. There are many who are not married, but who are not living in the state of singleness. They have resorted to depraved methods of avoiding loneliness outside of marriage, contrary to God's intent and purpose for human relationships. Outside of marriage, it should be celibacy. Celibacy is not just the condition of being unmarried, but also implies abstinence from sexual intercourse, especially by reason of religious or spiritual vows. It is clear from the Word of God that the alternative for celibacy is marriage between a man and a woman. Any other form of alternate lifestyle is outside of God's will.

Loneliness

Loneliness can be defined as the felt, unwanted experience of being alone. It is finding yourself alone when you wish otherwise. Loneliness can be a forced choice imposed by circumstances, your personality, rejection, abandonment, and inability to form and maintain meaningful relationships with others. Solomon, in Song of Songs 2:11-13, painted a portrait of the beginning of a relationship or the honeymoon that he compared to the spring when the flowers are burgeoning, and the birds are singing, and the turtles are heard. It is the time when the fig tree and the vines let out the perfume of their fruit. However, what precedes the spring is the winter—the winter of loneliness when the sun is not shining much, and it's cold, and it's hard to keep warm. There does not seem to be much life out there other than the impatient waiting for something to happen to give life and energy and the desire to venture outdoors. This gloomy picture of loneliness and depression is the painful reality that many men and women are currently experiencing because they have neglected to develop meaningful relationships. It is with much pain that I remember conversation after conversation with people who, while tears are flowing from their eyes, describe how painful it is not having someone to turn to, no one to give your heart to, and no one whose heart you would love as your own. Some are experiencing regrets for mistakes they made in lost relationships and for having taken for granted the joy of sharing their lives with someone who would be devoted to them.

Loneliness, as the Creator has declared, is not good. It leaves the person in a state of disappointment, depression, bitterness, frustration, and unhappiness. Many people who claimed to have chosen a life of solitude have eventually demonstrated that it was not their choice to be lonely, and that they would jump at any chance to get out of the pit of their loneliness. Often people who have married in their 50s and 60s have discovered that the gift of celibacy that they thought they had was for somebody else. Others who are not so fortunate often openly confess to the feelings of despair. They are ravaged inside with feelings of being all alone with no one to care for or to love. This usually happens when the career they have chosen over relationships is completed or is no longer enriching or satisfying. Perhaps the possessions they have accumulated at the expense of meaningful companionship are no longer fulfilling. There are a number of cases where people who have become more mature reminisce over missed opportunities and experience a lot of regrets. You often hear, "I could have married so and so or I should not have been so picky." Sometimes people start out with criteria that are not realistic and at times totally superficial. With maturity even some of the criteria they once held so sacred are set aside out of despair. It has been observed that the list of criteria becomes shorter and shorter as the years go by. Some lists that began with twenty or so characteristics or non-negotiable qualities have been reduced to only two: breathing and moving. The point of the matter is that solitude can be a good thing when voluntarily chosen. Celibacy can be well lived without being a pretext for justifying or masking feelings of loneliness.

Loneliness and Singleness

It must be noted that singleness does not necessarily mean that you have to experience loneliness or that marriage is an automatic cure for loneliness. Obviously, God has remedied the problem of loneliness that he observed in Adam by creating a suitable helpmate for him. It is clear that God's solution to Adam's loneliness was to create Eve and to marry them in the garden. Therefore, marriage must always be looked at as the most legitimate and most fulfilling way of coping with loneliness. Certainly, opportunities for interactions with others in society and in the body of Christ can alleviate, to some extent, the pain of loneliness. Nevertheless, they will never surpass nor replace the joy of mutual love, mutual commitment, mutual sharing, and devotion that can only be found in a marital relationship. It is unfortunate that today some people take cheap shots at marriage as a way of justifying or appeasing their experience of loneliness.

Contributing Factors to Loneliness

There are many factors that contribute to the state and the experience of loneliness. They include developmental, psychological, familial, social, and spiritual issues. Many people find themselves single and lonely because of one or more of those very factors. Yet, they are not always aware of them. They often ignore the way in which such factors could affect their choice to embark or not to embark in this enjoyable journey called marriage. Often you will hear people claim to have the gift of celibacy, or that they have made a decision not to get involved in seeking a mate when deep down, they are craving the companionship and the love of someone with whom to spend the rest of their life. Others won't even admit how much life circumstances and negative experiences have contributed to their decision not to pursue marriage. Certainly they have made a choice, but it is a "forced" choice, in that, it is a choice imposed by others or by issues that they have failed to acknowledge and resolve in their life.

While choosing not to get married can be a very legitimate and noble decision, it must be an informed and well-calculated decision, and consistent with the will of God for one's life. Otherwise, it will leave a bad taste in your mouth when your lips are saying one thing about being single and your heart experiencing something else. The Bible is clear that singleness can be a gift from God to certain people. However, not everybody who is single has received such a gift. In fact, the devastating moral effect of imposed celibacy in the Roman Catholic priesthood is well known. The scandals have certainly proven that many, not all, who found themselves forced to remain single, also found themselves in serious moral struggles in order to maintain the purity that the Bible requires of all of us. The gift of celibacy will come with the grace of living it out, and the contentment of being in that state for the sake of God's kingdom. If your choice to remain single is paired with feelings of guilt or remorse over failed relationships, and if you struggle with feelings of bitterness over betrayal or missed opportunities for relationships, then perhaps you don't really have the gift of celibacy.

The efforts to suppress or justify the feelings of loneliness and even the restlessness of resorting to inappropriate and immoral means of meeting your social, emotional, and intimate needs may well be good indicators that you have not received the gift of celibacy. In such a case, it might be worth it to explore the factors and issues that contribute to being single and to deal effectively with them. Thus, the choice to remain single or to get married may be truly your choice and not forced upon you by circumstances, mistakes, victimizations, or other such factors.

There are factors and issues that contribute to the decision to marry or not to marry that should be considered. These include developmental issues, psychological issues, dysfunctional families, and religious or spiritual factors.

Developmental Issues

Retracing one's life story to early childhood development has often been regarded as suspicious of tendencies to blame adult behaviors on parents and to fail to ascribe responsibility to individual adults. This is not the intent here. Every negative experience in relationships is not necessarily caused by childhood experiences; neither do childhood experiences determine your future, nor are they responsible for all adult decisions. However, to ignore the factors that might have contributed to certain traits and behaviors is to ignore a vital biblical principle that sees the parent-child interaction and the childhood experiences as critical in influencing your life even as an adult. In fact, understanding those experiences and interactions will enable you to take responsibility to confront and correct those issues through appropriate, God-given opportunities to grow and to change. The old adage "to ignore history is to repeat it" may be applicable here to some extent. For, when those issues are not acknowledged and dealt with effectively, they may be the very factors that contribute to negative experiences in relationships and impact your decisions. The truth might well set you free in that regard.

Most personality theorists have emphasized the role of the parent-child interaction in shaping and influencing our personality. For instance,

Austrian medical doctor and psychologist Alfred Adler (1870-1937) suggests that the child's social interest may be fostered or thwarted by the mother whose role is crucial in developing the child's social interest as well as other aspects of the personality. A child may grow up to look at others with suspicion and hostility, or with trust and cooperation depending on that vital interaction in childhood. Karen Horney, a German psychoanalyst (1885-1952), suggested that the parent-child interaction that is characterized by warmth and affection will facilitate a sense of security that the child will learn to display later on in interpersonal relationships. The opposite is also true. The lack of warmth and affection and parent-child interaction characterized by unfair punishment, promises not kept, ridicule, humiliation, and isolation are likely to induce hostility, fear, and insecurity. It is likely that if uncorrected, those experiences may contaminate the child's social life later on. Lastly, Erik Erickson, famed German-born psychologist, has shown that the baby's interaction with the mother or the primary caregiver in the early years develops within the child a sense of either trust or mistrust that begins to shape their personality and impact their interpersonal relationships later on in life. Love, affection, and security if experienced consistently early in life are likely to be the basis for positive social interaction later on in life. When they are absent or inconsistent, they lead to mistrust, fear, suspicion, and difficulties in interpersonal relationships. In worst case scenarios, when they are replaced by rejection, inattention, and hostility, they form a bad recipe for any meaningful relationship.

This is not your blame-it-on-the-mother game. It is simply acknowledging that the things that we learn about ourselves in our developmental years, either through direct teaching, modeling, or experiences, if not altered or corrected, will impact our relationships later on. Some of the difficulties that people experience in forming lasting relationships may be related to those early experiences.

Even if the developmental theories are rejected, we must accept the fact that the Bible speaks of the influence of our childhood development and learning on our adult experiences. That's the point of Proverbs 22:6

in which the principle of early training/shaping and later development of the child is established by Solomon. The training of a child is not just by words or commands, but it also involves the experiences that children have in growing up with and observing their parents. Furthermore, Paul spoke to the fathers and gave them two directives when it comes to child rearing. In Ephesians 6:4 (KJV), we read first that we do not provoke the child to wrath. It is an admonition against bringing the child to a deep-seated anger. The word hostility comes to mind. The way children are treated as children may contribute to deep-seated hostility and bitterness, which are later projected or displaced in the world in interpersonal relationships. Daughters' relationships with their father and sons' relationships with their mother have been found to influence their choice of a spouse later on in life. Deep seated anger or hostility can be fostered by inconsistency or lack of demonstration of affection, harsh punishment, absence, lack of involvement, etc. Second, Paul offered a positive directive to nurture or to feed physically, emotionally, and spiritually. It means to provide for with tender care all the developmental needs of the child.

So it is not just developmental theorists who see the importance of the role developmental factors play in affecting our social behaviors later on in life. The disagreement with the theorists may be to the level of our view or interpretation of them. One aspect of this discord may be whether or not those factors contribute or determine our social and interpersonal relationships and to what extent they can be reversed. We believe that those factors contribute positively or negatively in affecting our capacity to form meaningful relationships. They tend to form the foundation of our social interest, security, expectations, suspicions, fears, hostility toward others, and capacity to give and receive affection. We certainly affirm that those factors can be altered, corrected through personal growth and emotional corrective experiences, and spiritual maturity through the work of the Holy Spirit in our lives. But, they must be acknowledged, confronted, and dealt with effectively in order to avoid the negative impact they might have on our ability to form meaningful, lasting relationships and avoid the pain of loneliness.

Psychological Issues

Living in an imperfect world with imperfect people (including families and friends) and being imperfect ourselves make all of us susceptible to experiencing certain ill treatments, rejection, setbacks, betrayals, and disappointments that leave us with feelings of bitterness, apprehension, and distrust. One would agree or at least acknowledge that those issues do not make good provisions for meaningful, long-lasting relationships. In fact, many folks who are single have stories to tell that reflect at least one of those ill issues. Many who are married and miserable continue to show the scars of some of those same issues. Those factors are certainly reversible through appropriate interventions. Nevertheless, their contribution cannot be underestimated.

Rejection

I know a young man who felt so betrayed upon learning that the girl he was going to marry decided to marry someone else without saying a word to him. This happened a few weeks before he was going to officially, according to the custom of his culture, ask her hand in marriage. He was so disappointed that he quickly resolved that he would never trust any woman again. For him, at that time, it was a "clear signal" that the Lord did not want him to ever get married and that he should concentrate on studying since he was in seminary. As such, he resolved to concentrate on the books and to prepare himself for the ministry and never look at another woman as long as he lived. However, with the help of a Christian psychologist friend, as well as concerned advisors, he was rescued out of this emotional dump that would have crippled his life and ministry. He needed healing from this terrible experience that could have forced him to choose to be single against his true will and God's will for his life. This young man has been married now for twenty-four years and is enjoying such a wonderful journey with a beautiful and God-fearing soul-mate that he dares to write about it in a book like this.

His story is not unique. Some of you reading these lines may relate to them to some extent. The question is whether or not you would seek healing from the disappointments and betrayals that might affect your decision and force you against your will to experience the pain of imposed solitude and loneliness.

Most of us have experienced some level of rejection in our lives. However, being rejected by someone you love is hard to swallow. It is not something we want to re-experience. We often carry the wounds and the scars of rejection with us for the longest times without being aware of their influence on our actions and reactions, especially in the area of relationships. As a result, we may act in a way that predisposes us to be rejected by others thereby adding to our fear of being rejected. It is not unusual for a person to feel that they are a perpetual victim of rejection without realizing that they are playing a role in those experiences. People who have experienced rejection often find it even where it does not exist. In our approach, we often project to others those negative feelings that we have cultivated out of our bad experiences. Since we expect to be rejected, we end up rejecting them in our attitude and actions which, in fact, cause them to reject us. Because we anticipate rejection, we unconsciously attempt to reject them before they do it to us. Their rejection becomes a self-fulfilling prophecy.

Another ill effect of rejection is the tendency to overcompensate for it in the choices that we want to make, just to prove to ourselves that we did not deserve it. Sometimes those we choose to marry or want to marry may have a lot to do in our overcompensating for it. At any rate, rejection can cause us to build a lot of resentment, hostility, and mistrust in the process. Those feelings tend to be generalized and to attribute to well-meaning and good, prospective relationships. In counseling situations, I have worked with people who resolve not to get married as a result of rejection experienced in break-ups. I have dealt with couples who carry the wounds of rejection in their marriage and thus decrease the level of intimacy they should experience because of their own reluctance and suspicion.

Family Dysfunction

Another condition that affects the choice to marry or not marry is growing up in dysfunctional homes. Being exposed to constant disputes, abuses, quarrels, threats of separation, or the separation itself all have detrimental effects on children's perception of relationships and greatly impact their decisions about them later on in life. As such, many children of dysfunctional families carry the scars of those relationships with them and often make decisions based on those experiences. There are a number of children who decide early not to get married lest they should experience what they see their parents go through. Children of divorced parents often resolve not to get married because of what they have witnessed in the home. Those experiences often impact their social life, their choice of a suitable mate, and their decision to get married or not to get married. Those who had a good relationship with particular parents of the opposite sex often look for the same traits in a potential mate, and when they find those similar traits, they tend to overlook some important issues by focusing too much on the similarities. Others who have not had a positive relationship with parents tend to look for mates who reflect the opposite traits. For instance, if a girl lived with a harsh, cold father, she would compensate by marrying someone who is open, caring, and communicative; however, she doesn't know how to reciprocate, and therefore ends up chasing that person away. Often she ends up marrying someone who is just like the parent that she resents because of the dynamic with which she is familiar. As such her nightmare comes true, and she ends up experiencing her own heart-break in divorce, separation, or emotional abuse in the marriage. If she stays in the marriage, she'll often find herself reproducing the pattern she has lived through in her childhood.

Because of childhood experiences, unresolved hostility, disappointments, and unresolved conflicts, people develop unrealistic criteria and expectations that often result in missed opportunities to develop healthy relationships. I often joke with some folks about the list they take with them in social situations and in relationships. Many times the things that they look for in a mate are based on their wounds, their fears, their unmet needs, and their wish to compensate for their own emotional deficiency. Girls often look for a husband who will take the place of the father they never had, and boys want to marry someone who is just like their mothers or vice versa. People may find it unhealthy to look for a spouse who has the qualities or the characteristics of their mother. It depends on those qualities and the level of objectivity involved in the criteria that is used whether or not those qualities should be pursued. While this may be a noble testimony and compliment to the parent/s, it may cause rejection of some good prospects because the criteria used are too subjective or restricted. Admittedly, children who come from healthy relationships where true love and commitment were modeled for them are often more optimistic about the prospects of their relationships. However, we need to weigh those criteria objectively. The criteria that should affect the choice of a spouse will be discussed later. Let's say for instance that her father had a good sense of humor or her mother was very industrious. While those characteristics may have been great in their relationship, the absence of such qualities should not deter a person from wanting to develop a relationship with someone who does not possess them. They may, in fact, have other and perhaps greater qualities than their father or mother possessed. While looking for those things desired in a person, a lot of other and sometimes more important qualities or characteristics may be overlooked that would most likely affect the decisions made. These characteristics may be both negative and positive.

One more thing must be said about the list of criteria that may affect our decision to look for Mr. Right and avoid Ms. Wrong. If we are not careful, we might end up looking for the wrong thing in Mr. Right or Ms. Right. Everybody wants to marry the right person. Who doesn't? After all, marriage is for life. Who wants to spend their life with a loser and in misery? There is nothing wrong in looking for Mr. Right or Ms. Right. The problem is in the definition of "right." If "right" is defined as perfect, then we have a serious problem for two reasons. First, Mr. or Ms. "Perfect" does not exist. Second, if they did exist, we would not deserve them because we are not perfect. Marrying someone like us would be their first mistake because they would fail to see how imperfect we are and how imperfect we would make them if they were to be involved in a relationship with us. There is a difference between marrying the right person and marrying Mr. or Ms. "Right." The meaning of finding and marrying the right person will be discussed in Chapter 3. As for now, we must acknowledge that we often let go of the right person too soon because we are focusing on the wrong criteria or the wrong expectations. Using the wrong criteria and having the wrong expectations have caused many couples to marry someone for reasons that will no longer be important later on in life. They were looking for someone to meet some particular needs based on some superficial criteria that has no lasting values and/or are no longer important to them as the years go by. Some criteria may be important for a time, such as looks, style, height, family origin, etc., but compared to spiritual maturity, true love, devotion, and spiritual values, they will not weigh much in the balance of life, especially when faced with all of life's challenges.

So far, as we have seen, the reluctance to be actively involved in the process of finding a spouse and the indecisiveness that many experience in making the choice is related to fear. The fear of marriage that often results in loneliness may also grow out of the fear of being rejected.

Fear of Marriage

In reality, the fear of marriage is related to the fear of getting hurt. Feelings of abandonment and feelings of betrayal experienced either in dysfunctional homes or interpersonal relationships tend to cause a person to be overprotective lest they should relive the same experiences. Albert Bandura, professor of Social Science in Psychology in Stanford University, and others who have studied children's behaviors related to parental modeling suggest that parents tend to be the models for most of the behavior of their children. As such, one can establish at least a relative link between the fears of marriage and parental divorce as well as the scars of the wounds caused by marital disputes, threats of separation, open distrust, and resentment that divorcing parents express and share with the children.

Having witnessed, lived through, or experienced the emotional abuses of dysfunctional homes, children often at an early age resolve never to allow someone to inflict those pains upon them. They become sensitive to pain. Any hint of being misunderstood or any tendency of emotional distance tends to scare them away. Sometimes, even the slightest sign of conflict, which may be part of any healthy growing relationship, would cause them to remember their past experiences and to make sure they protect themselves from getting hurt again. As such, there are people who have great capacity to love and be loved, but who are crippled by their past experiences and who find themselves lonely because of what some person or people have done to them or to someone they know.

When children are torn between parents in cases of divorce and separation, they experience a great deal of confusion and ambivalence. The lack of balance in children of divorced families related to which parent to be loyal to and which one to resent makes it very difficult for them to develop and cultivate proper relationships in adult lives. Often there is on one hand an unhealthy attachment to the remaining parent that is developed by fear of abandonment or feelings of sympathy, and on the other hand, unresolved anger and resentment toward the other parent. This tends to create serious difficulties in forming relationships with others. Being torn between two parents can cause a child to develop indecisiveness and difficulties in making a commitment in later relationships.

Religious or Spiritual Factors

There are people who are single and lonely because of their religious and spiritual beliefs or convictions. One's spiritual and moral convictions may cause someone to consent to a life of singleness and even loneliness when the opportunities for relationship are not consistent with the will of God for their lives. Among those are strong Christians who accept living alone and who will experience the pain of loneliness instead of violating their spiritual and moral convictions. I will never forget the testimony of young lady who refused to marry a non-Christian in spite of the pressures of family members and friends. Her statement still rings true to my ears: "I'd rather spend the rest of my life alone than be unequally yoked to a non-Christian. What can I have in common with a non-Christian and why should I dishonor the Lord by committing my life to someone who does not know him as his Lord and Savior?" To my knowledge, she has never married, nor has she regretted it even once. There are a number of people who have found themselves in such a predicament, not because of lack of opportunities, but because of their spiritual convictions. For instance, some people who are divorced and do not meet the biblical criteria for remarriage may endure the pain of loneliness against their will. Those who find themselves in this situation have decided to honor the Lord and to accept the suffering of loneliness rather than disobey the Scriptures to avoid it. Others may experience loneliness because of the death of their spouse. The grief process for many can be a very complicated process thus making it difficult to engage in any meaningful relationship. Many widows and widowers continue to be too emotionally attached to the deceased. I worked with a lady once who considered it a betrayal to consider marriage after her husband had passed away many years before. She started feeling guilty as though she was contemplating an affair whenever she was approached by a gentleman on the subject of relationship. Others have begun relationships and often sabotaged the process because of complicated grief or other unresolved issues related to their previous marriage.

The religious or spiritual factors are related to someone's understanding of and adherence to the teaching of their church on the issue of marriage, celibacy, divorce, and remarriage. People develop spiritual convictions that often determine whether or not their relationship or status will be approved by God or whether it will be supported by families or friends from the church. There are people who are often torn between their biblical or spiritual convictions and their needs. They end up experiencing a great deal of turmoil when their feelings of loneliness and their convictions clash. Those who choose to go against the teaching of their church often experience disciplinary measures, as well as feelings of guilt and the rejection of friends or leaders who do not support them or their decision. These situations include marriage to non-Christians, remarriage that does not meet the biblical criteria, and marriage to a divorced person. Others who choose not to violate those convictions and who decide not to get married are often faced with the dilemma of wondering if it's the will of God to remain alone for the rest of their lives or whether or not God would change their situation by providing the right circumstances for them to meet someone and marry again. When that does not happen, the feelings of loneliness can be very painful and difficult to reconcile with God's plan for their lives. They end up questioning those convictions and can become quite bitter toward their religion or toward God.

There are others who will maintain their convictions joyfully and learn to trust God to meet their emotional needs through the love and the support of friends and families in the body of Christ. These people, therefore, do not compromise their spiritual convictions by entering into a relationship that does not meet the biblical criteria for their lives. They find the grace of living out their singleness in a way that glorifies the Lord without necessarily experiencing the pain of loneliness.

Among those who remain single against their will and end up experiencing the pain of loneliness are people who have a misunderstanding of the teaching of the Word of God on the subject of celibacy. This will be discussed in the next chapter as we look at the Lord's teaching on celibacy in Matthew 19 and Paul's teaching on singleness in 1 Corinthians 7.

DECIDING ON THE JOURNEY,
PART II: CELIBACY AND THE BIBLE

Many years ago, in the early 80's to be exact, a friend of mine who had been divorced invited me to attend a conference on singleness. The speaker was a well known Christian psychologist in the area. The title of the seminar was "One is a Whole Number." He made an excellent presentation on how to live a full life while being single. The audience was eating from his hands. I noted the nods and the interrupting ovations he received. The audience apparently received much needed encouragement to live life to the fullest. I remember experiencing some discomfort. I felt the speaker was elevating celibacy over marriage to the point of using illustrations of failed marriages to encourage celibacy. The attendees, nonetheless, including my friend, could not agree with him more. Today, I experience the same discomfort when I see the same tendency to justify being celibate by denigrating the marriage institution. I think we can encourage people to enjoy their choice to remain single and to live life to the fullest, whatever that means. Nevertheless, it should not be done at the expense of the honorable state of the marriage institution.

In the previous chapter, we discussed a lot of factors that contribute to the decision whether or not one should consider marriage. Among them we briefly touched on religious or spiritual factors that could affect the decision that people make. Such decision is often based on their understanding of Christ's teaching in Matthew 19 and Paul's admonition in 1 Corinthians 7. This chapter will attempt to clarify some of the misunderstandings and interpretations that might lead some people to the conclusion that God wants them to remain single against their will while they burn with the desire to do otherwise.

Christ's Teaching in Matthew 19

Matthew 19:1-12 deals with the subject of marriage, divorce, remarriage and celibacy. In speaking with his disciples, Jesus says, "Not everyone can accept this word, but only those to whom it has been given. For some are eunuchs because they were born that way; others have been made eunuchs; and others have renounced marriage because of the kingdom of heaven. The one who can accept this should accept it" (Matthew 19:11-12). However, the context is crucial in understanding this critical issue as it relates to a person's choice to remain single or to accept the fact that not everyone will have an opportunity to be married or has received the gift of celibacy.

The verse is within the context of a sensitive discussion on divorce and remarriage provoked by the questions of the Pharisees. It must be noted that divorce and remarriage was a sensitive topic to address during that time frame. It even had political and vital ramifications. John the Baptist had just been imprisoned and killed. Herod had put him in prison because John had denounced as unlawful the marriage of Herod to his brother's wife, Herodias. Herodias' daughter, Salome, prompted by her mother, asked Herod for the head of John the Baptist as a recompense for pleasing Herod with her dance before the spectators (Matthew 14:1-12). So, it's fair to say that the topic of divorce and remarriage was a hot one, and the Pharisees wanted to put Christ on the spot and place his life in jeopardy.

From the religious viewpoint, there were two different schools of thought promulgated by two leaders of the 1st. Century, Rabbi Shammai and Rabbi Hillel. The Pharisees wanted to trap Christ into a theological controversy and find some way to discredit him. Their question stemmed from Deuteronomy 24:1-24, which dealt with Moses' regulations against the abuse of divorce and remarriage with a view to protect the victims. The followers of Rabbi Shammai were the "conservative" group. They believed that "something indecent" referred to adultery and took the position that a man could divorce his wife only if she was unfaithful, i.e. if she had committed adultery. The followers of Rabbi Hillel were the "liberal" group. They believed that "something indecent" referred to anything that displeased the husband, giving him the right to divorce his wife for any cause, hence the question of the Pharisees.

The discussion on the issues of celibacy began by what I would call the disciples' reactive concessions. They were reacting to Christ's response to the Pharisees on the subject of marriage, divorce, and remarriage. In light of what Christ had to say, they conceded, but they apparently had some feelings of dejection and almost despair, in that they felt it would be better for some one not to marry (Matthew 19:10). So the conclusion of the disciples came at the end of a long discussion between the Jesus and the Pharisees on the subject of divorce and remarriage. As the context indicates in verse 2 of Matthew 19, the Pharisees asked Jesus a question as a trap to test him and set him up against the major teachings of the time on that subject.

In his response, Christ went all the way back to the beginning, to Genesis 2:18-25. His answer was to reaffirm the institution of marriage as well as the indissolubility and permanence of marriage. The Pharisees rebutted. They raised the issue of the certificate of divorce. Christ responded by saying that the reason behind Moses' concession was because of the hardness of the heart and again referred them back to the beginning, thus reaffirming the permanence of marriage from the Creator's viewpoint. Christ added that the permission to divorce was only on the basis of adultery and concluded that remarriage would be adultery.

The disciples followed the discussion closely and with great interest. Apparently Christ's teaching hit them pretty hard. They understood that marriage was intended to be a permanent bond between a man and a woman. They also understood that finding a cheap and quick way out was against the Creator's intent and purpose for marriage. In light of Christ's teaching about marriage, they concluded: "If this is the situation between a husband and wife, it is better not to marry" (Matthew 19:10).

In their concession, the disciples demonstrated their understanding of the seriousness of the commitment. They further affirmed that celibacy is a viable option only for those who are unable to make such commitment. In addition, the disciples' soberness about marriage clearly outlines the fact that it is not something to go into without reflection, soul-searching, and careful study. The implication here is that if you are not ready to make that lifetime commitment, don't be in a hurry to marry; wait a while or wait indefinitely. What are the disciples not saying? Well, if you take their statement out of context you might jump to conclusion that the disciples are placing celibacy above marriage and that it is better to remain single and not to marry. That is not the case at all. The first part of the statement must never be detached for the concession: "If this is the situation between a husband and wife, it is better not to marry." In other words, if marriage is for life with no way out, if this is a lifetime commitment with a very limited alternative, it is better to remain single. Upon their reply, Christ introduced the issue of celibacy and proceeded to talk about the eunuchs.

Note the beginning of Christ's first statement: "Not everyone can accept this word . . ." (Matthew 19:11). It seems plausible in the light of Christ's teaching to take "this word" as referring to the disciples' conclusion about marriage: that it is better to remain single. It is unlikely that Christ would be saying that not everyone can accept the Creator's intent and purpose of marriage as though it was an option. God's rules, intents, and purpose for marriage are binding to all, with no exception. The option has to do with entering or not entering the institution.

"Not everyone can accept this word." What did Christ mean here? A simple word study will help us understand this portion. The word "can" here, which may also be translated "is able," is the Greek verb *dunamai* or noun *dunamis* from which we get the English word dynamite. Here it denotes the physical and/or moral power and ability, as residing in a person or thing. The meaning here is: "not everybody has either the moral and/or physical capacity to remain single or not to marry." While celibacy might be a viable option, before considering it, we must check our capacity, our strength or power either physically or morally to handle being celibate.

Now, let's study the second part of Christ's reply: "... but only those to whom it has been given." The second part introduces a category of people who have the gift-capacity to remain celibate or not to marry. The teaching here points to celibacy as a gift that involves either the physical or the moral capacity to remain celibate. Christ proceeds to describe those who fall into that category by introducing the concept of eunuchs. He identifies three kinds of eunuchs: 1) those who are eunuchs by birth, 2) those that were made eunuchs by man, and 3) those who have chosen to become eunuchs for the sake of the kingdom. Before describing each of those three kinds of eunuch, let's understand what a eunuch is.

Eunuchs

A eunuch is by definition a castrated male, someone who is emasculated. In other words, a eunuch is a man who does not function as a male in the physiological and sexual sense of the term. He may or may not possess all the physical reproductive physiological organs or desire to function as a man in relation to women. This definition gives us, at least, a partial understanding in defining eunuchs. The following description will further clarify the issue for us. But, provisionally, the context of Matthew 19 strongly suggests that it can be used as a metaphor for celibacy.

The first kind of eunuchs—*"those who are born eunuchs."* We have to allude to the biology of childbirth in order to understand the notion of "born-eunuchs." It seems to refer to some congenital defect in the development of the baby in the mother's womb whereby the child does not develop all the necessary organs or hormones to be fully functioning as a male. Although rare and unusual, genetic accidents in physiological development, just like congenital blindness, do occur. We have children who are born with extra chromosomes and others who lack the necessary hormones. In a fallen creation, those things are prone to happen. We know that male physiological formation is different from that of female. God made us that way for a particular reason. We learn from biologists who have studied the reproductive system that normal human cells have forty-six chromosomes. When fertilization takes place, the normal inheritance consists of twenty-three pairs of chromosomes, one of each pair being from the mother and one from the father. Twenty-two of the chromosome pairs are called autosomes, and they are involved in general anatomical and physiological characteristics. The remaining pair, which consists of the sex chromosomes, determines the individual sex as well as other characteristics of a person. To be a girl, both of these sex chromosomes, one from each parent, are designated as X chromosomes. In other words, a female's chromosomal make-up would be designated as XX. In the male, the sex chromosome from the mother is an X and the sex chromosome from the father is designated as Y. Thus, the boy's chromosomal make-up would be designated as XY.

In very rare cases, there are chromosomal anomalies that sometimes result with a child having an extra chromosome from either parent. For instance, in Down's Syndrome babies, there is a trisomy, that is, instead of two chromosomes, the child has three of one autosomal pair. Then it's XXX. In Klinefelter's Syndrome, there is an extra X added to the XY make-up thus producing a male who lacks some masculine traits and possesses some feminine traits. Then it's XXY. There are cases as well where the males have an extra Y making it XYY. In addition, to chromosomal anomalies, there are also hormonal imbalances that may affect the characteristics of males and females. Such seems to be the case with eunuch-born individuals.

While we may not know for sure what their exact chromosomal or hormonal make-up is, we understand that there may be an anomaly or deficiency that might influence their decision to marry or not to marry. So Christ's statement about eunuch-born must be understood that there are people who have the capacity to remain celibate because they are born that way. They have this capacity because the physiological response or interest in the opposite sex is not there. Celibacy comes naturally to them as a gift. With such absence of physiological response, they would not be burning with desire for the opposite sex. Therefore, they would have the capacity to remain celibate.

There is a false notion permeated by those who want to support the practice of homosexuality that the term "eunuch-born" refers to homosexuality. Nothing can be further from the truth. Being born eunuch in the context expressly indicates that those people are born with not just a lack of interest in the opposite sex, but a lack of interest in sex period. It was clear that from the Pharisees' questions and Christ's response reaffirming God's design in Genesis 2:18-25 that marriage was between a male and a female. The absence of interest in the opposite sex meant no marriage, therefore no sexual relationship for that individual because he was born that way. To use this to justify homosexuality would be to not only reject that God's design for marriage is between a male and a female, but also to make Scriptures support sexuality outside of marriage. This would be blasphemy, since the Bible clearly describes sex outside of marriage as fornication and adultery, which are condemned throughout Scriptures.

Furthermore, the context here strongly indicates that men or women who are born with a physiological defect with regard to their maleness or femaleness should refrain from marriage since they are not fully equipped physiologically to form a relationship with the opposite sex. Therefore, celibacy, not same sex relationship, is the proper response to the congenital defect.

While we must concede that in very, very rare cases in a fallen creation, biological defects or genetic accidents do occur. These are consequences of the curse of the Fall, not an excuse for further damages. For instance, we also have children who are born blind, or born with intellectual deficiencies. Their conditions are abnormal. As a society and as families we support them and accommodate them and provide for them with the same worth and dignity as any other member of society. But we never do so at the expense of moral and social conventions. For instance somebody who is born blind may still have a burning desire to drive. We have set rules and laws that regulate the ability to drive motor vehicles, and we would not violate them just because we want to fulfill the desire of someone who has a strong and natural desire to be independent and drive. It would be irresponsible to give them a license to drive since it would jeopardize theirs and our physical safety. It would not only be irresponsible but even wicked to encourage them in that sense. If we as humans can set and respect such rules for the benefit of society how much more can the Creator of the universe set rules and boundaries for the moral preservation of society, the families and ultimately for his glory? Christ in his response to the Pharisees clearly evokes the Creator's rule for marriage between one man and one woman. Those for whatever reasons have a deficiency that disqualifies them from marriage should abstain from it. Such is the case for the eunuch-born who by virtue of his biological deficiency has the capacity to remain unmarried and therefore asexual.

The second kind of eunuchs—*"others who were made that way by men."* Here the definition of eunuchs as a castrated or an emasculated male seems applicable. In ancient cultures, it was customary to castrate some of the male servants in order to free them from sexual distractions and the ability to reproduce, such as the men who presided over the king's harem. They were in charge of the management or care of women's chambers. They were castrated to make it impossible to have sexual relations with the women under their care. Those emasculated chamberlains, as they were called, could not function as males in regard to sexual relations with the opposite sex. Consequently, they could not consider marriage since it would be impossible for them to function fully as a male in the relationship. They would be sexually impotent to fulfill their duty toward their wives as Paul would admonish later on in 1 Corinthians 7.

The third kind of eunuchs—*"those who choose for the sake of the kingdom to become eunuchs."* In this category, we find two kinds of voluntary eunuchs. The first type involves those who like Origen of Alexandria, a theologian and biblical scholar of the early Greek church (185 AD-253 AD), have castrated themselves in order to avoid having feelings for the opposite sex and therefore find themselves with no desire to be married. Even when the desire is present, they have already made it impossible to consider marriage because of lack of physiological capacity to fulfill the needs of the opposite sex. The second type involves not the physical castration, but the moral decision to abstain from marriage and from sexual relationships. These people have made a vow to give priority to the kingdom of God thereby sacrificing all sexual and marital pleasure in order to be devoted entirely to the service of the Lord. Both "physical" and "moral" eunuchs in this category have received the capacity-gift not to enter marriage. God honors their decision by empowering them with the ability to refrain from sexual relations and to glorify him fully through their chosen ministry. These people can do so while quoting Paul in Philippians 4:13: "I can do all things through Christ which strengtheneth me" (KJV).

As such, the physical eunuchs, either by birth or emasculation, either voluntary or not, have the capacity not to enter marriage because of their physical or their physiological condition. The "moral eunuchs" have received the moral gift-capacity to remain celibate and not to enter marriage.

Paul's Teaching in 1 Corinthians 7

Paul elaborates on Christ's teaching in 1 Corinthians 7. Although in a different context and for different reasons, he addresses the issue of celibacy. As expected, Paul's teaching in 1 Corinthians 7 is consistent with Christ's teaching in Matthew 19. The similarity and consistency in teaching are remarkable. The teaching of both Paul and Christ about celibacy is in response to man's failure to live up to God's standard for marriage. Just like the disciples, the Corinthians wrestled with the idea that someone might be better off not being married.

The Corinthians were living in a culture in which relationships between men and women within and outside of marriage were inconsistent with their new found understanding of the Creator's will. Since they did not fully understand how to react in light of their new found faith, they wrote to Paul and asked him a few questions about sexuality, marriage, and celibacy. Like the disciples, they were reacting to what they were experiencing, i.e., the struggle between honoring God and living with their desire to be involved in a relationship with the opposite sex. Paul responded by affirming Christ's teaching in the following points: first, one should consider celibacy if he or she has received the gift. This assumed the physical and/or moral gift-capacity to remain celibate without violating God's principles for purity both in and outside of marriage. Second, celibacy can be chosen for the sake of prioritizing one's ministry over one's sexual needs or the needs for a relationship. In that instance as well, the moral capacity to remain celibate without violating God's principles for purity is assumed. Paul quickly adds that if a person is burning with sexual urges, i.e., if a person does not have either the moral or the physical capacity to remain single, then they should get married. It is clear from both Matthew 19 and from 1 Corinthians 7 that anyone who has not received the physical and/or moral strength to remain single or the capacity to choose celibacy over marriage should consider praying about finding a suitable mate. No one should pretend to have received the gift of celibacy while burning with the desire to get married.

Neither Paul nor Christ has denigrated marriage nor elevated celibacy over marriage. Their teachings are in response to man's reactions and concessions in light of their failures and weaknesses, as well as the "present distress" that incurs as a result. The Creator instituted marriage between one man and one woman to respond to man's loneliness and to meet his needs for companionship and intimacy. It is the intention of Christ that man should have the joy of sharing his life with his soul-mate. Unfortunately, because of man's sinful condition, the hardness of his heart and his failure to uphold God's standard, many questions have been raised on the subject of celibacy and marriage. Nonetheless, God's intent, purposes, and standards remain the same in spite of man's dilemma to follow them.

It is a complete misunderstanding to suggest that Paul was prescribing celibacy or elevating it over marriage. Such misinterpretation of the passage results from the failure to note that Paul's inspired opinion was a concession in light of the current distress brought about by man's failures and sins. It was in light of this dilemma and the struggles that the Corinthians were experiencing that Paul writes. In 1 Timothy 4:3, he denounces the false teachers who were forbidding marriage. Later on in 1 Timothy 5:14, he makes it abundantly clear that he wants the younger women to marry and to have children and not to give an occasion to the adversary to speak reproachfully. In Hebrews 13:4, the author of the book reaffirms the honorable state of marriage. No one has to disparage marriage in order to justify their inability to follow the right path to marital happiness. One does not have to pretend to have the gift of celibacy when in fact they are craving for a relationship with someone.

Celibacy as a gift or as a choice can be very fulfilling, especially to those who are engaged in ministry. Single people are not necessarily lonely and miserable. There are or should be opportunities in the body of Christ to have meaningful, God-honoring relationships that should alleviate the pain of loneliness. In fact, the one-another principles found throughout Scriptures, especially in Paul's epistles, do not apply only to married people. As children of God, we are called to love one another, to support one another, and to care for one another. No one in the body of Christ should suffer the pain of loneliness whether in or outside of marriage. However, the Creator's plan remains. His ideal answer to loneliness from the beginning is to find someone to love and to commit their life to through thick and thin. There is nothing like having a soul-mate to be there with you in good times and in bad times. Many years ago, my former pastor, Dr. Mariot Valcin said something to me that I will never forget, especially after it has been confirmed over and over again. When I was considering going to seminary, he asked me about my plan for marriage. Upon hearing my nonchalant response to the idea that I should take some serious steps in that direction, he said, "There are certain joys in life that can only be experienced in an enriching relationship with your spouse and in the context of healthy family interactions." Many times I have rehearsed that sentence with a smile, and said to myself, "You were right, Pastor." I just needed to find the right person, and for that I am grateful.

Remaining single instead of getting married can be a very legitimate choice, but it must be a personal, well-calculated choice, and not a forced one. The issues that were raised in this chapter might have served to open your eyes on the factors that might contribute to singleness against your will. They included psychological and personal factors that resulted from familial upbringing and personal experiences as well as spiritual factors that might cause someone to look at celibacy as a legitimate choice. We propose to address those factors more fully in Chapter 3. The reality is that the past experiences, unresolved issues, and conflicts may create a lot of unnecessary fear and trepidation about marriage. Often relationships are sabotaged and opportunities are lost because of a person's past experiences, upbringing, and poor choices.

The decision to embark or not to embark on the journey is each person's right. But the choice must be theirs. They should not let the past or someone else make that choice for them. They should not have to apologize for their desire to get married. They should not have to suppress their need to find someone with whom they can spend their life. These feelings and desires are natural. Every person was created as an emotional and social being with needs and desires for affection, intimacy, and companionship. God intended those needs to be met in a marital relationship.

As I write these lines, there are images of those who are lonely and hurting through no fault of their own. They have trusted their lives and their hearts to someone who turned against them and abandoned them to face life and its difficulties alone. They were abused either physically or emotionally, and now for companionship, they only have the scars and the tears that flow at the remembrance of those painful days of mistreatment. There are others who are ravaged by guilt while paying the consequences of foolish decisions of breaking viable relationships they could have preserved with a little bit of perseverance and forgiveness. Still others are facing life alone because they have lost their lifelong companion to death. One of the hardest things is to say good-bye, to cry over the coffin of a soul-mate. As this is read, the scenario of each person may not show up in these lines, but the void and the pain are no less real. Whatever a person's situation may be, the hope that this book is offering is that they can make the decision to experience or re-experience the joy of companionship, provided that it is within God's parameters of relationship.

In Ecclesiastes 4, Solomon decried the fate of the one who is crying with no one to comfort him. He also confronted those who fail to give priority to human relations over work and material possessions. To accumulate riches with no one to share it with is futility. Yet people are seen devoting a lot of time pursuing their education, pursuing ministry, and pursuing advancement in careers while neglecting their social life and opportunity for fellowship. Many of them are content with passing pleasures, flirts and temporal flings. Since they never take the time to cultivate meaningful relationships, they experience break-up after break-up that leaves them more scared and more hardened than they were to begin with. They will never know the joy of someone who has committed their life to them while they reciprocate. They will never know the intimacy, the trust, and the love that can only be experienced in a marital relationship. At the end of their life, they will look back with regrets and remorse, and the pain of loneliness will be even greater than they had ever experienced it.

After describing the pain and futility of loneliness, Solomon proceeded to expound on the value of a shared life. His affirmation that two are better than one is a summary of all the joys, the advantages, and the blessings of having a life companion. Working together toward the same goal is better than doing it alone. The mutual support, the companionship, the warmth, the embrace, and the care of lifelong commitment in marriage cannot be matched by the riches of this world. The mutual encouragement, the accountability, and the capacity to face life's difficulties with someone who loves you unconditionally and whom you love in return in the same way have no comparison.

As indicated earlier, the choice to be single for legitimate and biblical reasons will be honored by the Lord, and the choice of this commitment will give opportunity to glorify him. That choice may be because a person has decided to prioritize Christ's kingdom over their needs, or it may be because a person has decided to remain single instead of violating God's moral and biblical standards. In such cases, one can be confident that their heavenly Father will honor and reward their commitment to him. These noble decisions may be the cross that some may have to bear in order to follow them. Following the Master will never be a point of regret. The whole purpose of this chapter is not to discourage a person from making a biblical and spiritual decision about marriage or celibacy. This decision should be a well-calculated, prayerful, and personal one, and not a pretext for justifying unwanted celibacy.

Again, if a person has not received the gift of celibacy, they can be actively involved in the journey. If any of these issues raised seem to be of concern, and seem to influence a person's decision against their God-given needs and desires, they may need to get help to experience God's healing and forgiveness. A person should not pretend or claim to be something that they are not. They should not try to act super-spiritual by ignoring or minimizing those needs. They should pray earnestly about their needs to find a life companion. If they have the gift of celibacy, they should celebrate it, enjoy it, serve the Lord with it, and thank God for giving them the moral or physical capacity to remain single. Still, one should not be lonely. But, if they have not received the gift of celibacy, they should not feel embarrassed about their needs, nor be afraid to embark on the journey; they are not alone. There are instructions, guidelines, and recommendations, such as those provided in this book, that would equip a person to make the marital journey more enjoyable than they think. All that is needed to make the choice is a clear understanding of the Designer's blue print for the journey.

❧ III ❧

BEGINNING THE JOURNEY
WITH THE DESIGNER'S BLUEPRINT
AND GOD'S PURPOSE AND PLAN

The first time I learned how to use a map was when I was leaving Wheaton, Illinois where I had completed my pre-doctoral internship and half of my post-doctoral residency to move to Massachusetts and work at Cambridge Hospital. The map was so detailed that it not only gave me directions to my final destination, but also highlighted major key points along the road and even the approximate time I would get to each point and how long it would take me to complete the journey. Here I was, driving on I-80, going through various states and cities with no major concerns because I was following the map. Nowadays, we use MapQuest or even GPS to guide us along the way with detailed instructions and guidance in our journeys. In fact, using a GPS is so incredible that even if a person got lost, it would recalculate and use different directions to get them back on the right track to their final destination.

I spoke to an engineer friend of mine about road construction. He revealed to me that the first step to building any road begins with a blueprint. The blueprint is purposefully designed to help travelers embarking on a journey. Every aspect on the blueprint is important, even the curbs are designed in a way that is consistent with the designer's intent, purpose, and methods.

Well, marriage to some extent is like a journey. The only difference may be that a person doesn't have to wait for a final destination to enjoy it. There are many key points along the way that make it enjoyable. Choosing to follow the right path will make the journey enjoyable, and we will deal with more than just a map, MapQuest, or GPS. We will look at the Designer's blueprint. We will go right to the conception of the journey, the plan for the journey, and the Designer's intent for the journey. In short, we will deal with God's blueprint for the marital journey. While there are universal principles or pathways that one can follow to experience a certain degree of joy or happiness in their marriage, it is almost impossible to reach the ultimate destination of the enjoyable journey apart from God's blueprint for the marriage.

Back to the Basics

One of the things that I admire about great athletes is the constant reference to the "Fundamentals." I take it to mean that a person cannot be successful in the sports if they ignore the foundational elements of the game. All the fancy stuff a player can do on the field or on the court will mean nothing unless they keep going back to the basics. The same is true of the marital relationship. Many couples fail to experience the happiness they wish in their marriages because they keep running away from the fundamentals. In order to enjoy the journey, we need to go back to the fundamentals of the institution. Those fundamentals or foundational elements are found in Genesis 1:26-27 and Genesis 2:18-25, where both the creation of man and woman and the institution of marriage are given.

Use of the Fundamentals by Jesus and Paul

Jesus was confronted by the Pharisees in Matthew 19 with a question on the issue of divorce and remarriage. While the Pharisees wanted to take him back to Deuteronomy 24 which was the focus of the contemporary debate on the issue, Jesus took them to the beginning, back to the basics or the fundamentals found in Genesis 2:18-25. Much of the debate on the subject of the marriage institution would be resolved if only politicians, legislators, the church, and the general public would go back to the foundational elements of the institution. Unfortunately, the liberal and post-modern thinkers prefer to deal with the here and now and ignore the fundamentals. However, as Christians, any serious conversation about marriage must imitate what the Lord himself did, i.e., go back to the basics or the "beginning."

That's exactly what Paul did. In his discussion of husbands and wives and their relationship, he beautifully compares marriage with Christ's relationship with the church by referring to the fundamentals: "For this reason a man will leave his father and mother and be united to his wife, and the two will become one flesh." Ephesians 5:31 In 1 Corinthians 6:16-17, Paul denounces the practice of sex before and outside of marriage by referring again to the basics where he briefly commented on the meaning of the one flesh principle.

Like Jesus and Paul, it is important to go back to the fundamentals of the institution found in the Chapters 1 and 2 of Genesis where God's blueprint depicts those entering into marriage as male and female, the number of parties in the marriage, the nature of the marriage per se, the intimate quality of the marriage, and the duration of the marriage. His blueprint for the marriage begins with his definition of marriage, and his intent and purpose for the marriage.

Marriage is God's institution. As such, it is regulated by God's principles apart from which there can be no true or lasting happiness. As the Designer, God sets the pathway to follow and the parameters that must be respected. In order for the journey to be enjoyable, a person must follow the roadmap God provides to achieve any level of happiness in the marriage. In other words, the choice to be happy in marriage begins with the choice to understand and obey his principles.

The Creation of Man and Woman in God's Image

The starting point of understanding God's blueprint is grasping the meaning of the creation of man in the image of God as male and female. It is clear there is a close relationship between the nature of man and the institution of marriage. A simple observation will help clarify that point even before delving any deeper into the subject. Genesis 1:26-27 states that God created man in the generic sense, in terms of humanity as composed of both male and female: "in the image of God he created him; male and female he created them." This simple yet profound statement found in the first chapter of Genesis is clarified in detail as to the timing, the intent, and the sequence of that creation as stated in Genesis 2:18-25. In other words, Chapter 2 gives us the description of the event stated Chapter 1. One cannot separate the two accounts. However, in order to offer further clarification on both, we will deal with each separately. Then we will synthesize the overarching principle of the passages as they relate to the institution of marriage.

"Then God said, 'Let us create man in our image, in our likeness' . . . so God created man in his own image, in the image of God he created him; male and female he created them" (Genesis 1:26, 27). For centuries theologians have debated over the meaning of the image and the likeness of God. In his article, *Male and Female Complementarity and the Image of God*, Bruce A. Ware provided an excellent overview of the various historical interpretations of the meaning of the image and the likeness of God, from Iraneous in the second century to Anthony Hoekema. Doing a survey of those views is like describing the elephant. In an old time tale, a king is said to have asked six blind men to describe an elephant. Each one described it according to the part that he touched. The elephant was not fully understood until all the parts were put together. Various descriptions give the following elements about the image of God in man: intellectual capacity, reason, volition, spiritual endowments, self-consciousness, dominion, emotions, and functional holism. Functional holism is the ability to carry out the responsibilities God has given man and to act as finite representatives of God's own nature in relationship with him and with each other. Most, if not all the thinkers, would affirm that the image of God in man is comprised of these three basic elements: intellect, will, and emotions. These elements are crucial in understanding man's capacity to relate to God and to form meaningful relationships with one another. The relational dimension of the meaning of the image of God is adopted and emphasized in this book. This aspect of the image of God in man has received much support from theologians and Christian thinkers over the centuries.

According to two major church theologians, Thomas Aquinas (1204-1274) and John Calvin (1509-1564), the image of God is located in man's reason and man's soul (both heart and mind), which habilitates man to know and love God. As such, they implicitly support the relational dimension involved in being created in the image and the likeness of God. It can be further implied that man's capacity to know and love God will result in his ability to know and love his fellowman, especially one's wife or husband. This consequential aspect of knowing and loving God is well known to the reader of the Epistle of 1 John. In this epistle, it is clearly taught that to know and love God is to love one's fellowman, which is culminated in the love for a husband for his wife and a wife for her husband. By the way, that's the summary of the Law of the prophets, according to Christ, "'Love the Lord your God with all your heart and with all your soul and with all your mind.' This is the first and greatest commandment. And the second is like it: 'Love your neighbor as yourself.' All the Law and the Prophets hang on these two commandments" (Matthew 22:37-40). Marriage between a man and a woman provides the greatest opportunity for the highest expression of the relational dimension of the image of God in man.

Among other proponents of the relational dimension of the image of God is church theologian Karl Barth (1886-1968), who sees the image of God as comprising the relational and social nature of man. Accordingly, the male and female relationship is the manifestation of the image of God in man.

It must be pointed out that as we advocate the relational dimension of the image of God, we are not implying that it is the exclusive manifestation of the image of God. Even outside of a meaningful relationship with God and his fellowman or in a husband and wife relationship, man still retains the image of God. However, as Bruce Ware indicated, it is in the use of the other capacities such as reason, soul, and volition in relation with God and others that reflects most clearly what it means to be created in God's image.

Although not a theological treatise on the meaning of the image of God, one cannot touch on any aspect of creation in the image and the likeness of God without raising the question as to how the Fall affected the image of God in man. As clearly taught in Scripture, particularly in Genesis 9:6 and James 3:9, man retains the dignity and the nobility of the image of God. However, man's capacity to reflect that image at any level was tarnished and distorted by sin. As such, in the relational dimension, man's capacity to know and love God and consequently to know and love his fellow man has been distorted and misdirected. Instead of knowing and loving God, man becomes self-centered, loving himself above and apart from God. Consequently, his capacity to love his fellowman as God would have it is corrupted by selfish ambition and pursuits. Instead of engaging in the pursuit of the happiness of our spouse in the marriage, we are looking for our own happiness—often at the expense of our husbands or wives. In the pursuit of our own happiness, we manipulate, we destroy, and we become self-protective and self-centered. In so doing, we discover that we become more and more miserable. As we will discuss further in this book, the choice of being happy in marriage is a mutual pursuit of the other's happiness in the marriage.

Just like one cannot speak of the image of God in man without talking about the effect of the Fall, by the same token, one cannot speak of the devastating ruin of the fall on the image of God without appreciating the wonderful restoration of redemption. Whatever we lost through the Fall can be regained through redemption—gradually, but certainly. Whatever we have lost in Adam, we are regaining through Christ Jesus in all dimensions of our lives. That's what spirituality is all about. Through the blood of Christ and the power of the Holy Spirit, we are gradually being transformed into the likeness and the image of Christ thus learning to know and love God more and more, and as a result, loving each other more and more.

Image of God and Marital Relationship

The commonly accepted elements that comprise the image of God in man are specifically relative to the male and female relationship in marriage. Although there are various interpretations of the meaning of man's creation in the image and the likeness of God, there are three basic elements that are agreed upon by most if not by all theologians pertaining to the image of God. These are the intellect, the will, and the emotions.

Intellect

The intellectual dimension involves man's capacity to process, learn, reason, think, and understand. Man has the capacity to know God, to know his will, to apprehend the truth of God, and to also know himself and his fellowman—to know and be known. He has the capacity to understand and explore the rest of creation, which further reveals the truth of God. As man gets to know God through his general revelation, that knowledge will also cause him to discover God's love. His goodness is also more deeply grasped through the special revelation of his Word and through Christ. The more a person knows God, the more they learn to love God. The more they love God, the greater their capacity to love their fellow man, and especially their spouse.

Will

If the intellectual capacity habilitates man to know and to reason, the volitional capacity enables him to act freely on that knowledge. Man has the capacity to choose, decide and act freely based on what he knows. As theologians, a person would have a field day with this as to the meaning of free-will, the bondage of the will, and God's sovereignty. It is not our intention to engage in such debates here. One thing is clear, man has the capacity to make choices and to act freely, especially in the area of choosing who to love and who to hate and when to love and when to hate. Granted there are a number of factors that may influence our will and affect our choices. Many of those factors are sometimes done unconsciously. We do have the capacity to choose, and to choose to love and to choose to be happy. Marital happiness is a choice. It is not a blind choice; it is a well-informed choice based on the knowledge of God, the knowledge of his will, the knowledge of ourselves and our spouses, and the choice to act on that knowledge.

Emotion

All the elements are intertwined and impact the relational dimension of the image of God. There is interrelatedness of the intellectual, the volitional, and the emotional dimensions of our being. However, among them the emotional dimension stands out. It is through our emotions that we demonstrate the capacity to feel, to love, to relate, to give and receive love, to share feelings, to empathize, to show compassion to others and be subject to the affection of others toward us. In other words, the emotional dimension allows us to manifest the capacity to love and be loved. Through this we learn to receive and be penetrated by the love of God. We learn to love God in return and to grow in his love. Thus, we increase our capacity to love and be loved by others. This is so crucial that a little more time should be devoted to it. As write this, I am mindful of the effect of sin on that very capacity both subjectively and objectively. The first thing Satan did was to cause man to question God's love for them by questioning why a loving God would restrain them from eating from the tree of the knowledge of good and evil in the garden. He then directed them to take matters into their hands and to seek to provide for themselves. Disregarding God's command and at the expense of the loving relationship and fellowship they have with God, they do as Satan says. Therefore, because of sin, our capacity to love and be loved has been terribly affected, thus leaving a lot of damaged emotions with regard to our ability to love and be loved. As I write this, I feel a knot in my stomach for the many individuals and couples who are miserable because their capacity to love and be loved has been seriously compromised.

I am thinking of a little girl whose father divorced her mother when she was still an infant and whose mother died before her thirteenth birthday. Not only has she given up on the idea of ever being loved by someone, she has become distrustful of any attempts by others to love her. She does not think that anybody has the capacity to really love her for a long period of time. Her lack of capacity to be loved has inversely affected her own capacity to love, always thinking that she will end up getting hurt again, thus restraining herself from truly loving anyone, lest they should love her in return. Although she is an adult now, she continues to be haunted by the negative experiences of her past that diminish her capacity to love and be loved. Yet, as you talk to her, you discover that there is inside of her a loving person ready to come out, but restrained by hurt feelings, anger, and frustrations experienced in previous relationships.

There are a number of individuals who have suffered the pain of rejection, physical and emotional abuses, and the pain of failed relationships, divorce and separation. Deep inside, they continue to experience the need to be loved and the capacity to love, but are being hampered by bitterness, lack of forgiveness, and lack of resolution of the unfortunate experiences of the past.

I remember a desperate husband who came to me with tears in his eyes explaining how his wife would not let him love her. Upon talking to the wife, she confirms that he is a good husband and that he has made a lot of efforts in their marriage. She admitted that she does not know how to respond to or to reciprocate his love. Upon further exploration, it was discovered that her heart had become callous or even hardened by bitterness resulted from years of abuse, mistreatments, and past relationships. It was also discovered that although she was a Christian, she did not fully understand what it means to be loved by God. There was a fear of God, but not in the reverential sense. It was a fear that any moment, God would zap her, destroy her, or kill her for any sin she might have committed. Because she has not fully accepted God's forgiveness through Christ, she has not freed herself to love and forgive others. She was miserable even in the arms of a loving husband.

Still, because of our creation in the image and the likeness of God, we have the capacity to love and be loved. If sin has damaged these capacities, one of the marvelous results of redemption is that we can experience God's love, grace and forgiveness. One of the passages that I like reading in the Old Testament is Deuteronomy 30:6 where the Lord promised to circumcise our hearts, and as a result, we will be able to love him. That's what happens in regeneration. According to Ezekiel 36:26-27, at conversion, we receive a new heart. The heart that was damaged by sin, unforgiveness, and bitterness—that heart of stone has been removed and replaced with a heart of flesh, capable of loving, and being loved. We can choose to use this capacity to love God and love one another as we allow ourselves to experience God's love for us as well as the love of others, especially our spouse.

The Image of God and the Nature of Man and Woman

It is clear from Genesis 1 and 2 that both males and females are made in the image of God. No confusion or debate should exist in the fact that both Adam and Eve were equal in their humanity. Both were distinctly created as independent and distinct individuals. The fact that Eve was taken from Adam's rib did not make her less of an individual. If the logic of where she came from would make her less than Adam, that logic would completely destroy Adam's nobility for having come from the dust. It did not matter where they came from or how they were formed with regard to their dignity. What matters is that they both were created in God's image and in his likeness. The other confusion that we need to avoid is the idea that Adam was incomplete without Eve, and that Eve was created to complete Adam. Although this may sound interesting in wedding sermons, it has no biblical support. The only comment God made about Adam was that it was not good for him to be alone. He said nothing about his being incomplete. Being alone or being single does not make one incomplete, although vital relationships are important and crucial, as we have shown in the first chapter. Any potential confusion on that point should be elucidated with the statement found in Genesis 2:24 that the two, i.e., the two individuals, male and female, should become one flesh. It was not two halves, but two separate individuals, two separate genders, both created in the image of God who would cleave together to become one flesh. Male and female created in God's image speak of their equality in essence. Essence does not negate differences in terms of the body, function, ability, and responsibility in the creative order. However, in spite of these differences, there are equality, similarity and complementarity, and compatibility factors that make the marriage both interesting and enjoyable. The beautiful mystery of becoming one flesh to which Paul alluded in Ephesians 5 serves as the best analogy *(toute proportion gardee)* for the relationship of Christ with the church. You cannot go higher than that.

Male and Female Equality/Similarity

Maleness and femaleness in the image of God not only supposes equality but also similarity in many respects. First, they are equal in essence and attributes. As such they are also equal in worth, dignity and importance as well as accountability in the eyes of God. They are also equal in the Fall. Both had to respond to God and inherited the consequences of their sin, although at different levels. In addition, they are equal in their redemption (Galatians 3:28, Colossians 3:20-21) and become co-heirs with Christ (Romans 8:16-20, 1 Peter 3:7). Both male and female have the responsibility to reflect God's glory in their lives and in their relationships, and they go through the same spiritual process of regeneration, justification, sanctification and glorification. However, equality and similarity do not mean that the male and female are identical. God intended some differences for the purpose of marriage and his plan for creation. In fact, identical people should refrain from marriages since they violate the very idea and purpose of marriage. The word that is used to describe Eve as being a "suitable" helper speaks to some extent of the non-identicalness of their characteristics. Suitability does not mean sameness. It rather implies two different entities that have been formed or built to fit each other. This is physically demonstrated in the formation and nature of the sex organs of male and female and the sexual relationships between husbands and wives. They are designed to fit and accommodate each other. While they are equal and similar in many respects of their physical attributes, they are vastly different in their anatomical and physiological make-up in many other respects. However, these differences are there so that the male and female can adapt and adjust to each other in such a way that they can become united as one.

Male and Female Differences

Vive la difference! The difference between men and women is what marriage is all about. It ranges from the chromosomal and hormonal differences to the psychological and functional differences. Science has helped us understand how those differences begin even in the womb. For instance, males have XY chromosome; females have no Y chromosome, but two X chromosomes. There are also anatomical differences. Female and male pelvic bones are shaped differently. Their reproductive organs and genitalia are different. Males and females differ also physiologically. Their hormonal balances are not the same. Their metabolic functions and rhythms are different. Women menstruate during portions of their lives; men do not. Women go through menopause, men do not. There are other obvious physical differences that are rooted in the biological differences. God intended those differences for the marriage and the different roles and functions that men and women would play. Even the psychological differences in terms of experience and expressions of emotions were designed by God. Women are generally more tender, more sensitive, more nurturing than men. Although not limited to this particular task, God fashioned women this way, in my opinion, to prepare her for motherhood, to provide the nursing and gentle care. A mother is more prone to create the kind of affectionate climate a child would need to experience love, tenderness, and compassion that is so crucial to his or her upbringing. In Isaiah 49:14-15, the Lord illustrated his love for Israel by using the picture of a nursing mother. But men shouldn't feel left out. The Lord also used the compassion of a father to demonstrate his mercy for his children (Psalm 103:13), but obviously we know there is a difference between the care of a mother and the care of a father. Just ask your children, especially the small ones. I remember how Jean Abede and Jonathan made me feel when I stayed home with them for a couple of days when they were small. Even though they were subtle about it, I got the message when they kept asking me when Mommy would be coming home. I have to admit that I could not wait for her to come home either. What if babies could talk?!

In addition to biological differences, there are others, such as neurological and psychological differences that can be explored in literature, but which will not be dealt with in this book. The Bible expressed that difference in 1 Peter 3:7. Peter admonished men in terms of how they should treat their wives. He used the expression "weaker vessels" to warn husbands about how they should treat their wives. The word "weaker" is not used in a pejorative sense. It refers to the observable physical and emotional fragility of women who are more delicate in many respects. The exhortation here is while Peter is affirming the woman's spiritual equality with the man as co-heirs with Christ, he is warning the husbands about how to treat their wives. The male and female differences are what define marriage. God intended those differences not only for the reproductive roles, but for the complementarity of the marital relationship. He intended the physical attraction of a male to a female or vice versa to be the natural course. He intentionally created not another Adam, but Eve to be his counterpart. In fact, as we see in Genesis 2:19, 20, he allows Adam to experience the need for that counterpart in naming the animals, which apparently were in pairs of males and females. Adam not only did not have anybody who resembles him, he did not have the right counterpart. He lacked not only a companion, he lacked a female companion, and God met that need by creating Eve. That's the natural order; that's what God intended and did, and that's what makes a marriage a marriage. Anything else is un-natural and an abomination in the eyes of the Lord. The so-called same sex marriages clearly violate God's intent and purpose. But beyond that, it violates the laws of nature both in the animal and the vegetable kingdoms.

To understand the nature of marriage, we must understand the nature of man's creation. Man (in the generic sense) was created in God's image as male and female: two individuals equal in essence, but distinct in their biological, physiological, and psychological make-up, who are suitable for each other to form the bond called marriage. Genesis 1:26-27 is the key to understanding Genesis 2:18-25. One cannot and should not engage in any discussion about the institution of marriage without referring to man's creation as male and female in the image of God. Provisionally, we can affirm that according to the creative order, marriage should be between one male and one female.

Understanding God's Design

God's design for marriage as referred to by both Jesus and Paul is outlined in detail in Genesis 2: 18-25. Having understood the creation of man and women in the image of God from Genesis 1: 26-27, we now can understand the sequence, the manner, and the purpose of that creation. To be sure, it must be pointed out that although the sequence of their creation in no way affected neither their essence nor their worth or value, it did reveal different levels of responsibility in the relationship. Furthermore, the sequence should not be interpreted as to imply that Eve's creation was an afterthought. God's plan for creation was not apparently to continue to create, but to facilitate his creatures to be fruitful and to multiply. Fruitfulness and multiplication are terms that can be replaced by expressions such as reproduction or procreation. God created both the animal and the vegetable genre with a reproductive system by which the earth can be replenished. God's creative plan for humanity all along was that there be both male and then female. The sequence, in my view, was intended for us to understand the care, concerns, and the degree of importance that were involved in the creation of Eve. She was not an afterthought but an indispensable counterpart of Adam in order to fulfill God's design. As many commentators point out, God wanted Adam to realize this by asking him to name the animals and to experience his own need for a suitable mate since according to Genesis 6, for each male animal, there was a female animal. There was a suitable mate according to each kind. However, for Adam, until the creation of Eve, there was no suitable mate. As such, the creation of Eve from the first would be consistent with that creative order for procreation and reproduction. Although her role would be more than "being barefoot and pregnant," her gender as female was certainly necessary to fulfill God's initial command to be fruitful and multiply. God's statement about Adam's loneliness was a clear indication that his intention for Eve was to be a companion for Adam before being his sex partner for reproduction. But God intentionally wanted that lifetime companion to be a female not another male. He created a suitable, not an identical mate for him. By suitable, he meant another creature that would correspond to Adam. The word suitable here must be taken to imply equality in essence and worth, as well as complementarity and reconcilability of differences.

Adam's Reaction to Eve's Creation

One does not have to be a genius or a poet to imagine what Adam felt when he woke up from that sleep. For me it's easy. I just have to remember the time I first met my wife and the first night of our honeymoon. On both occasions, I almost spoke in tongues, without having the gift. Adam would not stop talking: "Bones of my bones, flesh of my flesh," meaning "She is in many respects like me, yet different from me." Adam noticed something that he did not notice in the animals—someone with the same essence, the same nature, and same characteristics as his. Still, he did not call her another man or Adam II. He gave her an identity—woman. The reason for Eve's identity is also given: "Because she was taken from man." There are strong indications here that this appellation related to both Eve's similarities and differences with Adam. The identity seems to convey both similarities and distinctions. The similarities were as striking as the differences were sharp. Adam noticed in Eve something that was different yet compatible to him. So when God, acting as "the first Father of the Bride" brought her to him, he immediately realizes the suitableness of their union. Note that Adam did not see another of himself. Eve was not his alter ego, but someone to whom he could relate. There was something in Eve that could meet his needs, and he had something that could meet Eve's need.

In conclusion, the first step in studying God's blueprint is to understand the nature of the people who are to enter marriage. They must be male and female with the potential to be fruitful and multiply and with the capacity to become mother and father within that union. Unless one rejects the whole account of creation of man in Genesis, we must subscribe to this principle. One cannot separate the creation of man as male and female in the image of God and the marriage institution. In fact, God certainly had the marital relationship in mind when he created Eve. A careful reading of Genesis 2:18-25 would reveal that Eve was not created to just co-exist with Adam; she was created so that Adam could have a suitable helpmeet. By the way, the word helpmeet or helper does not convey any pejorative connotation as though she was just there to give a hand to Adam. The same word is used to describe the Lord in other passages of Scriptures, such as Psalms 33:20; 70:5 and 115:9 where the Lord is clearly described as our helper. There is a tendency to avoid the idea that Eve was created for Adam as the Bible teaches in 1 Corinthians 11:8, 9, "For man did not come from woman, but woman from man; neither was man created for woman, but woman for man." That does not sound politically correct because of the potential misinterpretation and misreading of the text to suggest somehow that woman is inferior to man. This is preposterous! Inferiority and superiority of a thing depend on its nature and essence. Eve was made of the same essence as Adam and both were created in the image and the likeness of God. Because she was created for Adam does not make her any more inferior to Adam than Christ would be to us, since he came to earth, was born, and died for us. The idea here is that Eve's creation was intended by God to be a relational counterpart of Adam. That's the intent of the creation of male and female. God created one woman for one man. That's the Creator's blueprint.

✦{ IV }✦

BEGINNING THE JOURNEY:
THE DESIGNER'S BLUEPRINT AND
THE NATURE OF MARRIAGE

One of the experiences that I will cherish for the rest of my life is when the OBGYN handed me a pair of scissors and ask if I would cut the umbilical cord when my second child Jonathan was born. For me it represented the physical detachment from the mother to become attached to both of us emotionally. Although children continue to depend on parental care and protection, they have to be separated from the mother and receive outside of her what they need to develop normally. It represents the first detachment a child must go through in order to be fully functioning. The second detachment is usually when they leave to go to college. That separation is sometimes partial and temporary. For others it is permanent. Some keep coming back, others never return. I remember how my wife and I were hoping that our son, Jean Abede II would move back home for at least a year before he would leave for good. That second detachment is often necessary to develop their own sense of self, independence, and exercise of freedom to choose, to decide on their values, and to determine their priorities and course of their lives. Although it may provoke a lot of feelings of apprehension and anxiety for both parents and adventurous teen-agers, it is crucial and necessary leading to the next separation: the separation from the parents' tutelage, protection, and provision in order to be united with one's wife or husband. It involves not only physical detachment, but also emotional detachment. In order to cleave to their spouse, the individual must become independent enough from the parents to be able to form any meaningful relationship with his wife or her husband. The mutual cleavage requires a double separation whereby both the man and the woman leave their parents in order to become one. It is often difficult for some children to detach and for some parents to let go of their children. Many parents experience a fear that they have not done enough and that their child may not be ready to be completely detached from them. Those feelings, however natural they may be, should not prevent the normal process of separation. It must be anticipated and accepted. If parents have not done enough by the time children are ready to enter marriage, it's rather too late to try to add anything or correct any mistakes they might have made raising them. As I am experiencing alongside many parents, a person will always be a parent with the love, care and concerns for their children at whatever age they may be. However, the role of parents must vary with ages and stages of the child's life. When the time for leaving comes, it must be welcomed and adjusted to like any other stage in life. The detachment does not mean total severing of every tie with the parent. Care, love, affection, and honor to one's parents continue throughout life. However, in terms of priority in the marital relationship, they become secondary to the need to cleave to one's wife or husband.

The Meaning of Leaving

Before delving deeper into the meaning of the subject, it must be pointed out that there is an implicit definition of not just marriage in the passage but of the family as a whole. Leaving here has to do with leaving one's father and mother suggesting that God not only defines marriage as between one man and one woman, but also in so doing defines the family as composed of a father, mother, and at least one child.

Physical Separation

It should be obvious that physical separation is intended in the statement "man shall leave his father and mother." As stated earlier, the double separation is necessary for the mutual attachment between husband and wife. When the man leaves his parents' home to take a wife, he is demonstrating his independence from the parents' care, protection and provision, and the capacity to care, to provide, and to protect his wife. The wife, in turn, leaves the protection, care, and provision of her parents to enter the marital relationship in order to love her husband and to receive from him the care, protection, and the provision that her father was known for before the marriage. In both cases, the leaving is necessary since it demonstrates a level of independence and maturity that must be demonstrated by both parties. Leaving involves leaving the paternal roof to be on your own so that the process of becoming one flesh can be facilitated. In premarital counseling, it is necessary to help the fiancés assess their capacity for that physical separation. A lack of independence and maturity on that level may well indicate a lack of readiness to enter the marital relationship. Inasmuch as it is possible, parental cohabitation with newly-weds should be avoided. There are rare and unusual circumstances whereby a temporary shared living arrangement may become necessary. In such circumstances, open discussions of the boundaries should be considered to avoid any interference and/or disruptions in the cleaving process of the married couple. Too many marriages have been compromised, sabotaged, or even broken as a direct result of those interferences. In any case, they leave deep wounds that may take years to heal in all parties involved. The physical separation may be a difficult choice, but it is an important choice for the experience of happiness in the marital relationship.

Emotional Detachment

If physical detachment is not always possible, emotional detachment is critical with or without physically leaving the parental home. The couple must become emotionally independent of the parental bond and emotional attachment in order to cleave to one another. The emotional detachment does not in any way shape or form the filial affection and the natural love that children have for their parents and vice versa. However, in order to cleave to one's spouse, the love and affection of that spouse must take precedent over any other natural bond. The love of or for a parent will not be the same kind of love in the marital relationship. The emotional dependence that a child had with regard to the needs for nurturance and affection will take a new dimension in the marital relationship. In any marriage, if the affection toward a father or a mother is stronger than or even equal to the affection that a wife has toward her husband or a husband to a wife, something is terribly amiss. The habit of running to Daddy or Mommy when one has a booboo must stop when they get married. Any attention or support that Mom and Dad can provide will be in addition to what a spouse is providing and not as a substitute for the marital bond between husband and wife. Dad needs to know that his little girl is a grown woman now in the arms of a loving and caring husband who will now serve as her protector, provider, caretaker, and lover. Hopefully, Dad has done a great job preparing her for her new role as a wife. The tradition of giving the bride to the groom in the marital ceremony is a great analogy of both the physical and the emotional detachment. As one of the Cosby shows in the TV series demonstrated, Dad stood there and proudly answered the question, "Who gives this woman in marriage to this man?" His answer was "Her mother and I do." You have entrusted her care to the loving arms of the young man for life. This is not a loan, you can't expect to have her back or have her run to you whenever something goes wrong in the relationship. You may intervene if solicited by mutual consent, but you may never interfere in that relationship. The same goes for Moms. You should be proud to have raised a fine young man whom a lady has found suitable to marry and into whose hands she is going to entrust her life. Your work is done. Whether she feeds him pepperoni or tofu, whether he gains weight or not is no longer your responsibility or your business for that matter. If invited, you may visit them or offer any solicited support within the boundaries they have set. You may never interfere in their relationship to correct or undo any damages that might have been caused or created. Allow your son to develop his total affection and devotion to his wife who has now become her primary source of love and affection besides God. She has also become the primary object of his love besides God. Although children will continue to love and honor their parents throughout their lives, they should not be expected to have the same level of attachment and commitment as to their husbands and wives. While the spouses forsake the dependent ties that bind them to their parents, they are able to become inseparable from their husbands and their wives. A man or a woman whose 'umbilical cord' has not been severed is not ready for marriage. Often the parents are ready to let go, but some children for one reason or another are not ready to leave. A lack of readiness for leaving is a clear indication of a lack of readiness for cleaving. There must be a personal decision and readiness to leave. In Genesis 24:57, we have the example of Rebecca. When asked if she was willing to leave, she consented by saying: "I will go." It was a voluntary decision to leave her parents and travel many miles to be with a husband. In order to cleave, one must have the moral capacity and emotional maturity to leave and detach themselves from their parents. There are too many "Mama's boys and Daddy's girls" out there who cannot be the wives or the husbands God calls them to be because of their inability to detach themselves emotionally from their parents and to cleave to their spouses. Just like Rebecca, one must travel from their parent's home to embark on another journey, the journey of being glued together with their spouse and travel the wonderful journey of life together.

The Meaning of Cleaving

The verb to cleave has been translated from the original Hebrew *dabaq*, which means to cling, to keep close. Many commentators have rendered it as to stick or to glue. As such the husband and wife have become so attached or so "glued or stuck" together that their separation is inconceivable. Any way you look at the word, it conveys the meaning of intended inseparableness, attachment and permanence at all levels emotional, physical, and spiritual.

Emotional Attachment

When two people are married, there is passion; there is desire; there is need for each other. There is burning passion inside for each other, not a passing flame, but a deep longing to remain close to that person. Their hearts are so much devoted to each other that even temporary, physical separation does not diminish their attachment to each other. They are in each other's minds, thoughts and feelings. As I write these lines, I am at friend's house in Atlanta, Georgia while my wife of twenty-four years is in Boston. But, I can picture her in mind, sleeping, smiling, praying, and doing other things. I miss her, and knowing that she misses me makes me miss her even more. I cannot wait for her to board the plane and join me in a few days. That is, in part, what I think emotional attachment is—being so connected inwardly with the person that they invade all the dimensions of your life. This emotional glue that binds husbands and wives also involves the desire to share yourself with that person and to be interested in knowing what is going on in the life of that individual. That emotional attachment takes precedent over all other relationships. There is nobody else who is worthy of such devotion and attention in your mind. The emotional energy devoted to one's spouse is not shared by anybody else. Although one can become attached to a good friend, a parent, or even a child, the intensity of that energy is exclusive to one's life partner. This notion should be familiar to anyone who has been in love. You should remember well how it was when you were dating. What has been described in many cases as "butterflies in your stomach" could well have been the beginning of such emotional attachment, unless it was just the usual passing flame that burns for a moment until it finds another incendiary victim. Some would go as far as saying they cannot eat or drink thinking about the person. I have to confess, that when my wife and I were dating, she was in New York while I was at Dallas Seminary.

I would be sitting in class, and while the professor thought I was writing every word that came from his mouth, I was in fact writing love letters to her. I was emotionally attached. The best line I have ever read on that emotional attachment came from the French: *J'entends vibrer ta voix dans tous les bruits du monde."* Roughly translated, it reads: I hear the vibrations of your voice in all the sounds around me." We all have experienced these at one level or another during the dating process. Certainly the emotional attachment takes other dimensions as, over time, both of us mature in our love. Still, in order to cleave, the emotional attachment must exist between husband and wife. While many would admit having had that initial attachment at the beginning of their relationships, the greatest struggle for them is to either maintain or regain that attachment that characterized their union in the beginning.

Physical Attachment

The leaving of the parents' home to become attached to one's spouse clearly involves the physical movement and attachment toward each other. Physical attachment is the most obvious and visible meaning of the cleavage, yet it is often not respected in the marriage. Husbands and wives must live under the same roof, share the same bed, and literally be in each other's arms inasmuch as it is possible. There are circumstances that rarely mitigate against that, such as illnesses, military service, and migratory experiences. Those are unusual, uncontrollable and temporary life circumstances to which couples often have to adjust. However, physical attachment to one's spouse is the norm. The self-imposed physical separation of couples often reveals that other considerations have become more important at the expense of the marital relationship. Although not limited to it, the sexual union of the couple involves the physical attachment. In 1 Corinthians 7, the Apostle is very clear in his admonition against prolonged physical detachment even for spiritual reasons. Both emotional and physical attachments are implied in the cleavage between husband and wives. That level of attachment can only be broken by death, hence the meaning of "till death do us part." I remember a husband begging God to grant him at least another year with his ailing wife. The thought of her imminent death, the thought of being torn physically from her by death was unbearable. But realizing that she was suffering terribly from an incurable disease, he finally accepted God's will to take her to be with him. His attachment to her was so strong that he could not imagine being separated from her.

Spiritual Attachment

As a divine institution, marriage does not just involve our bodies and emotions, it also involves our faith, convictions, and spiritual commitment. The choice of a spouse, the understanding of the marital vows, and the conduct of the spouse within the marriage often reveals one's level of spiritual maturity. When the glue that cleaves the spouses together is not spiritually binding, it becomes difficult to experience the full joy of marriage as God intended it. The spiritual attachment involves the mutual understanding of God's expectations, instructions, and rules for marriage. When either one or neither one of the spouses lacks spiritual commitment, then the marriage is at the mercy of circumstances and social or cultural pressures. Spiritual attachment involves shared spiritual values, disciplines, and practices. Many years ago, a friend of mine preached a sermon that I will never forget. He said that the most romantic scene in a marriage is when a husband and a wife are both on their knees holding hands and praying together. Making time for prayer, worship, study of the Bible together, and sharing spiritual insight with one another would definitely put a big smile on the face of God.

Becoming One Flesh

In Ephesians 5 verses 30-31, Paul alluded to the concept of being one flesh analogously to our union as Christians with Christ. He then calls it a great mystery. It is indeed a mystery that can only be unraveled by the Spirit himself. According to Ephesians 5: 30, we have become members of Christ's body, his flesh and his bones by the Spirit of God. Eve, who is of Adam's flesh and bones, became one with him when she was joined in marriage to him by God. The two had become one. In answering the Pharisees' question on divorce, Christ not only referred to Genesis 2:18-25, he further commented on this phrase not found in Genesis: "They are no longer two, but one" (Matthew 19:6) Obviously, Christ's emphasis was on the permanence of their union or the inseparableness of the bond between husbands and wives. They were two at first, but now they had become one—no longer can two be made out of one. Once they have become one, they can no longer become two, only two halves. To accentuate this point, Christ strongly gave this admonition that I believe is addressed to husbands and wives, state officials, and church ministers, and other interested parties: "What therefore God hath joined together, let not man put asunder" (Matthew 19:6, KJV). Thus the one flesh principle conveys the idea of a permanent and lifelong union and intimacy between a man and a woman joined by God himself in marriage. The oneness that needs to be achieved affects all the dimensions of our being as individuals: emotional, spiritual, physical, and volitional. Such a wonderful mystery must be understood before embarking in the journey.

A Divine Act

Many explanations have been given to the expression "The two shall become one flesh." I think of all the interpretations given, the one that Jesus points to in Matthew 19 is the one that I would adopt. "*What God has __joined__ together . . .*" The underlying verb "join" is the best way to understand how two people can become one. They become one because they are joined together. One is not added to the other, but joined to the other. It is by virtue of the cleavage that they are able to become one. Note also that it's two—a complete male and a complete female—that are joined. Also, as previously discussed, the idea that they were incomplete like two halves and needed to be married in order to be complete is inconsistent with the biblical narration of the creation of

Eve. She was created a complete woman and a complete woman in the image of God and his likeness. Otherwise, unless someone is married, they would not be a complete person. According to Christ's teaching in the New Testament, it is the Creator himself who joined them in marriage. Marriage is not only God's institution, but a sovereign act by which the husband and wife are joined together to become one flesh. This sovereign act implies that when a man and a woman enter the marital institution, they are united in God's eyes according to his intent and purposes. This does not mean that God approves all marriages. Only those who follow his blueprint meet his approval and fulfill his plan for marriage. When God's ministers, either from the State or the Church, perform the marital ceremonies in the presence of witnesses, they act as God's agents in joining a man and a woman in marriage. They are acting under God's sovereignty, on his behalf to administer the oath of marriage. Since marriage is the Creator's institution, all parties involved in it should be sure to follow his blueprint in order to meet his approval. The sovereign act of God in joining a man and a woman to become one flesh is not devoid of human responsibility.

A Human Responsibility

Although the joining is done sovereignly by God, the parties involved play a significant role in the process of becoming one flesh. Note that we use two terms in talking about becoming one flesh: an act and a process. The joining is the act by which the two individuals are no longer separate; they have been made one. They are one in God's sight. But since the word "become" also conveys the idea of a process, it takes time for the union to be solidified and to manifest all the characteristics of that unity. It is the same concept of the "already" and the "not yet" that are often used when we talk about salvation and sanctification. A Christian is already saved, justified, and sanctified, but sanctification leading to glorification is the process of a lifetime. The same is true for becoming one flesh. By virtue of their union or their joining, husbands and wives are one, but being fully united takes time, personal responsibility, and choice to fully enjoy the process of that unity. The process begins with the necessity of leaving and cleaving in order to become one flesh. It takes both the detachments and the attachments discussed earlier to achieve beginning and then processing.

Emotional Interdependence

The idea of one flesh conveys among other things the concept of intimacy. True intimacy requires emotional interdependence. As discussed earlier, having created man with the capacity to love and be loved, God decided that Adam's need for intimacy was to be met by a suitable counterpart called Eve. Adam not only realized that need but also its fulfillment in God's wonderful creation of the one who was flesh of his flesh and bone of his bones. God's intention was that Eve's needs would be met through Adam and Adam's needs through Eve. That's what I call emotional interdependence; that's my definition of true intimacy— when both man and woman use their capacity to give and receive love in the relationship.

Interdependence, in my view, involves both the concepts of independence and dependence. As an individual created in God's image, man is endowed with the ability to reach out, to love, and to meet the needs of his partner. However, he himself has a void that he cannot fill on his own nor she on her own. He depends on someone else who has the same ability to reach out to him, to love, and meet his needs. In other words for true intimacy to develop, and in order to become one flesh, husbands and wives must choose to depend on each other. A lack of emotional interdependence in the relationship makes it difficult if not impossible for true intimacy to be achieved or experienced.

Unfortunately, there often is an imbalance in the relationship. Some spouses are in the relationship to receive not to give. They are the takers or the consumers. They get married to be taken care of by someone. They never see themselves as capable of meeting someone else's needs or with the idea that someone might depend on them to have their needs met through them. They resort to manipulative tactics in order to have their needs met. They don't give just for the sake of giving; they give in order to receive. Their idea of marriage is "quid pro quo," you scratch my back and I'll scratch yours. In many instances, marriage, even at the emotional level, becomes like a business arrangements; you do this for me, and I'll do that for you. That idea is often conveyed with the erroneous notion that marriage is 50-50. Emotional interdependence implies that each spouse makes the choice and takes the responsibility to meet the need of their partner while allowing them to do the same. Although mutuality should be expected in the marriage, it should not be confused with conditionality. As I write this, I am mindful of a wonderful statement found in Acts 20:35 attributed to Christ by Paul: "It is more blessed to give than to receive." I cannot think of a better concept than for those truths to be more evident in a marriage whereby a husband devotes his emotional energy to meet his wife's needs and for the wife to choose to do the same. The blessing or the happiness that ensues from that process would make the journey definitely more enjoyable and less painful. The emotional independence must be cultivated by dependence on God to meet our needs and using the resources that he has already invested in us to meet the needs of our partner.

Some spouses are too dependent emotionally in the relationship without realizing the dependence of the other partner on them to have their needs met. There are also some spouses who are too independent, unwilling to allow themselves to become dependent enough on their spouses to have their own needs met. It is not that they don't have a need for the other spouse, but for some reason, they suppress their needs and are not willing to appear too dependent. Often, behind the suppression is a fear of being too vulnerable, a fear of rejection, and a fear of their needs being frustrated. A husband confided once to a marriage counselor that he has ceased to rely on his wife to have his needs met because of repeated experiences of inconsistency, rejection, and frustration. Rather than continuing to be disappointed and frustrated, he has resigned himself to "get what I can when I can get it, expecting nothing." The tone of his voice and the choice of his words betrayed the resentment and the bitterness that characterized his feelings about the relationship. The choice to be less dependent in the relationship might have been learned through negative experiences either before or during the marriage.

In order for true intimacy to exist at any level or domain in the relationship, there must be emotional interdependence whereby both spouses realize how they are indispensable to each other in the relationship. When there is proper equilibrium of dependence and independence, the process of becoming one flesh is facilitated. When imbalance exists, it hinders the process and affects the quality of the marital relationship.

Oneness

Oneness is not achieved haphazardly or by itself. It involves a personal choice and a constant voluntary effort to become one. It requires both gains and losses. If you want to remain yourself, it will be difficult to become one with someone else. In order to become one, we must be willing to lose a little bit of ourselves in the other person while gaining whatever they bring to us in order to become united. People who are self-sufficient and self-satisfied don't need to get married. By the same token, people who want to keep what they have without giving up some of themselves will not only be miserable in marital relationships, but will also make certain that anyone else is miserable. The beauty of the relationship is in mutual self-abandonment and self-giving. Self-absorbing individuals are not ready for marriage and may not be able to experience the oneness that marriage requires. Nevertheless, being married does not mean losing your personality, losing your values, or losing yourself. It does mean that as you grow closer to each other, and as you adapt to each other, some of your personality and personal attributes will be modified or even altered in order to become one with your spouse who hopefully is moving toward you as well. Oneness requires voluntary movement on the part of each party to move toward the other.

Oneness requires the ability to reconcile the differences. The most common reason for divorce nowadays is "irreconcilable differences." Whenever I hear that expression, I think of two selfish individuals who should have never gotten married to begin with. The differences were supposed to be what attracted them to each other. Certainly, having certain key values in common, sharing the same faith, and having key spiritual convictions are important and sometimes necessary in order to have a good marriage. However, being different from each other is what marriage is all about. Just like you would not want to wake up seeing another you in the bed, however repulsive that image is, you would not want to marry someone who is exactly like you in all aspects of your life and domain. It is the reconciliation of those differences that makes the marital relationship worthwhile.

Oneness requires acceptance of each other. Often in the marriage, oneness is not achieved because of the lack of mutual acceptance. There is a lack of knowledge of each other because of the refusal of letting that person inside. True oneness is difficult to achieve when the spouses are not open to each other. There are several factors that constitute barriers to the oneness in the relationship. First, lack of trust is often the primary barrier to oneness. It takes a certain level of vulnerability to allow someone to know you. Second, the fear of rejection often is what is behind the lack of trust. Openness is always risky when there is no assurance of being accepted. The underlying questions which couples often ask themselves can be expressed as follows: "Can I really trust you with myself, my deepest needs, my weaknesses, and my past? What will you think of me when you discover who I truly am? Will you ever use that knowledge against me in the relationship?" The lack of openness in the relationship not only affects the progress of becoming one flesh, but it causes the relationship to be superficial and creates a certain insecurity that threatens the stability of the marriage. Trust is built over time, and becoming one flesh is a process which develops gradually through experiences both positive and negative in the relationships. Openness is necessary for true intimacy. As the couples get to know each other, they learn to trust each other more and become more accepting of each other.

Oneness requires self-acceptance. The fear of rejection and the lack of trust often begin with self-rejection. While vacationing in the Dominican Republic, I had a chance to interact with a wonderful couple who had traveled from Europe to spend some time alone to work on their relationship. After applauding the man for taking such a responsible initiative, I offered them a free counseling session since our hotels were not far from each other. They were in love with each other, and they both wanted to experience whatever possible happiness they could in their relationship. After a few minutes of conversation with both of them, I realized that their main issue was related to lack of trust. Behind the lack of trust that threatened to destroy their relationship was a terrible fear of rejection. The woman was being haunted by a past of which she was not proud. Although she believed that God had forgiven her and restored her life by giving her a loving and caring husband, she could not completely trust him. Her problem was not that her husband was not trustworthy. She continued to reject herself and projected her feelings onto her husband. Her problem was that she could not fully accept herself; she was too ashamed of her past. She had a difficult choice to make. She needed to choose to accept God's forgiveness, accept herself as one who has been redeemed and restored by Christ, and learn to trust her husband, who apparently was fully accepting of her and did not care much about her past. Self-rejection has the tendency to paralyze growth in the process of becoming one flesh. Lack of self-acceptance is a serious handicap to oneness and intimacy.

Sexual Intimacy

Most biblical commentators agree that becoming one flesh involves sexual intimacy. In 1 Corinthians 6:16, the Apostle Paul put the one flesh principle in the context of being sexually united in one body with someone. We will address the issue of sexuality within the marriage, but provisionally, we can affirm that Paul provided the best physical illustration of true intimacy. Sex between married couples is the bodily expression of the intimacy and the oneness that exists between couples. In fact, that's why I believe that the Bible condemns sex outside of marriage as well as before marriage. When two people, who are not committed to each other in marriage, engage in sexual activities, they make a mockery of true intimacy by using the expression of a reality that does not exist between them. That reality has to do with the commitment, the emotional interdependence, the oneness, the trust, and the intimacy that exist at the intellectual, volitional, moral, and spiritual level through cleaving to one another in marriage.

The expression found at the end of Genesis chapter 2:25 speaks a volume on the level of intimacy that must exist between husbands and wife. *"The man and his wife were both naked, and they felt no shame."* You cannot be more vulnerable than exposing yourself to someone. We are talking here of those of who have no respect for their body and are ready to expose themselves to anybody for fame, fortune, or illicit pleasure. A little bit of shame here should be in order. Unfortunately, there is no shame and no guilt nowadays with regard to nudity, self-exposure, and sexuality before or outside of marriage. What a shame! The expression *"The man and his wife were both naked, and they felt no shame"* Gen.2:25) means more than exposing their body to each other. They were innocent and pure in motives and actions; after all they had just gotten married. In the context of becoming one flesh through emotional interdependence and oneness, self-acceptance, and mutual acceptance, they were saying through their exposure that nothing is hidden, no cover-up, no hidden agenda, no rejection of either self or of you. Their transparency and vulnerability manifested the trust and the confidence of the relationship. They were fully accepting of each other. Both Adam and Eve were to some extent saying to each other, "Here I am, what you see is what you get, you take me as I am, and I take you as you are." That, my friends, is marriage. If you have to hide, make up things, pretend to be somebody that you are not as an attempt to impress your fiancé/e and force them to accept you, neither one of you is ready to get married. And if after getting to know your spouse in the marriage, you end-up feeling ashamed of them, you have not truly loved. Mutual acceptance before the marriage and during marriage is necessary for becoming one flesh.

I think Solomon expressed this mutual acceptance, self-giving, and oneness in the Song of Songs 2:16, "My beloved is mine, and I am his." What trust, what confidence, what security those words convey! I wish more husbands and wives could use such words about their marriage. Those words would not be uttered if there was any reservation about the oneness that characterized their relationship. In order to be able to express the same sentiment, there must be a mutual experience of emotional interdependence, mutual acceptance, and oneness at all dimensions that are also expressed physically and sexually in the marriage.

What then is God's blueprint for the marriage: a permanent and lifelong union between a man and a woman created in the image of God with potentials for reproduction and who are cleaved together to become one flesh in mind, spirit, and body through emotional interdependence, oneness, and sexual expression to the glory of their Creator. Anything outside of this blueprint is a violation of God's intent, design, and purposes for marriage.

BEGINNING THE JOURNEY:
CHOOSING THE RIGHT PARTNER

I was nineteen years of age and living more than 200 hundred miles away from my parents' home. For the first time, I was spending New Years Day by myself. I was depressed, sad, and dejected. Fortunately, there was a college professor of mine who had taken a paternal interest in me and who was living nearby. I stopped by his house unannounced. He graciously let me in and gently asked me, "How may I help you?" I jokingly said, "I stopped by to get my New Year's gift from you." He smiled and asked me to sit down. He offered me a glass of lemonade and a piece of special bread, which I enjoyed. "That's all I have," he said. I laughed and said, "I'll take it." Then he proceeded to say, "Before you leave, there is something else I would like to offer you." Once he said that, I knew I was in for a treat because, you see, this college professor was a very wise man and loved to share his wisdom with young people—young people like me who valued the advices, guidance, and instructions of more experienced elders. He offered me one of the best New Year's gifts I have ever had. He counseled me on the three most important questions in life. Even though today, I am a middle-aged man, much older than my college professor was at that time, even after many years of studies, teaching, counseling, and pastoring, his words still resound in my mind as though it was yesterday. Here is what he shared with me that night. The three most important questions in life are as follow: first, where will you spend eternity? Second, what will you do for a living? And third, who will you marry and live with for the rest of your life?

My college professor did not insist much on the first question. He knew of my faith in and personal relationship with my Lord and Savior, Jesus Christ. He brushed on the second question by simply stating that I needed to have a focus on my major and career. He added that, however important that might be, making the wrong career choice could be corrected since I was still young and with plenty of opportunity to change my mind and change the direction of my life in that regard. He then jumped to the last question and said, "Choosing the right person to marry is the most critical decision you will ever make in your life next to where you will spend your eternity. For before heaven, if you are going to heaven, you may spend a life in misery, regrets, pain, and bitterness for having chosen the wrong person for the wrong reason and have to live with her for the rest of your life."

I wonder how many people are reading these lines and nodding their heads in agreement with the professor. I also wonder how many of my readers have read those words with some tears in their eyes because of their current situation for having made the wrong choice of a life partner in marriage. The pain, the agony, and the suffering that marriage causes in our society, the heartbreaks of the children, and the emotional toll on those who are caught in a loveless misalliance are too much to even describe in this book.

Over the years, both at the clinic or at the church and even in casual interaction with friends and acquaintances, I have discovered how right my professor was. The choice of a marriage partner is the most critical question we must answer next to our decision to go to hell or to heaven either by believing or rejecting the Gospel message. At the time of this writing, I can picture in mind the many couples who have sat across from me pounding at the consequences of their decisions.

In my first year of psychological studies, I was given an assignment that included an interview interaction with three married couples. One of the couples admitted that they realized that they were not made for each other, that they had married the wrong person. They had been married for five years with two children. They believed that God would not approve a divorce and felt condemned to be miserable together for the rest of their lives. For the same assignment, I had a chance to interview a couple who had been happily married for fifty-five years. They were still holding hands and kissing each other in public. They confessed that it was the Lord who had brought them together.

What are the factors involved in choosing a mate? What are the criteria that determine a right or a wrong choice for marriage? Is it a matter of taking a chance or being lucky? How can I be sure that this person will make a good wife or a good husband? What should or will influence my choice?

First, we must stress the fact that marriage is a serious decision that demands time in planning and preparation. People tend to think of marriage in a very passive way. They fail to play a more active role in the choice to either remain single or to marry. Although they think of marriage, they view it as something that will happen if they are fortunate enough to meet the right person by chance or coincidence.

A lot of people approach marriage with a lot of fear and trepidation because of negative familial experiences or unresolved emotional conflicts resulting from previous relationships. There is often tension between wanting to get married and the fear of falling into the wrong marriage. Some people experience some confusion in terms of what to look for in a mate.

There are three kinds of knowledge one must possess in order to make the right choice for marriage: First and foremost, we must know what marriage is all about by having knowledge of God's blueprint for marriage. Before considering the journey and with whom to embark on this journey, we must know what the journey is, what is expected of you and your partner, and where the journey leads. That will help you determine whether you or your potential life partner has the right resources and the equipment for the journey. God's definition for marriage, his intent and purposes, and guidelines are critical not only for you but for the person that you think you can embark with on this journey. There must be a way of assessing that person's understanding and acceptance of God's blueprint for the journey. Otherwise, you might find yourself either stuck on the road or going on a solo trip after the journey has already begun. What a nightmare that would be!

The second kind of knowledge that you must possess before considering the choice of a partner is the knowledge of yourself. This is crucial because we are often aware of the true motives behind the choices that we make in life. There are a lot of personal factors and psychological issues that are involved in our choices. We need to be aware of them and how they will influence our choice so that we may make a more or less objective decision of a life partner.

Third, we need to have at least some knowledge of the person with whom we plan to embark on this wonderful but challenging adventure called marriage. It is difficult to know everything about anybody since getting to know your partner is a lifelong experience with all the changes and stages of life. However, there are certain things you need to know about your partner before making a commitment or asking him or her to make a commitment to embark in this "chemin de non retour" (no turning back journey).

Knowing Yourself

In my training as a psychologist, a lot of emphasis has been placed on background information. In addition, one of the things I emphasize in teaching psychological testing and personality assessment is that no psychological evaluation would be complete or even valid without a thorough review of relevant information about the individual to help interpret the tests results. One of the assignments that I enjoyed in one of the Doctor of Ministry classes at Dallas Seminary is the life story exercise. It was interesting to note how many things we can discover about ourselves just by taking the time to retrace our history in terms of our experiences, defeats, successes, trials, disappointments, happy occasions, encounters, break-ups, accomplishments, and failures. An honest inventory, whether personally undertaken or through the help of a trained professional, would reveal so much about ourselves, our fears, apprehensions, unmet needs, desires, motives, and many important factors that contribute to our character and shape our attitudes about life, relationships, and the choices that we make.

In case you wonder whether the art of knowing oneself is psychological babbling, let me remind you that in many instances the Bible encourages us to take a personal inventory. For instance, on many occasions, the leaders of Israel take the time to retrace their stories to bring them to a better sense of their present and their future. There are many other instances God's people are encouraged to bring to mind concerning the experiences of life's journey with the Lord. The reason is to better understand their current circumstances and approach life differently than they would normally do without the reference to their life stories.

When it comes to personal relationships, it is even more crucial to take that personal inventory before embarking on the road. As you contemplate entering the marital relationship, you must bear in mind that you are going to share your inner self with someone whom you will expect to do the same. It is important for both parties to engage in that personal inventory to discover who they truly are. People often experience disappointments in relationship as though the person waited until the marriage to reveal their true self. Often, it is not out of dishonesty; it's rather a lack of awareness of who we truly are. We present ourselves in a socially desirable manner in order to be accepted by others and end up making choices on the same basis. Many marriages are broken because they were founded on superficial attributes that do not hold true in the marriage. Most often, the decision was based on lack of knowledge of ourselves and of the other person. The place to begin is a personal inventory like a life story assignment to get to know ourselves and use some of the same criteria to get to know others around us.

What would a personal inventory reveal and how can we use this information appropriately to make acceptable decisions about ourselves and for ourselves? Usually, a personal inventory would reveal a series of patterns in our life, especially in the area of relationships in terms of experiences and the kinds of people we have encountered, how we have dealt with difficult situations, things, and people who have positively or negatively influenced us. It helps us to look at mistakes that we have made in past relationships and areas in which we were successful as well. We might also want to evaluate what we were looking for in those dating relationships. What criteria did we use and which ones are still important or relevant to us. A personal inventory should reveal to us the values—personal, familial, cultural and spiritual values that are non-negotiable in choosing someone to marry.

Another important piece of information that a personal inventory might provide is in your area of strengths and weaknesses in dealing with someone of the opposite sex, especially in communication, conflict, resolution, restoration, and reconciliation, etc. It is also important to assess your real needs and your station and direction in life. This is particularly relevant to those who have already decided on a particular career choice or vocation and their hopes and aspirations. For those who have not yet done so, they should carefully assess the level of flexibility they must have or should expect from their potential life partner.

Although this might be difficult to do on your own, an assessment of past relationships with the significant others in your past might be very helpful. Relationship with people such as parents, friends, and co-workers might have shaped your thinking over the choice of a partner for the journey. There are decisions that we make in life that are forced or shaped by negative experiences of the past. There are deep wounds that may need to heal before considering contaminating someone else with them.

As previously discussed in the Chapter 1, there are experiences that even as children force us into making decisions on whom we will choose to marry. For instance, children who grow up with abusive fathers may resolve to avoid such men in their life, thus vowing not to relive the same experience. The danger in such cases might be the tendency to project that father image onto all good potential candidates who might not be abusive at all and who have other good qualities that we tend to overlook. The reverse is often true. We tend to look for those traits that are contrary to our negative experiences while overlooking some that are important and may pose a greater challenge to our marital relationship. While we may run away from any sign of harshness that reminds us of the abuses that we have suffered, we miss out on the honesty, the caring, and the responsible leadership that may be behind what seems to scare us. By the same token, we may be deceived by the softness and kindness of a mate while overlooking the lack of important convictions and decisiveness that will be necessary later on, especially in times of crisis or other difficult situations. Through personal inventory, you might also discover that there are certain needs that you are trying to compensate for in the choice that you are making or have made. There are a number of people who marry above their station of life to compensate for feelings of inferiority. Others marry to compensate for failures in previous relationships to show that they can do better this time around. They may just want to appease their own consciences over the break-ups in an attempt to convince themselves that it was not their fault; it was the other person who could not appreciate who they truly are.

As you can deduct from all this, there may be a lot of things about you that you don't take time to know. Those things affect everything that you do, your thinking, your feelings, and your attitude about the most important decision that you will make after salvation. All of us have a past—we grow up in a sinful world; we are not perfect; we grew up with imperfect parents, however well-meaning they were; we make mistakes; and we have been hurt at one level or another, some more so than others. Hopefully, we have been healed and restored from those negative experiences. However, if the personal inventory reveals anything in your life that needs to be addressed before deciding on a life partner for the journey, take some time to address those things. They are not only likely to affect your choice one way or the other; they will continue to affect your relationship in the marriage in ways that you may not yet imagine.

A couple of years ago, a young man came to me and expressed his desire to marry a particular girl. She was beautiful, talented, and attended a good evangelical church. In his eyes, she was a catch. However, based on what he shared with me about himself and this girl, I strongly advised him to delay the marriage and to separately seek individual counseling as well as premarital counseling to address certain issues that would definitely have an adverse impact on their relationship. Unfortunately, he did not have that kind of time. I wish I could say that my advice to them was unnecessary.

Knowing yourself involves making an assessment of who you are. The person that you are today may not necessarily be a product of your past since we believe in God's power for restoration and redemption, but they are things that you make you who you are that will take time to reverse, if ever possible. Redemption from sins does not always eradicate all the consequences of our past experiences. Even when it does, it is a process that may last a lifetime. There may be areas in your life, in your personality, and even in your character that you may need to address before asking someone to share some of the baggage of these things.

Personal inventory helps you be honest with yourself and with the other person. You don't have to pretend to be somebody you are not. Certainly, you have some wonderful qualities that make you worthy of someone's love and partnership. Even if you have blown it in the past, you don't have to continue to live a life of hypocrisy hoping someone would not discover. Your family background, your entourage, your social status, your education, or your cultural and ethnic heritage do not have to be suppressed or denied in order to earn someone's hand in marriage. No one is worth so much effort or pretense, and being found out may cause disappointment, loss of credibility, and lack of trust and respect. Those things are hard to regain once you have lost them, especially in relationship.

Personal inventory helps develop true love. When you are superficial, then the love itself is superficial. You don't want someone to fall in love with the mask that you are wearing. When the mask is removed, the love will go with it. I love the title of the song "Just As I Am." One of the reasons I love the Lord Jesus Christ so much is the fact that his love for me is real. He took me just I was and loved me anyway. I know no one will ever love you or care for you like Jesus, but you will not know until you let them love the real you. You are not perfect, but you are lovable. Let the person make a real decision, a real choice of you based on who you are and not what you pretend to be. It begins with knowing yourself and learning to accept yourself for what God will make of you when he is through with you.

As stated earlier, knowing what the journey entails and knowing who you are will help you decide on the resources and equipment that you need for the road but also who would you want to travel with you. Does that person have the right resources for the trip? The choice is critical for the journey. The partner you choose will determine whether it is enjoyable or not. Even if you follow the right path, if the partner does not follow the same path you are traveling, certainly it will be a long and arduous trip to nowhere enjoyable.

Knowing the Partner You Want to Choose

It is often said that you can never truly know someone. If someone wants to fool you, they will. The examples of those who have been fooled by pretenders are numerous. How can we expect to know anybody when we don't make the effort and often do not want to know ourselves? How can we expect others to be honest with us when we are not even honest with ourselves much less with them? My training in psychology is geared toward helping people discover the truth about themselves in order to deal effectively with what is behind the issues that land them in my office. It is always interesting to note how often defensive and resistant people can be when confronted with the truth about themselves. It is difficult to know people, but honesty begins in the first person. Honesty with yourself allows you to be authentic and transparent with others. Although they may not always reciprocate right away, they eventually discover that they don't have to pretend around you. Your acceptance of yourself makes it easier for them to accept you and to expect you to accept them as well.

The key to knowing people is to know yourself and use the same honest criteria to evaluate their behavior and attitude. The basic truth about yourself is that you are not all that you think you are. You are a sinner saved by grace, redeemed by the blood of Jesus Christ, and indwelt by the Holy Spirit who is producing Christ-likeness in you through the ministry of the Word in the body of Christ. That's what it means to be a Christian. It is true for you as well as the other person you want to consider for the lifelong journey. Granted not everybody is at the same pace on that spiritual journey; in fact, not everybody in the church necessarily meets the above definition. That's why you need discernment. In fact, one common complaint is that there are too many fakers in the church. It is often asked of me how I would know if someone is spiritual or not. My first answer to the question has always been "It takes one to know one." Often people are looking for a spiritual person to marry when there is no evidence of spirituality in their own lives. If you are living a spiritual life as defined by the Word of God, then you will know how to identify the things that make you spiritual in someone else. In other words, the same criteria that you use in your honest personal inventory, your life story, and how you deal with those issues from your past should be a good place to start when you want to get to know someone. Through that process, you will come to know what issues need to be addressed and to be resolved, and how the past experiences affect their current attitudes and behaviors. You will also discover how honest they want to be about those issues and whether or not they are willing to seek help in dealing with them. If you perceive any resistance on that level, you know you are dealing with a pretender. Watch out! Any information that was relevant to you in your personal inventory should also be relevant in your attempt to get to know that person, and you should not dismiss it.

In order to know whether or not you have the right partner for the road, there must be the beginning of openness at some level that facilitates a more or less well informed decision to venture on or to put the trip on hold at least for now or as far as that particular person is concerned. However, you don't have to wait until you are ready to consider the marital journey to start planning or making preparation. It may take years of experiences and preparation. Ability to form relationships, especially lasting ones, is not something you improvise overnight. It is a long process that involves time, energy, and wisdom along the way. The process of getting to know a particular someone begins with getting to know people in general and narrowing it down to someone else. You should always be distrustful of someone who has never been in any meaningful relationships, who never has someone they can call their friends, and who all of a sudden wants to make you their best friend for life. You will be an experiment, not a true friend. You get to know yourself and people through interaction, exchange, resolution of conflicts, communication, and trials and errors in relationships.

The AFDEM Theory

In that regard, I have developed a theory that can be used as a process from A to M. It represents the stages of the dating process. I call it the AFDEM theory.

+ A stands for *Acquaintance*
+ F stands for *Friendship*
+ D stands for *Dating*
+ E stands for *Engagement*
+ M stands for *Marriage*

Each letter represents a stage and each stage has different levels and subcategories. I will summarize the meaning of each one in the following lines, but before delving into them, I would like to point out that God created us in his image according to his likeness, and with the capacity to relate to him and to others. We have clarified the relational dimension of our essence in Chapter 2 of this book. Our ability to relate to others before marriage and even outside marriage can be a good indicator of how successful we will be in the marriage. We don't become all of a sudden sociable. We are social beings, and our ability to relate to other people must be demonstrated over time through insignificant relationships building up to the most significant relationship on earth: the relationship with our wife or husband. We must be available to form and to seek those relationships by which we can know through feedback and learning how to prepare ourselves for marriage. We can cultivate valuable friendships through fellowship with other believers, even with the opposite sex, in a way that honors God and prepares us for our future life partner.

The Acquaintance Stage

An acquaintance is someone with whom you are familiar because you know the person through personal information and have had some level of experience with that person. It can be because of work or church related activities. You may even have some personal interests in common and share some activities. Your interaction with that person is usually related to those shared interests or activities. In the Acquaintance Stage, there are intimate details about the person's life that you do not know. You would not share too much personal information with that person either. Neither would you be interested in knowing more about the person. You share a level of kindness, courtesy, and preference toward that person when among strangers or those with whom you are not so acquainted. Certainly there are different levels of acquaintances depending on opportunities for interactions, exchanges, or shared activities. You can have any number of acquaintances, some of whom you may even call friends and who may consider you as a friend. But in reality, friendship goes deeper than acquaintance. Having acquaintance with both sexes is a good thing; the interaction and socialization process can be very nurturing, providing you with much information and perspective from both sides. Human relations of any sort are very enriching and can progress to even more meaningful ties. Many good friendships begin as casual acquaintances that progress over the years to inseparable ties and some to even deeper levels. As social beings, we need to engage actively in developing those relationships with other fellow human beings.

The Friendship Stage

A friend is someone beyond the level of just acquaintance whom we know through personal contacts and personal information. We have some common interests and common activities, but beyond those mundane or spiritual interests, we are interested in each other as a person. With acquaintances, it is the activities by which you relate to one another, but as friends, it is the person that is the object of interest. It is someone you love spending time with and with whom you share from your heart. There is in the other person a level of mutual acceptance and trust as well as confidence to the point that you may risk certain vulnerabilities. Certainly there are various levels of friendships. Friendship with the opposite sex is very good preparation for marriage when the people are mature enough to cultivate an open, honest, and pure friendship that does not compromise their respect and trust in each other. They respect each other enough not to jeopardize their shared moral and spiritual values. They are able to disagree without being disagreeable and learn to deepen their friendship through resolutions of conflicts, appropriate confrontation, and open communication. During the Friendship Stage, having several friends of the opposite sex can be very enriching. Through these intimate interactions with members of the opposite sex one can learn a lot about oneself and the other party, especially when the trust level allows them to show their weaknesses and strengths through difficult situations or crises in the friendship itself. That would be ideal. Unfortunately, nowadays, the world has become so corrupt that not even outsiders could trust two people from the opposite sex to cultivate a meaningful friendship without being suspicious of inappropriate behaviors. We have become so uncivilized that we can't love each other without compromising our virtues, even as Christian brothers and sisters in the Lord! Because of that fact, people usually jump from acquaintances to dating, ending up focusing on carnal relationships that are usually broken or end in marriage without proper preparation and often for the wrong reasons. It is often sad to see people leave those they have known all their lives, with whom they grew up and with whom they were familiar, but have now entrusted their future into the hands of a complete stranger that they have known for only a few months. Often they feel they are not impressive toward nor impressed by those they have known. They are more apt to fool and be fooled by a stranger than to learn to accept each other and to allow the friendship to progress into a more meaningful relationship. Admittedly, it is sometimes a risky proposition to ask a close friend to develop a closer relationship with you. Most often, the fear of rejection and of losing the relationship entirely makes it more difficult to envision such progression. However, it is a risk worth taking compared to going into a life journey with someone that you don't know as well as you know your friends. Ideally, out of the many friends that we have, there would be one or two whom we might consider or desire to spend more time with, and whom we would like to know better and would start dating.

The Dating Stage

The term is not used here in the sense of going out on a date with someone. There is nothing wrong in two friends and even two real good acquaintances from the opposite sex to share a meal together or attend a concert together. Mutual respect and trust from two mature Christians and civilized people should allow for these kinds of outings without any concern, suspicion, or criticism from themselves or others. As Christians we should not let what is going on in the culture intimidate us from respectfully enjoying the fellowship that God allows us to have in the body of Christ. We should be able to set the tone and to serve as models of true friendships and meaningful dating patterns for the world. Every stage of the process of my A to M theory falls into the category of getting to know one another more and more. The Dating Stage is the level at which friendship takes a more exclusive turn. While you both can continue to enjoy the friendship and the fellowship of others, you have decided to take your friendship to a more serious level of getting to know each other. Either at friendship or dating level, there must be a commitment for mutual trust and respect and a level of openness that allows for disagreements, conflicts, resolutions, and getting to know oneself and each other in the process. All through the process, personal inventory and assessment of the relationship can be conducted to determine whether or not another level might be worth exploring. It is unfortunate that often boundaries are not set or they are overstepped forcing the couples into premature decisions about marriage before they are ready or when they should not consider marriage at all. But all things being equal, the Dating Stage can lead to consideration of the other person as being worthy of a lifetime commitment. Although it might raise a number of questions in the mind of on-lookers or cause the couple themselves to question each other's judgment, dating is more of a social road that may lead to proposal and engagement.

The Engagement Stage

After praying, soul-searching, and carefully seeking advice from respected others, and careful examining of both personal and interpersonal resources, the couple may now enter the Engagement Stage, which is almost the last step, but not the last. Granted that a public commitment and announcement are made, the two people are not yet married and should not consider themselves to be so or to behave in any way shape or form like married couples. Many engagements have been broken, and the harm done to one or both individuals either social and/or personal can be repaired. Even during the engagement, the couple is still getting to know each other and may decide at any point during that period to call off the wedding, even if a date has been set or the caterer retained. The Engagement Stage is more emotionally binding than anything else. It is survivable. I'd rather have ten broken engagements or even more, than one broken marriage. A broken marriage is like cutting a person in half while they are still alive whether they stay in the marriage or get divorced. Reparation is possible, but complete restoration is uncertain. As a twice divorced husband told me, "People are never the same after a divorce, and as a several times divorced Hollywood actor stated it, it always hurts to the core." But if everything works out well, then the couple will embark on the wonderful and adventurous journey called marriage, with all the joy and the blessings that God intended them to experience. That is what this book is all about. There you have it, from "A to M" (AFDEM) or "Alexandre's Theory for the Dating Process."

Using the Process

The first thing to be learned from the process is the need to take responsibility and to play an active role in search of a life companion. The process is designed to help you get to know the person you would be interested in for the marital journey while doing your own personal inventory. Before and during the process, you might want to learn to realistically formulate and prioritize what you would be looking for in a spouse. You need to make sure you separate fantasy from reality and trivial pursuit from the necessary ingredients for a marriage. Too often we find people establishing criteria that has nothing to do with the reality of their own lives nor does it measure up to things that are lasting or that will make or break a marriage. There are certain things that may be a preference but not a priority in any relationship. Wishing to marry a tall woman might be nice, but that won't matter much in times of crisis and in conflict resolutions. Marrying someone because they speak well may later on mean that they can articulate well the insults that they will throw at you when things go wrong in the relationship or when you act "stupidly." The muscles that make you go "gaga goo goo" may be used to break your jaws ten years from now. I know you are laughing, but seriously, don't make life decisions on trivial or passing attributes. Be serious, you deserve much more than that.

A lot of people build criteria for marriage on soap operas and romance magazines. There are certainly more profound values and virtues than these to look for in a man who will be, whether you like it or not, the designated spiritual leader of the home. There are certain qualities and virtues that you should look for in a woman, such as those found in Proverbs 31, that should be more important to you than her height or her weight or her skin tone.

Praying for the Right Mate

What about prayer? Whenever you think of prayer, whether for a mate or for anything else, think of two terms that are paradoxical but reconcilably represented by the two sides of the same coin—divine responsibility and human responsibility. As Christians, we should trust in and depend on God for everything, i.e., every aspect of our lives. Nothing is too small or too big for us to bring to the Lord in prayer. In fact, I deplore the fact that we don't spend more time in prayer for a mate. We pray for every thing else: houses, college education, jobs, etc., but we neglect to pray about the most important decision of our lives after salvation. As mentioned earlier, you rarely hear someone ask for prayer in public or in private, especially women, about finding the right person to marry. I was thrilled one day when one of my daughters in the faith came to me and said, 'Papa, I don't think I have the gift of celibacy. I need you to pray for the right guy to come along," and she added half jokingly, "Quick!" Well, the Lord has not been as quick as we both would like, but we are still praying. There is no shame in taking our needs for a life companion to the Lord in prayer. But prayer is not a substitute for taking responsibility to play an active role in finding the right person through the steps outlined above. While asking the Lord to send the right person, and I believe that He does more often than we think, we need to pray for wisdom and discernment in discovering the right person whom the Lord would want us to embark with on the journey.

What We Have Not Yet Talked About

We have gone through an entire chapter about choosing a life partner for the journey without saying one word about love. I am sure you were questioning that. What has love got to do with it? Love has everything to do with it, but not in the sense that you think. If there is one thing that you need to know from reading this, it is that love is not a feeling, although there are a lot of feelings related to love. Love not only is not a feeling, it is a decision that permeates the process at all levels, taking different dimensions and proportions during this process. It is a decision that grows overtime through experiences, getting to know oneself and the other person. It grows with values, experiences, priorities, and the choices that we make along the way. What about physical attraction and attributes? They are great as long as they come with more lasting virtues. They are like the gift-wrap—what is inside is what we should be interested in. It is great when the gift-wrap is not worth more than the gift itself or serves as an indication of the value of the gift. But we know too well the disappointment of a nice package that is well adorned on the outside but with a cheap gift inside, something of no value for which we have no real use. We say "Thank you" to be polite, but in reality we wish it was not so well wrapped, creating an anticipation that turns out to be deceptive.

Many years ago when in my 20s, I preached a sermon on 1 Samuel 16:7, "*But the* LORD *said to Samuel, 'Do not consider his appearance or his height, for I have rejected him. The* LORD *does not look at the things people look at. People look at the outward appearance, but the* LORD *looks at the heart.'*" To illustrate the message, I brought two gifts, one wrapped in a beautiful box with a little ribbon around it, the other was wrapped in a piece of paper I picked up from somewhere. I placed them in front of me and said, "I have two gifts here; whoever gets to either one of them first can keep it." I made sure to place a real gift in the dishelved (*chiffronen*) gift, and I placed a piece of rock in the nice, well-adorned box. Several people who were sitting up front rushed to the box, and a lady took it and raised it in the air proudly. I felt bad. Only one person picked up the real gift. I wanted them to know that the Lord looks not on the outward appearance, but into the heart, and he can give us wisdom to do the same. Don't get me wrong, physical attraction is great. If you were to see a picture of my wife, you would know what I mean. In Genesis 12:11, the Bible says that Abraham's wife Sarah was a beautiful woman. However, true beauty is inner beauty. It's a particular grace when you can find both, but in the absence of outward beauty, you should go with the one that will last—inner beauty.

The marital journey is an enjoyable journey if you follow God's blueprint and have the right partner for the road. Finding the right partner is not a mystery. It is a very serious endeavor that requires time, energy, prayer, and wisdom. However, when led by the principles and the guidelines of the Designer, it becomes easier. He can equip you with the right resources for the journey and allow you to find the right companion to take with you on the journey and to experience all the joys and blessings he has in store for you!

~{ VI }~

ENJOYING THE JOURNEY:
FOLLOWING THE RIGHT PATH

I remember how I reacted to the title of the best-seller book *Happiness is a Choice* written by my former professors, mentors and benefactors, Frank Minirth and Paul Meier. I thought to myself, "If happiness was a choice, then everybody would be happy. For who in their right mind would not choose to be happy?" Actually, many years later, I am paying for thinking this way. I get the same reaction when I announce to people that I am writing a book entitled *Marital Happiness Is a Choice*. Perhaps, even you had the same reaction when you first read the title of this book. Some might even react against such a title, knowing how hard they have tried to be happy in their marriages and yet end up being miserable. A husband said this to me once, "You don't know how hard I try. We have gone to counseling; we have read books together; we have gone to retreats, yet the pain of living together is so unbearable that sometimes I wish one of us was dead." I can't count the number of times I have sat down with couples and individuals who are disillusioned about the whole concept of happiness in their marriages. Both as a clinician and a minister, my heart aches so many times for people who want to be happy in their marriages and yet are agonizing over the fact they may never experience the degree of happiness they were hoping for in their relationships. Some wish they were never married, others are hoping for a miracle. Still, the tears that flow from the cheeks of couples sitting in counselors' offices, at home, in pastors' studies, or court benches are enough to make a river—not mentioning those who are suffering in silence with no one to turn to, with the ache cutting them inside like a knife, digging deeper and deeper every day and every passing moment. Many years ago, a man told me that it was easier for him to be in Vietnam because there he was fighting a known enemy. In his marriage, he said that he was fighting an unknown enemy, someone who was supposed to be his best friend. A wife told me that she has been married for almost thirty years, and she can count on her fingers the number of days of joy and happiness she has experienced in her marriage. These painful stories have motivated me to write this book with a view to alleviate the pain and the suffering registered.

If you were to ask people what they want out of their marriage, most of them, if they are honest, would respond simply, "I want to be happy. I want to live in peace and harmony with my spouse and family and have joy." Everybody wants the story of their marriage to end with this line: "And they live happily ever after." Yet, if you were to ask them what would make them happy in their marriage, the answer would vary from one couple to another. While everybody aspires to happiness in life and in their marriage, they don't pursue it the same way, nor even have the same definition of happiness. It becomes an ever elusive concept, and all are left to wonder with the Psalmist in 4:6 "Who will shew us any good?" (KJV).

What is happiness anyway? The Declaration of Independence of the United States teaches that the pursuit of happiness is our "inalienable right" along with life and liberty. However, we are not told what it is or how to pursue it. How will we recognize it when we see it? As soon as we begin to define it, we discover how wrong we are. For instance, one would think that having fame, pleasure, and fortune would make someone happy. No sooner do we think that than some famous and rich person is dead from a drug or painkiller overdose. We see people getting married and seeming to be happy, and before you know it, they are in a divorce court vowing never to speak with one another as long as they both shall live separately. Happiness is one of those concepts that are difficult to define and even harder to experience as a condition. While you may be happy in one domain, you are miserable in another. For many, it is partial, temporary, or altogether non-existent on this earth. Yet, we are pursuing it like a hunter going after prey in the forest. It does not take a rocket scientist to know that pleasure, entertainment, and euphoria are not happiness. Those are transient, passing experiences that last only for the time they are being enjoyed and brings no lasting joy.

There are three roots to consider when one attempts to understand the concept of happiness and how it relates to your marriage. The first one comes from the Latin root *beatus*. In the first section of the Sermon on the Mount in Matthew 5, we become familiar with the word beatitude because of the term "blessed" that Christ uses. The word beatitude itself comes from beatify or to make happy. The Latin root *beatus* speaks of consummate bliss or blessedness. It denotes a general satisfaction, contentment, and abundant joy. That's the first idea of happiness, a state or condition of general satisfaction and contentment. The second root, which is found in the Greek, is the word makarios, meaning blessed. This originally described the transcendent happiness of the gods, happiness beyond care, labor, tears, and even death. It describes a state that transcends circumstances. The third root comes from the Hebrew word *'esher* or blessed that speaks of an abundance of happiness and/or joy. Taken together all three roots for the word happiness strongly support the idea of blessedness, satisfaction, and contentment. When studied in many biblical texts, whether in Psalm 1:1, Psalm 32:1, or Matthew 5:3, being happy or being blessed is the state or the outcome of doing what is right or the condition that results from being or doing what is consistent with God's will and righteousness. Those who are pronounced blessed or happy in the Word of God are those who are living right, whose sins are forgiven, and who have demonstrated the character that is consistent with God's kingdom. Vincent's Word Studies, which discusses the etymology of Greek words, considers happiness or blessedness to be the principal element in the New Testament. Happiness or blessedness gives a sense of God's approval founded in righteousness that ultimately rests on love for God. As such, happiness is not something to pursue; it is a state to be found and something to experience as the result of pursuing the right thing. Marital happiness begins with the choice to follow God's blueprint, guidelines, and principles with regard to the marital relationship. Those principles are in many respects universal and can be applied by anyone under common grace. That's why even some non-Christians can experience some degree of happiness in their marriage by acting in a way that is consistent with God's design, intent, and purposes for marriage. However, since happiness is related to being in and acting according to God's will and glory, there are some experiences that should be unique to those who are committed to honor God and glorify him in their relationships. It is unfortunate, however, that because of sin and disobedience, the rate of divorce for Christians is almost as high as it is for non-Christians. To our shame some non-Christian husbands treat their wives better than Christian ones, and some non-Christian wives do a better job in accepting the leadership of their husbands in the home. In light of that, the following points will be discussed in this chapter:

- Marital happiness is God's ideal and purpose, but may not be achieved apart from his principles.
- Marital happiness is a personal and continual choice. Each individual must enter the marriage with the purpose of making the other person happy while cultivating their own happiness.
- Marital happiness is sacrificial: the sacrifice of one's self, one's selfish motives and one's unrealistic expectations.
- Marital happiness may be cultivated and preserved by each spouse. When each spouse makes the commitment to honor and glorify God in the relationship by ministering to each other, they can achieve true marital happiness.
- Marital happiness should be but may not be mutually experienced.
- Marital happiness is related to emotional and spiritual maturity.
- A degree of contentment and satisfaction can be achieved by being obedient to God and seeking to glorify him even when it does not bring immediate results.

+ Marital happiness <u>does not mean</u>
    1) All my needs have to be met by my spouse.
    2) My spouse will always understand me and will work to make me happy.
    3) Marriage is 50/50; therefore if I do my 50% and she does her 50% in the marriage, we will be happy.
    4) I will be happy only if my spouse is happy in the relationship.
    5) You have to have money in order to do the things that will make your marriage happy.

Marital Happiness is God's Ideal and Purpose

One of the attributes of God that is displayed in creation is his goodness and his loving-kindness toward mankind. He created a wonderful universe and handed it over to man for his enjoyment. The only thing of all creation that was not good was man's solitude, and he again intervened miraculously to meet that particular need so that man lacked nothing. Marriage was instituted for our enjoyment: to have a best friend with whom to laugh and play, someone who would be there with us and for us through thick and thin, someone who would love and care for us, someone whose company we could enjoy with the blessing of the Lord, giving praise and glory to his name for being such a thoughtful, generous, and benevolent God. Boy, have we fouled things up! The source of joy became the source of pain and suffering. We have turned the blessing into a curse by turning our back against his design, intent, and purposes. According to Romans 11:36, everything that we receive from God, whether in creation or in redemption, is by his grace and for his glory. Our marriage is also a gift from God to be lived for his glory. As we follow his principles and obey his rules for the marriage, we enjoy the blessings that ensue, and his name is glorified. When we experience those blessings and are happy with our spouse and demonstrate our gratefulness to him for such gifts, God's name is glorified. When as Christians, we live with our spouses in such a way that demonstrates to the world what it means to love and be loved, his name is glorified. In order to glorify him, we need to go back to his blueprint as discussed in Chapters 2 and 3.

Marital Happiness is a Personal and Continual Choice

Each individual must enter marriage with the purpose of making the other person happy while cultivating their own happiness. The choice that we make to follow God's path for a blessed marriage does not end with just finding the right partner and entering marriage. Certainly, as we have demonstrated, it does not happen haphazardly or passively. It's a process that requires a personal, informed decision and active engagement to follow the path God has laid out and to begin the journey with the right partner. It also requires consistency and continuity. So often we find couples who start out well, but who, in the middle of the road, start to rethink their commitment and when faced with some hurdles on the road are ready to give up or stop altogether. It takes a constant renewal of the initial decision and commitment to continue to experience the happiness that God intends for us to have in the relationship.

One of the impacts of sin is an attitude of selfishness and pride. Since Adam and Eve looked for their happiness and enjoyment outside of God's will by focusing on their needs, self-centeredness entered their hearts and ours. So instead of focusing on God and on each other to have our needs met, and instead of letting God meet our needs his way, we take matters into our own hands looking for our own happiness at the expense of the glory of God and of the needs of our spouses. If each couple were to focus on the happiness of the other person and the glory of God, things could be much easier for us. Most of the complaints in marriage have to do with blaming the other for failing to meet "my needs." As we will see later on in the discussion of the marital vows, each spouse makes independent vows to meet the needs of the other person with no strings attached. I have never heard a spouse say on the wedding day: "to have and to hold IF . . ."

Marriage works best when the husband focuses on doing the things that would make his wife happy instead of looking for areas where she fails to make him happy and vice versa. Certainly reciprocity should be expected, but not as a condition to act in certain ways toward one another. When two people are married, there is a mutual expectation that is expressed in those terms. "I am going to do everything that I can to meet your needs while I am going to leave it up to you to decide on how you are going to meet mine."

It is always risky to trust your happiness into the hands of someone else. If that person means well, then you have nothing to worry about. However, there are spouses who have learned the hard way not to trust and depend on their partner to meet their needs. Repeated experiences of neglect, inconsistencies, and selfishness on the part of either spouse leaves a lot of unmet needs. There is a terrible continuing that ensues because unmet needs lead to frustration. When frustration is prolonged, it turns to resentment. When resentment is not dealt with, it leads to bitterness. Bitterness destroys intimacy and turns the marriage into what a French columnist called the marriage of Prince Charles and Princess Diana "a loveless misalliance." We all know the public and private pain that this couple experienced when their marriage was broken. The glamour, fame, and fortune that characterized their position and lifestyle could not save them from the misery and agony of heartbreak. To avoid or break this cycle, each couple must be conscious of the other spouse's needs in the marriage and honor their commitment to meet those needs inasmuch as the Lord has allowed and commanded them to.

It is often said that marriage is give and take. It's true, provided that the giving is not conditioned by a contingent upon the taking. Happiness in marriage is a shared experience when each spouse finds joy in meeting the needs of the other person. The question that is often raised is this, "What if I married a selfish person who is in the relationship to take and who has not learned to give?" The joy you experience in giving would at least meet your need partially. If you stop giving at all because there is no reciprocal activity toward you, then you would contribute to the miserable cycle above. God has made marriage in such a way that our needs can be at least partially met when we meet the needs of the other person. For instance, if you are married to someone who loves to talk and does not like to listen, you will have at least a chance to know what they think just by listening, and that in turn may modify what you were about to say or give you a new perspective on it. The best example is in the area of sexuality. Even in this a person may be reluctant to give in the act, but your needs would be met to some degree as you focus on giving your partner pleasure. Certainly, full bliss is achieved when both parties focus on meeting each others' needs in all domains of the relationship.

In addition, there is a level of satisfaction that you can experience just by being obedient to God and doing what you are supposed to do. Your Father will be glorified by your obedience, and you can be sure that in his own way, he will see that eventually your needs are met—just continue obeying and honoring him in the relationship. Sometimes we become discouraged and give up too soon. Remember that the Apostle Peter in addressing his exhortation to the "daughters of Sarah" in 1 Peter 3:1-6 urges the wives who are married to non-Christians or disobedient husbands to live in such a way that they may win them over through their chastity, meekness, and quiet spirit. Paul seems to make the same implications in 1 Corinthians 7:16 when he commanded that the non-believing spouse is "sanctified" by the believing spouse, and that the believing spouse should not leave the non-believer if he "be pleased to dwell with her." The principle here is applicable to both husbands and wives in the sense that the spiritual, obedient, or Christian spouse should continue to display in the relationship the virtues of godliness even when there is no reciprocity. We need to trust God on that. We need to learn to cultivate our own happiness in the marriage without being self-centered. While we seek to do everything in our capacity to meet the needs of our partner, we also need to trust God for our own needs and rely on him to do what is necessary in the relationship to meet our needs. The happiness that comes through obedience to Christ can bring you the joy that you are seeking. In John 15, Christ in speaking to his disciples admonishes them to abide in him and his Word and to keep his commandments. In verse 11, he states: "These things have I spoken unto you, that my joy might remain in you, and that your joy might be full." (KJV) True happiness or the fullness of joy is found in obedience to Christ's teachings and commands. That is not a cliché.

There is a feeling or better yet, a sense of contentment that comes with pleasing your Master that surpasses any pain that you may experience out of deprivation of someone else's attention. A lady shared with me the joy she experienced in forgiving her husband who had mistreated her so badly that her family thought she was crazy for reconciling with this man. She said that she had stopped making her happiness dependent on how he treated her. She found joy in doing things for him just because she knew that Christ was pleased with her. That's remarkable!

Marital Happiness is Sacrificial

Hopefully by now, you have realized that happiness is not only possible in your relationship, but you can experience it as a result of choosing to do the right thing. In other words, your choice to do the right thing in your relationship will help you know what it feels like to be happy as you travel the journey of life with your partner. Making the right choices is not always easy. Well, forget "always," they are never easy. It takes sacrifice. Often the choice that you have to make is between your needs and your spouse's needs, between your feelings and their feelings, between your rights versus their rights, between pride and humility, between forgiveness and bitterness, between your family and their family, between your career and their career, and between your parents and their parents. I could go on and on. Each one of those choices is difficult to make. It will take a lot of grinding your teeth, shaking your head, or pacing the floor. However, to do the right thing that is consistent with God's will is never easy, but always rewarding.

Often in marriage, people realize that they have to make sacrifices in order to bring a certain level of happiness to themselves and their spouses in the relationship. They are willing to sacrifice time, energy, money, career, and even ministry opportunities at times. But they are unwilling to make the greatest sacrifice of all, the sacrifice of self. The self with its pride, rights, needs, and preferences is the one standing in the way of your happiness most of the time. It is self that holds us back in choosing to let go of certain things in order to move on with our lives together. We tend to be too sensitive, too protective, and too pitiful of the self. Self-sacrifice is just what it is, the sacrifice of the self for the benefit of the two of you in the relationship. However, it's always easier to go along with self than to oppose its tendencies or to discipline it into making the right choice.

A pastor shared with me an experience that he had one night with his wife. They had a habit of praying together and kissing each other good night before going to bed. A habit they had maintained for over fifteen years of marriage. However, one night there was a heated argument, and he felt that he was right and his wife was wrong, except that she would not admit it. After arguing for a while, they finally decided to call a truce since they needed to go to sleep and wake up early in the morning. He had to preach the next day. His heart was still heavy when they "prayed" and kissed each other good night. He pulled himself onto one side of the king-sized bed and left his wife on the other side. A river could run in the middle. He was not able to sleep. There was no intimacy. He agonized for about a half-hour telling himself that his wife was the offender; she should make the first step in getting closer. After a few more minutes of wrestling with himself, he almost literally had to grab his right hand with his left and drag himself across the bed, so he could place it on his wife's shoulder. He discovered that his wife was just waiting for him to respond. That set the stage for a much more enjoyable time together. After that, he was able to have a good night's sleep and woke up refreshed and ready to preach one of his best sermons. He then realized that it was the smart choice. Sometimes a simple choice to stay on your side of the bed might determine a restless night, interrupted sleep, and cold shoulders for days. He had to overcome self.

I am sure you can come up with many stories like that one. You get the picture. The choice might be simple but not easy to make because of self. The more you worship self, the less you will be capable of sacrificing it for the betterment of the relationship. The key to sacrificing self is the understanding of the one flesh principle—you are no longer two. Since you have become one flesh, then the self has to be sacrificed for the benefit of both of you. If you insist on pleasing self at the expense of the two, you will soon realize that self will be miserable being by itself. The best thing you can do for self is to submit its needs to the needs of the marriage. The benefit far exceeds the cost.

Marital Happiness is Related to Emotional and Spiritual Maturity

In Chapter 2 of this book, we spoke of the image of God as involving the capacity for relationship, the capacity to love and be loved, and the capacity to understand what it takes to be in relationship with someone else. It is true for all human beings. However, not everybody is at the same level of the continuum. Sometimes spouses behave in such a way that it is questioned whether or not they should have ever married. They act in such a selfish and childish way that they are not even aware of the other person much less their feelings, their role, and their contribution to the relationship, and how their behavior might affect the other party. It takes both emotional and spiritual maturity to experience marital happiness.

Emotional maturity is the ability to manage one's emotions and to express them appropriately when necessary so as not to cause damage to self or others. The emotionally mature individuals are very much aware of their emotions. They do not deny, suppress, or even repress their emotions. They allow themselves to experience those emotions without acting on them. They are not impulsive, but rather exercise self-control. They know when to listen and when to speak. They know when to respond and when to delay their response to avoid causing more damage in crisis or volatile situations. They have the capacity to challenge, question, and learn from their emotions. They don't always justify their emotions nor their reactions because of the way they feel.

Among the abilities that the emotionally mature possess is the awareness and sensitivity to others' emotions. They avoid causing the same offense over and over in relationships. When they are wrong, they are secure enough to admit it and to make amends whenever possible. Emotional maturity is important in marriage to help manage conflicts, facilitate communication, and navigate through difficult waters of the relationship. Emotional maturity is demonstrated in language, actions, expressions of feelings, and capacity to compromise and make concessions in order for both parties to be satisfied in the relationship.

There are various scenarios of both wives and husbands acting immaturely in the relationship and fighting over trivial matters and issues that are not worth fighting over. There are times that all people need is to grow up a little. For husbands and wives to have conflicts over which suit or skirt should have been worn to a particular event, or the scores on a particular sporting event is ridiculous. Often, those discussions are symptomatic of other issues in the relationship. The need to be right and the need to feel that you have the upper hand in everything can be behind a lot of silly arguments. You should learn to save your energy for more important fights like where the kids are going to school and whether or not we should move out of town. Fighting over McDonalds or Burger King is unnecessary. Both are fast food places that will affect your health if you abuse them.

One of the ways to understand emotional maturity is to think of its contradistinction. When you think of emotional immaturity, think of children. The most common attribute of emotional immaturity is selfishness. The younger the child, the more selfish they are. Babies don't care about anyone else but themselves. They have no understanding of delayed gratification. When they want something, they need it now or else they will fuss, cry, throw tantrums, or make a scene until their needs are met. They don't care how tired you are or whether you had time to eat yourself. They just want what they want at the expense of everybody else. Do you know anyone like that? It may not be the one you think. It may be the one that occupies your chair or stands in your shoes. A lack of awareness and sensitivity to your spouse's needs is a sign of emotional immaturity.

Another characteristic of babies or children in general is lack of self-control. I remember the embarrassment of some parents during a dedication service. There they were, proudly dedicating their baby to the Lord before a congregation of a thousand people on a Sunday morning. The pastor, I guess, held the baby too close to his portable microphone, and everyone heard an interesting noise that resounded loud and clear in all the church speakers. It was hilarious. Well, that's what babies do! It does not matter when or where. In the same way, immature individuals are not always aware of their surroundings or the timing of their outburst. They need to learn to manage their emotions in their relationship instead of constantly living with frictions and conflicts that are sometimes unnecessary.

Spiritual maturity and emotional maturity are closely related, but are not the same. Their manifestations may be similar in many respects. Many of the things described above about the emotionally immature can also be said of the spiritually immature. Emotional maturity is achieved through practice, learning, and experiences. Spiritual maturity is the work of the Holy Spirit in the life of the believer. Spiritual maturity also requires practice, learning, and experience, but cannot be accomplished solely through those things. Both emotional and spiritual maturity requires time, effort, and energy. None is achieved passively. Paul was indeed indignant in admonishing the Corinthians for fighting over trivial matters when they should have been grown up and dealing with more serious stuff. (1 Corinthians 3:1-3) His indignation was based on their failure to use the opportunity they had to grow. The author of the book of Hebrews also helps us to understand what spiritual maturity is also about. In Hebrews 5: 11-14, we discover some of the symptoms of the spiritually immature: dullness of hearing and the need to learn the same basic things over and over again. They keep making the same mistakes dealing with simple issues in relationships. They have an inability to grasp or understand substantial information about themselves and others, but they prefer the simple stuff. It is often said that some people major on minors and minor on majors. They fight over trivial issues while neglecting more important issues in the relationship. The reason for their immaturity is their refusal to apply the basic principles and to grow. They continue to repeat the same mistakes and have not learned to practice the things that would improve their relationships.

One of the characteristics of the spiritually immature is lack of judgment or discernment. They are not able to distinguish what is constructive from what is destructive to their happiness in the relationship. They are easily influenced by negative sources. They listen to what feels good to them and not what is good for the relationship. They are usually insecure and dependent with diminished capacity to contribute substantially to the relationships. They always blame others for what happens to them. They also lack the capacity of introspection, of examining themselves, and of learning from their mistakes. In fact, they are incapable of even questioning themselves and their reactions.

The spiritually mature person is not selfish; he does not walk according to the flesh (self), but according to the Spirit as described in Galatians 5:19-23. The spiritually mature person has the capacity to discern the will of God for the relationship. They seek to do what is pleasing to God in all aspects of their lives, and they are able to display the fruit of the Holy Spirit in their lives.

The spiritually mature person also has a servant attitude and seeks to minister to the other party instead of waiting to be served. Marriage provides the first and greatest context and opportunity to demonstrate the servant attitude that Christ expects of all his disciples. If we are called to wash each other's feet in meekness and humility displaying the love of Christ to one another in the church through our attitude and ministry, we should begin with our spouse. It takes emotional and spiritual maturity to be a true servant anywhere—beginning first in the home. There are still opportunities to grow for those who might have started the journey with the wrong map or without the knowledge of the divine blueprint for the relationship. The journey can still be enjoyable if we are willing to use the Creator's principles and apply his teaching along the journey. The path is clear for those who seek to honor and glorify

God in their relationship and experience his blessing as a result. The choice to do so is the choice of marital happiness.

What Marital Happiness Does Not Mean

"All my needs have to be met by my spouse." One of the sources of disappointments as well as overburden in the relationship is the notion that once a person gets married, all his needs will be met in the relationship. First, it is necessary to distinguish your needs versus your desires because even the Lord never promised to satisfy all of our desires. In fact, according to James 4:3, one of the reasons the Lord does not answer our prayers is because often our requests have more to do with our lusts and desires than our real needs. In addition, even those things that we need, we don't always get right away. The Lord often teaches us to be patient, to wait on him, and to learn to do without the things we think we need.

Second, even though the needs are legitimate, to expect a human being to be able to meet all our needs all the time is definitely unrealistic. Marriage, however, does provide the context for our needs for close intimacy, partnership, and exclusive ties to be met through our spouse. There are certain needs that can and should be met within the marriage. Obviously, the need for intimacy must be only met within the marriage; otherwise, according to Hebrews 13, it would dishonor the marriage bed with grave consequences. The need for fellowship with other friends and brothers and sisters in the body of Christ should continue to exist after marriage. No one should become isolated from the fellowship of other Christians because they are married. Men will need to meet with other men in the church for fellowship, sharing, mutual encouragement, accountability, and mutual sharpening as indicated in Proverbs 27:17. Women will need to do the same with other women for the same reasons.

A word of caution is necessary here about having other needs met outside of the marriage. It should never be a substitute for the marital relationship nor at the expense of marital harmony. It should never pose a threat to the security and the stability of the marital relationship, however innocent it might be. There is grave temptation to use outside sources to meet our needs when they are frustrated in the home in whatever capacity and at what ever level it might be. A lot of people think that because they are not having an affair, its okay to have their needs met outside of marriage. They engage in "innocent" activities to appease and reduce their frustration level and get whatever they cannot get at home. It might not be so innocent if it distracts you from investing what you should be investing in your marital relationship thereby making the spouse's role unnecessary. It could be anything like seeking personal approval from friends and family when the spouse is not supportive of one's decision or accomplishments. It could be eating at Mama's house when the home cooking is not so great. Or, it might be getting enjoyable compliments from other men when the husband fails to notice the sexy dress that you are wearing. It can happen at work, in church, in school, anywhere. Have you ever thought of how that would make your spouse feel? Your "innocent" little games may be like playing with matches.

Another fragile area to watch out for is making friends with the opposite sex. There is a basic rule that should be considered. Any friendship with the opposite sex that is not approved by your spouse should be eliminated, no matter what level. Having friends in common would be ideal when it does not pose a threat to the relationship. No friend should be important enough to fight over with your spouse. Letting go of family members and close friends you have known for years might be a difficult but necessary choice.

Even when the friendship is approved, you need to be aware of how much you are investing in it and how much distraction it might be causing. There is an emotional energy that you should never invest in anyone if it serves to diminish your need for your husband or for your wife. It might be a simple issue of asking someone else to do something for you behind your spouse's back that you have been waiting for them to do. It can be as "innocent" as asking the next door neighbor to cut your grass for you or trim your hair. Those "innocent things" may send the wrong message to your spouse and set a bad pattern for you. A small match has the potential for igniting a big fire. For the "spiritual one," it might mean asking a friend to come and spend times of prayer with you when your spouse is not the prayer warrior you hoped they would be.

In the age of e-mails, chatting, instant messages, texting, or even sexting, there are a lot of "innocent" and "not so innocent" opportunities to distract us from the emotional investment in our own marital relationship and pose serious threats to the security and stability of the relationship. You must not be naïve nor play dangerous games with your relationships. Some marriages are broken or are paying terrible consequences because of those little games. We need to establish strong boundaries both as individual spouses and as couples to preserve what we have.

There is a tendency to believe that what your spouse does not know will not hurt them. That's a very slippery road to travel, my friend. It may end in a terrible crash! Many people think that they are not being unfaithful or sinful if they have not committed adultery. Being unfaithful involves investing in something or somebody else what you should have invested in your wife or your husband. If the time you spend with that person, the messages you send, or the e-mails you exchange would make your spouse suspicious or feel unnecessary or even threatened, you have already been unfaithful to them, even if they never find out about it. If it meets a need for you that your spouse fails to meet, then you are unfaithful. Watch out for those outside of your marriage that love to make you feel appreciated when you feel so unappreciated at home.

I Will be Happy Only if my Spouse is Happy

True marital happiness must be shared by both parties in order to be fully enjoyed. It is hard to imagine a part of the "one flesh" being unhappy without affecting the whole. However, since happiness is a choice, one spouse may choose it while the other, for some reason, refuses to make that choice. There are many factors that may contribute to one's unhappiness beyond the marriage. Sometimes there are issues that precede the marriage or issues outside the marriage that cause a particular spouse not to fully enjoy the relationship, even when everything about the relationship is going fairly well. It can be lack of spiritual growth, emotional healing, personality factors, or just a persistent choice to be miserable and make everybody else around them miserable. What is the other spouse to do? You can be as supportive as you can; you can pray, and you can be patient. You may also resolve to experience some degree of happiness by doing what God has allowed you to do to honor him and glorify him in the relationship. Your joy will come from the knowledge of being obedient to God and caring and loving in the relationship, even when your own needs are not being met. Sometimes, in such situations, these may be the only answers you might get from God. First, he can strengthen you in the inner man so that you will be able to hang in there knowing that you can do all things through Christ (Philippians 4:13). Second, you may hear the only thing that Paul heard when he was going through a difficult ordeal: "My grace is sufficient for you" (2 Corinthians 12:9). Choosing his path is the only sure way to experience happiness—even when it is the hardest thing to do. You will never regret it!

VII

ENJOYING THE JOURNEY: APPLYING THE MARRIAGE VOWS ALONG THE WAY

Groom: *I, Previlon take thee Sylvania to be my wedded Wife, to have and to hold from this day forward, for better for worse, for richer for poorer, in sickness and in health, to love and to cherish, till death us do part, according to God's holy ordinance.*

Bride: *I, Sylvania take thee, Previlon, to be my wedded Husband, to have and to hold from this day forward, for better for worse, for richer for poorer, in sickness and in health, to love, cherish, and to obey, till death us do part, according to God's holy ordinance.*

According to historians, those original wedding vows found in The Book of Common Prayers were first published in 1549. Since then, with some variations over the years, they have been used in various languages as a binding oath between grooms and brides all over the world. Nowadays, many church ministers or wedding officials allow the couples to write and pronounce their own vows at wedding ceremonies. However, whether personally written vows or a varied version of the originals, they all commonly reflect the same sentiment and echo the same commitment.

What is always interesting to note is that there is no conditional clause in any of the statements pronounced by the groom and bride. Also, they repeat them separately, not together. It's personal and unconditional with no strings attached. Each spouse pronounced those words independently of each other. Each one is 100% responsible before God, society, and the church for his or her personal decision. That's why marriage is not 50-50. It's a 100% commitment to keep your promise to each other. Those words represent commitment based on extraordinary trust and love. They are made with confidence, and at great risk of their lives; they commit to each other regardless of the changes that the future may hold, and regardless of the changes that may occur in the other person's life, attitude, temperament, or personality. I don't know of a riskier proposition than that.

By taking this oath, a bride and a groom are taking a jump into the unknown. Although there are no terms or conditions attached, there is an implied expectation of reciprocity since they are both making those vows to each other. It's like putting your life into someone's hands as that person puts their life into yours. Nonetheless, the absence of reciprocity later on cannot be an excuse not to keep your part of the bargain.

A very famous French singer Sylvie Vartan made a declaration on her wedding day to the effect that she had said "yes" to her happiness with the certainty that she had signed her best contract. I am sure she was familiar with the word contract in the music industry whereby each party signs according to the terms of agreement. The difference between the marital vows and a contract is that there are no terms of agreement; there are no conditions in case the other person fails to honor their part of the deal; you are still responsible to honor and fulfill your part. That is why in the Bible in Malachi 2:14 states explicitly why God hates divorce— because it is a violation of the covenant. According to the Word of God, a covenant can only be broken by death. Actually, the word for covenant in the Bible comes from a word that means to cut, hence the expression "cutting a covenant." According to Genesis 15:9-17 and Jeremiah 34:18, a covenant was ratified by taking an animal and splitting it down the middle. After splitting the animal in half, each person stands in the two bloody halves of the animal with their backs to each other. Then they walk right through the bloody halves. It signified that the vow was deadly binding and each party is saying in effect, "May what happened to this animal happen to me if I break my oath to you." They expected to be split in half if the compact is broken, and the covenant is violated. That's how serious the marital vows are. Regardless of what your culture tells you about marriage, it is a binding covenant—"till death do us part."

What do the vows actually mean, how should they be applied, and what is implied when we repeat them?

I . . . take you . . . Marriage is an act of self-giving. When you enter marriage, you give yourself with no reservation to your spouse who in turn gives them self to you in the same manner. Each one then assumes the responsibility of taking the other. It is a tremendous trust that involves a tremendous responsibility. By saying "I do," you actually accept what has been entrusted to you with the confidence that you will have it and hold it as preciously as it was given to you. You are in effect saying to each other that you trust each other with your lives. I take the responsibility for your life and entrust you with mine. Other than God, my life is in your hands only, to live or die, to be miserable or happy, and to grow or to regress. At this point, there are three questions that need to be raised here. If you are not yet married, is the person you are considering worth being entrusted with such a heavy responsibility? Second, are you prepared to assume such a tremendous responsibility? And third, if you are married, what have you done to the life that was entrusted to you in marriage? The best way to look at the third question is to look at your wife or your husband now and conclude honestly that because of the relationship with you, they are a better person, a better Christian, and a happier individual. Are they more satisfied with their life because the two of you are married? While you ponder these questions, let's look at the next part of the vow:

. . . to have and to hold from this day forward. You have committed to accept the treasure entrusted to you and to continue to maintain it and hold on to it. There is no letting go of it. I remember the words of a song entitled "O Love That Will Not Let Me Go" that was written by a blind man whose fiancé abandoned him because of his blindness, and he had lost his scholarship to study. When his sister who was caring for him had married, he was left alone. He realized that the only thing he had going for him was the love of God that would not let him go.

A wife and a husband should be able to say or write the same thing about the love of their spouse, the love that will hold on to them, the love that will not let them go. It is for keeps, not just to have, but also to hold. The obvious meaning here is that "I will never send you away, no matter what. I will hold on to you even if you don't want me to hold on to you or stop holding on to me. I will never let you go." If only people would realize what they were saying, I wonder how many people would in fact repeat those words. How many people have turned those words into a lie? We live in a culture where we don't hold on to each other for too long. We tend to let go too easily.

. . . *for better for worse:* You mean these words are part of the covenant? I did not write them, I did not make you repeat them, but you did repeat them, didn't you? Often people repeat these words as part of their covenant in marriage and think that they apply to circumstances. It's true that they do apply to circumstances, and certainly circumstances will change. That's what life is all about, and you cannot predict the way they will change, or when or how they will change. That is unknown. Yet you are swearing that whether they change for better or for worse, your love will not let the other person go. That's a tremendous promise. For some it may mean that your dreams may be completely crushed and that the comfort you used to enjoy in your parents' home may be something of the past, or the freedom that you used to have may be difficult to maintain.

But circumstances do change—sometimes for the better, sometimes for the worse. However, "for better or for worse" may apply to the individual as well. There is a tendency to overlook certain weaknesses or character defects during the dating period with the hope that the person will change. We are growth-oriented individuals with the potentials to become better than we are. In fact being a Christian means that we are growing into the likeness of Jesus Christ. I believe strongly in the power of the Holy Spirit through the Gospel to change lives and to transform character. However, I have no guarantee that the person that you are taking to have and to hold will change for the better.

What do you do then if the change is for the worse? There is a lot of evidence that some people who were thought to be nice, kind, and courteous during the dating process were just playing "Mister Nice" until the marriage was over, the mask is removed, and the real monster shows up! That's your covenant. If you are in such situation, you need to remember your covenant and ask God to show you how you can continue to have and to hold in the relationship even if things are becoming worse.

A note of encouragement may be in order here. Before you throw the baby out with the bath water, you need to take a good look at your relationship. Usually circumstances or persons do not get worse in all domains or areas of life. Certain things may get worse while others get better. The person may not turn out to be all that bad. There are many areas in their lives that have gotten better while others have gotten worse. You need to count your blessings and focus on the areas that have improved in the relationship. They may have become a more caring parent or a more attentive spouse. Sometimes, if you look hard enough, you will find a lot of areas of improvement for which you should be grateful. At any rate, your vow was to have and to hold for better or for worse.

. . . for richer for poorer. In a materialistic world where we tend to value things, it may be hard to imagine this part of the bargain. Some people would rather say "for richer—yes, for poorer—no." Love that flourishes in good times when the economy is going well and dies down during recession is not true love. During the recession, people get laid off, lose their homes, and become deeply in debt. Accepting to lower your standard of living is not easy and can put a lot of strain on your relationship, yet that's part of the bargain. Even getting richer may pose a threat to the relationship. Sometimes it's the pursuit of riches, and material possessions that we have to adjust to in the relationship. Learning to prioritize the relationship over material possessions whether to have more or to live on less has been tremendously helpful in many of the cases that I have encountered. The love that binds you should be more precious to you than anything you might possess. It was an eight year-old girl that taught her parents a valuable lesson. While they were away on vacation, they came back to find their beautiful home burned to the ground and everything in it. The mother turned toward her husband, and sobbing said to him: "Honey, we have lost everything." The little girl

heard that and hugged both parents' legs and said: "Thank God, we have each other." We may have lost houses, finances, and jobs. Those things can come and go, and they can be replaced, but we need to continue to have and to hold each for richer or poorer.

. . . *in sickness and in health.* This is more common than you may think. Losing material possessions is one thing, losing one's health is yet another. Whether for a short period of time or for a long period of time, dealing with illness in the marriage is not easy. First, caring for a sick spouse not only requires a lot of patience and love, but worst of all, it may mean that your own needs are not being met. It puts a double strain on you. While attending to their needs, you have to learn to put your own needs on hold or suppress them altogether. The longer the illness, the more difficult is the adjustment period. In addition, in case of a prolonged illness, your responsibility might double all of a sudden when it comes to caring for the children or paying the bills. It's heartbreaking sometimes to see what some couples are going through when unexpected changes come into their lives in the form of illness. To continue to have and to hold in times of sickness is stressful. It sometimes creates a lot of insecurity and feelings of guilt on the part of the sick spouse who has become a burden to the other. The temptations to give up, to have your needs met outside of the home, or to give up altogether are tremendous. You will need a lot of endurance and faithful support from respected friends and family members as well as support from brothers and sisters from your church to go through a situation like that. But most importantly, you need to keep your word to your spouse to be there in good times and in bad times.

A couple I know is currently dealing with such a situation in a very exemplary manner. They were married only for a few years and had a beautiful little girl. They had projects, plans, and dreams. All of a sudden, the husband fell ill and had to undergo very delicate surgery. There is no quick recovery in sight. The wife continues to love him and care for him while carrying the burden of extra work and raising their little daughter. They go to retreats and church activities like any other couple. The wife is very active serving the Lord and coping with the situation with all the support she can get. She never complains, and she maintains her Christian testimony everywhere she goes. By the grace of God, she is hanging in there. She has taken him as her husband to have and to hold, for richer or for poorer, in sickness and in health, and that's exactly what she is doing. I am certain she is somehow being rewarded, or she will be.

On a less than encouraging note, I remember as a child hearing a friend of the family, who had been sick for a long time, praying and asking God to take her home to glory. She was tired of being a burden on her husband, and she had become resentful of being too dependent on him. I wonder what the husband had communicated to her either directly or indirectly during those difficult moments. It is important to know that while caring for a sick spouse, it needs to be done with a caring attitude and with love and respect so as not to create the feelings of resentment.

. . . to love and to cherish. The core commitment in the entire marriage covenant is a commitment to love. It is a covenant of love. The love that is of question here is not a feeling that comes and goes or varies with circumstances. It is a love of choice and of decision. The choice of happiness is the choice to love in good times and bad times whether or not feelings are present. It is a commitment-based love that will determine how you are able to have and to hold in poverty and riches, and in sickness and in health. It is a love that is constant because when the circumstances vary, it does not focus on the circumstances or on you; it focuses on the other person. You are concerned about the happiness of the other person instead of yourself. So when there is a change in the marriage or in the life of the other person, you do not resolve to self-pity, but see the challenges as opportunities to serve or minister to the other person in the marriage. It is the kind of love that creates feelings and does not depend on feelings. The feelings that are felt inside come as a result of acting lovingly toward the other person.

Too often people worry about falling out of love with their spouse because they don't seem to have the same butterflies in their stomach they used to have for that person. I often say to couples during marital retreats that in the absence of feelings of love, you need to make love. I don't mean going to bed, but making love in the sense that you don't have to feel love to act lovingly toward your spouse. Action can lead to feelings just like feelings to action. It is a principle that works most of the time with various individuals and even things. Take anything or any person, and start acting in a loving way toward them, and sooner or later you will discover that you will have feelings for them. That's how people become attached to any idol that begins as just an object, but any investment of time and consideration that is constant toward an object often leads to certain feelings of love. The love that we are dealing with here is not only an expressive love, but a demonstrative love. It is often said that love has various definitions dependent on the kind of words used in the Greek to discuss it. I think we can learn a lot from the original language about love, but the best definition we need is an operational definition, an acting kind of love that is not limited to feelings or limited to categories or context. It is the kind of love that is described in 1 Corinthians 13 in terms of what it does and does not do in whatever context, whether with friends, whether with brothers and sisters in Christ, or in the marriage. It is applicable in many contexts, but particularly in the marital context. It is the kind of love that helps us to have and to hold in good times and in bad times.

Besides love, the verb cherish is added. Cherish is the demonstrative kind of action that lets the person know that they are precious to you and that you truly care for them. It is not doing things for the sake of doing things for them, but doing them because you care about them. Cherish conveys the idea of tenderness and warmth. In other words, it means to make your spouse feel special. There are many creative ways you can demonstrate how much you cherish your spouse. The journey becomes more enjoyable when each spouse devotes time and energy to show the other not only how much they are loved, but particularly how much they are cherished as a treasure.

During several marital retreats conducted with hundreds of couples, the sponsor provided a list of things that they knew a person could do to make their spouse happy. At first, I was tempted to provide you with the list, but I don't want to spoil your surprise or destroy your own sense of creativity. I will venture to mention some universal ones like remembering to do something special for them on their birthday, initiating some things you would not normally do for them, and learning to find their particular likes and dislikes, maximizing on their likes and minimizing on their dislikes.

. . . to love, to cherish and obey. Note the slight variation in the vows between the bride and the groom at this particular juncture. The word obey is added. The politically correct thing to do would be to just ignore that little addition and move on lest some people should be offended. We will deal more thoroughly with this issue under the chapter that addresses the role of husbands and wives in the relationship. But provisionally, if you follow closely, the vows are based on a biblical understanding of what marriage is all about. Love and cherish are based on the admonition to husbands with regard to their relationship with their wife. In Ephesians 5: 25, husbands are urged to love their wife as Christ loves the church. If you skip a few verses and jump to verse 29, you will find that two verbs are added to illustrate how husbands are to love their wives: cherish and nourish. However, in regard to wives, they are urged to submit to their husband as the church submits to Christ. The word "submit," which may imply to obey, appears both in Ephesians 5:22-24 and in Colossians 3:18. However, in 1 Peter 3, Christian wives are expected to behave like "daughters of Sarah" and are urged to follow her example. In verse 6, the word "obey" is used: "Sarah obeyed Abraham, calling him lord." Ladies, don't close the book yet; you will love the chapter on the role of husbands and wives. Take it easy, for now. Oh, by the way, I don't know how Abraham felt, but I would faint if my wife called me that. She has called me many things: Honey, Sweetheart, Pumpkin, Cherie, Papito, and other names, but never "lord." Guys, I don't know about you, but all those names are just fine, however, "lord" doesn't sound too romantic to me.

. . . till death us do part. For some this may sound like a sentence; however, these are the most reassuring words in the entire vow. To hear a person give them self to you and take you with no reservation, to have and to hold in good times and in bad times, in sickness and in health, for

richer or poorer, and to seal that covenant before God with the words: *"till death us do part"* is indeed very securing. Those words are consistent with the meaning of the covenant itself, that only death would break the bond. It's a life commitment. Upon hearing these words, everybody should conclude: "I have nothing to worry about; they will be with me till the end; their love will never let me go."

These vows are the voluntary decision that we have made before God, parents, friends, and the body of Christ. Malachi 2 shows God as a witness to the covenant. To break these vows and turn them into a lie, whether you stay in or leave the marriage, will certainly cause a lot of pain and misery. You can choose happiness by keeping your word to each other before God. As shown in the second and third chapters of this book, marriage is God's institution and should be entered into and lived according to his blueprint. Happiness will be the result of obedience to his guidelines and principles for the marital relationship. The choice to follow God's will for the marriage is thus the choice of marital happiness. Marital happiness is found in loyalty to God and loyalty to each other in marriage.

Ruth's Loyalty to Naomi: The Best Illustration of the Marriage Covenant

The daughter of a friend of mine was getting married in New York, and I was invited to read a passage of Scripture at the wedding. It is customary to read 1 Corinthians 13, Psalms 127-128, and Ephesians 5:22-31, or some passages from the book of Song of Songs. To my astonishment, the young groom and bride suggested that I read from the book of Ruth. Actually, it was very comforting to me because it showed that they knew what they were doing by choosing the words of Ruth to Naomi to illustrate their covenant to each other. I have looked in the Scriptures, the encyclopedias, and the history books, and have not found any statement that paraphrased or resembled more closely to the marriage vows than these words from Ruth. In fact, Ruth's statement made it clear what the marriage covenant is all about. Yet, it was not even to her husband, but to her grieving mother-in-law. Yes, to her mother-in-law, if you can believe it! Actually, you should; it's in the Bible. Let's read those words: "And Ruth said, Entreat me not to leave thee, or to return from following after thee: for whither thou goest, I will go; and where thou lodgest, I will lodge: thy people shall be my people, and thy God my God: Where thou diest, will I die, and there will I be buried: the LORD do so to me, and more also, if ought but death part thee and me" (Ruth 1:16-17, KJV).

The story of Ruth is very fascinating. It takes place during the times of the Judges, a very somber period in the history of Israel. The people were living in an alternation of sin and repentance, of judgment and restoration. The last verse of the book tells the story: "In those days there was no king in Israel: every man did that which was right in his own eyes" (Judges 21:25, KJV). There came a famine. Elimelech took his wife Naomi and their two sons Mahlon and Chilion and went to live in Moab in search of a better life. The two sons fell in love and got married respectively to Ruth and Orpah. All three men died in Moab leaving three grieving widows—two sisters-in-law and a mother-in-law. I know some of you are probably thinking: World War III, but it was not the case at all. Those three women were knit together; perhaps they relied on each other for comfort. However, Naomi decided to return home to Judah and urged her daughters-in-law to return to their own families in Moab. For Orpah, Naomi did not have to say it twice. She kissed Naomi and left. But Ruth was determined to be loyal to her mother-in-law. In fact, she was so determined that neither Naomi's logic about not having anything to offer her nor Orpah's example of disloyalty could dissuade her to leave her mother-in-law. It was as though she was saying, "If I truly loved Mahlon, I must continue to love you even if he is dead; you are the one who brought him into this world, and I will love you in his place." Ruth was not about to leave her grieving mother-in-law by herself, but made the same commitment she apparently had made to her husband, Naomi's son when they married. Her words are powerful. Let's look at them and see how they relate to the marriage vows we just studied,

. . . for whither thou goest, I will go. Ruth was in fact saying to Naomi that she was willing to give up everything in Moab—her family, her comfort zone, her familiar surroundings, her parents, her gods, and her culture to follow Naomi. That sounds like leaving and cleaving to me. She also indicated in those words that she would follow wherever the journey might take her. Whether there are detours, hills or valleys, whether it is stony or smooth, thorny or clear, I will follow you wherever you go, wherever the road will take you. I will be there with you. That's what, in fact, you are saying to each other on your wedding day. You are promising to be the lifelong companion for the journey no matter what. You are committing to be at each others side in both good times and bad times.

. . . and where thou lodgest, I will lodge. Those words echo "For richer or poorer." The promise is that you will share your station in life. Whether you dwell in a castle or a hut, I will be with you. Whatever you choose to do for a living, I will share. I will never be ashamed of you, regardless of the circumstances of our lives. It was Loretta King who said it well. When asked how she was able to support her husband, the late civil rights leader Dr Martin Luther King, Jr., through all the ordeals, the threats, the character defamation, the assassination attempts, and imprisonments, she responded that she could support Martin and put her family through so much because she did not marry just a man, she had married a vision, and she had married a destiny. Many spouses wish their husband or their wife could see it this same way. When you marry someone, you also marry their aspirations, their dreams, and their calling. Whether in ministry, political career, military, mission field, teaching, nursing, medicine, cosmetics, or homemaking, you marry their vision. If you don't want to support or encourage them as you should, at least allow them to follow their calling and do not stifle their efforts or be a hindrance to their success. You take them as a whole package. You should have thought twice about it. Sometimes career changes occur during the marriage, and the spouse has to adjust to it—for better or for worse, at one level or another. While at Dallas Theological Seminary, I remember how heart-broken a friend of mine was when his fiancée decided to return

the engagement ring when he wanted to respond to God's call to become an overseas missionary. It was painful, but I was glad that it happened before they were married. His whole life would have been almost ruined if it happened after they had been married. I also remember how one couple came close to getting a divorce when the wife decided to go into nursing. The husband thought about the long hours at the hospital and decided that he could not live with that. Thank God, I was able to help them reach a compromise.

Sometimes the station changes. There may be a loss of career that means changes in the finances and the security that they were enjoying. I will never forget a couple who were doing so well in their careers. Because the husband was the primary bread-winner, the wife could spend less time at work and more time at home with the children. All of sudden, the husband had a stroke and was told that he would not be able to resume his career. I visited them one morning. The man shared with me the disability letter he had just received from the physician, detailing his condition and his handicaps. While he was battling with tears, his wife reached out and said these words: "Honey, don't worry, I will take over now. I will be your friend, your nurse, your caretaker. When you need a friend, I will be here; when you need a sister, I will be here; when you need someone to care for you, I will be here even to spoon feed you. You can always count on me." As I write these words, they bring the same tears that they brought to my eyes when I was listening to them for the first time. But my friends, that's what marriage is all about, a commitment to travel the journey together and enjoy each other's company even if the map is not always clear, and the course is not always sure.

. . . thy people shall be my people. In the third chapter, we insisted on the meaning of leaving—the necessary detachment that must occur in order to cleave. However, breaking the close ties that contributed to who you are must be a voluntary act. It should not be imposed by a spouse who, for some reason, wants to detach the other person from their culture, ethnic background, family heritage, and social status or station in life. When you marry someone, you also marry that which contributed in making them who they truly are. It's not fair to expect

them to reject their illiterate older aunt who baby-sat them when their mother had to go to work or school to provide for them. You cannot expect them to deny their background—who they are—in order to be with you. A rejection, whether it be of their family, their culture, their social status, and/or their background, is a rejection of them. Even when they feel forced to do so because of their love for you, they may resent it and live with feelings of rejection. There are people who for some reason end up marrying above or below their station in life or outside of their culture or even ethnic background. That's okay; love can overcome all sorts of boundaries, especially for those who are in Christ Jesus. But those issues may need to be clarified in your mind before you make a lifetime commitment and sign a covenant that will involve embracing some folks that you have never been around before in your life or go to a neighborhood you have never been allowed to visit before. That's marriage for you, my friends—"your people shall be my people." It means I will embrace and love your people as much as you love them without making you feel uncomfortable seeing me with them.

. . . and thy God, my God. When you marry someone, you marry into their religious as well as their spiritual aspirations. The repeated admonitions to the children of Israel and to Christians to avoid entering marriage with those who have rejected your faith, also anticipates the major risks and problems that result from mixed marriages. Religious affiliation and spiritual commitment are often the subjects of major conflicts in marital relationships. They have even contributed to separation and divorce. Those issues should be clarified, dealt with, and compromise must be reached; otherwise, they will threaten the stability of the home and the level of happiness the couple might enjoy with one another. Besides, religious affiliation and the church each spouse has joined may pose a problem, especially when the children have to take sides and have to be split between parents on Sunday mornings. Things can take a turn for the worst when one spouse completely opposes the other's faith, spiritual disciplines, and religious practices, whatever they may be. Every effort should be made, every arrangement should be mutually agreed

upon to facilitate a balance whenever there is a difference of opinions, beliefs, and practices.

. . . Where thou diest, will I die and there will I be buried. Ruth's loyalty was total; her commitment was without reservation or limits. In ancient times, the place of burial was very significant, according to Genesis 23; 25:9-10; 50:1-14 and Joshua 24:32. It designated ethnic and ancestral appurtenance. Ruth was not only devoted to her mother-in-law, but completely identified with her, her people, her faith, her station in life, her future, and her destiny.

. . . the LORD do so to me, and more also, if ought but death part thee and me. Does that remind you of *"Till death do us part?"* Ruth is making an oath for life and death. With God as a witness, she is swearing on her life never to break her promise or violate the covenant. *". . . To have and to hold from this day forward, for better for worse, for richer, for poorer, in sickness and in health, to love, cherish, and to obey, till death us do part, according to God's holy ordinance.*

The story ends with Ruth keeping her words to her mother-in-law, caring for her, and remaining faithful to her. God honored her commitment and loyalty and blessed her beyond what she could ever have dreamed or imagined. Because of her determination, loyalty, love, and devotion, because she kept her word and remained faithful to God and to her mother-in-law, this woman became the great-grandmother of David, whose offspring is none other than the Lord Jesus Christ himself.

God honors those who honor him. He will bless your commitment to honor him in your marriage. Changes will occur, circumstances will vary, and the roads will take detours—sometimes for the better, other times for the worse. No one can predict what turn it will take. But through the hills and the valleys, through the waters of life, and even through the fires of adversity, remember that you gave your word never to break your covenant. Death will be your only excuse. Sooner or later happiness will come to those who choose to honor God in their commitment in marriage.

VIII

ENJOYING THE JOURNEY: MEETING EACH OTHER'S SEXUAL NEEDS IN MARRIAGE

In the 1980s, during my pre-doctoral internship at one of the Minirth and Meier Clinics, a couple that I will call Pedro and Carolyn was assigned to me for marital counseling. They appeared to be madly in love with each other. They walked into my office hand in hand. They were almost on top of each other as they sat closely together on the sofa. I wondered, "What could possibly be wrong with these two lovebirds that seemed to be still on their honeymoon." The problem was they had been married for over a year and had not been able to consummate the marriage. Pedro's soldier was not marching—you know what I mean. When a soldier receives a command to march, he is supposed to stand straight and execute the order. Well, his soldier could not even stand straight, much less march. The wife was very supportive and understanding, but she was starting to get a little frustrated. They had saved themselves for each other, and now that they were married, they could not enjoy the physical intimacy. After assessing that there was no medical cause for his difficulties, I proceeded to try to understand what was going on with Pedro. He had all the right desires; he was sexually attracted to his wife who wanted him desperately, but could not fulfill his duty. He was getting depressed; he was feeling more and more embarrassed and guilty that he was not able to meet his young wife's needs.

Pedro had been raised in a very religious and "spiritual" environment where he had not received proper sex education. The only education that he received was that sex is dirty, that his sexual desires were all sinful, and that he should never think about sex if he wanted to be holy and not sin in his mind. As he was growing up, especially in his teen years, he resolved not to sin sexually. He even felt guilty about any thoughts of sex. He had very strong urges, but learned to suppress them by saying to himself this Latin phrase that a priest taught him, *"Vade retro, Satana"* that is translated, "Get thee behind me, Satan." In spite of his strong convictions, Pedro grew up thinking of sex as dirty and sinful. As a result, he conditioned both his mind and body not to respond sexually and to suppress his sexual desires lest he should sin. This feeling followed him in his marriage, and he was not able to use sex for which it was designed—in the loving arms of his wife. He needed to be reeducated about sexuality.

Strong convictions against sexuality before and outside marriage are good, but teaching that sex is dirty and sinful is wrong. Sex is a wonderful gift from God when enjoyed in its intended context and purposeful design. What makes sex dirty and sinful is not the act itself, but the context and the purpose of the act. As with all creation, Satan takes the good things that God created and perverts their use in such a way that the children of God may not fully enjoy them. As it is obvious today, those who are living in sin seem to have a better time enjoying God's gifts than those of us who should be enjoying them for the glory of God. Christians are ashamed and embarrassed to talk about sex in church. Some parents avoid the issue with their children all together or lie to them when the questions about sex come up. Some parents would even rebuke their children for daring to ask such questions. Sex education is relinquished to the schools, the streets, the magazines, or television shows. The kind of education that goes on through this media can hardly prepare anyone for sexuality as God intended it. Much of the information provided is distorted and inconsistent with the biblical teaching of sexuality between a man and a woman in the context of marital relationships.

Over twenty years of conducting annual marriage retreats, there are always questions about sexuality in the marriage. However, the only way I can get couples to ask any question about sex in the marriage is to have them write the questions down anonymously on a piece of paper and drop them in a box. Through these questions, I can hear the frustrations, the misinformation, and the lack of enjoyment of sex in marriage. Still, Christian couples should be the ones having the greatest fun together when it comes to sex because they are performing it in a context that honors and glorifies their Creator, who created them as sexual beings and established the context in which it is to be enjoyed. The Bible is not shy on the subject, neither should we be. In fact, the best sex education is found in the Word of God.

The Biblical Teaching on Sex

Physical/sexual attraction between a male and a female is normal

Sex is a gift from God. It begins in Genesis. As discussed in Chapter 2, God created Adam and Eve male and female, biologically and constitutionally different to attract each other and correspond to each other physically, morally, psychologically, spiritually, and sexually. God intended man to be attracted sexually to woman and vice versa although in different ways. God shaped them in such a way that they are suitable to each other physically. God had several purposes in mind for sex within the marriage However, we need to look at the rationale for the exclusivity of sex in the marriage. You have heard that sex before and outside of marriage is sinful. Perhaps you are questioning why something so natural and that feels so good between consenting adults can be regarded as sinful and even dirty. Isn't that what Satan has done, normalizes sin and makes those of us who hold to the biblical principles feel as if we are out of date or out of pace with the rest of the world? Sexual, sinful practices have become so common that parents, school nurses, and health centers are distributing condoms to under-aged children, lest they should get a sexually transmitted disease—as though that's the only harm there is to illicit sex. In fact, one former Surgeon General had suggested that we should put condoms on children's lunch trays. We have taught them that as long as they can avoid the physical consequences, they don't have to worry about the emotional and moral consequences of sex before and outside of marriage, and yet society is paying a big price for that through the degradation of the family and its impact on society itself.

It is important to note that man was not the only being created as male and female. The animals were also created as sexual beings, male and female. But note that while they were also created male and female, man was the only one created in God's image and likeness. The animals were just biological machines, capable of copulation for selfish enjoyment and for reproducing more animals each according to its kind. However, man, being created in God's image, has the ability to control his instincts, to act responsibly, to make rational choices, to evaluate the consequences of his actions, and to do whatever he does according to his ability for the glory of God. Reducing sex to its instinctual or natural tendencies apart from God's intended context and purpose is to reduce it to the animalistic level. It does not elevate us as people, it diminishes us. There is no pride in acting as animals and teaching our children to do the same. That's a misuse of our freedom as human beings. We are much more than our organs and desires.

Sex before and outside of marriage is sin

Fornication: The act of going to bed with someone before marriage in both the Old and the New Testaments In Deuteronomy 22:25-29, there are two instances of dealing with sex before marriage. In the first instance, if a man has sex with a young woman against her will, and she is engaged to another man, he had to be executed. That is called rape by today's definition. The reason that the young woman was not put to death was because she did not consent to it and cried out against it. Consensual sex before marriage was condemned. We are not advocating the death penalty for sex before marriage, but the point is that God's moral character does not change even if his methods of dealing with sin changes from one economy to another. In the absence of physical death, moral death certainly occurs even if our conscience chooses to ignore it.

We live in a society that is dead to its sins and is desperately in need of a resurrection through repentance and faith in the Lord Jesus Christ. In the second instance, if a man had raped a young woman who was not engaged to another man, he had to marry her and could not send her away. That's how serious it was. There's a tendency today to disregard the Old Testament as though its teachings were no longer relevant during the New Testament era. That is never an excuse for sin in any way, shape, or form. That's another debate in itself! But with regard to fornication, it is condemned in the New Testament as well as the Old. In Acts 15:20, the decision of the Jerusalem Council included abstinence from fornication. After admonishing the believers in 1 Corinthians 3:16, 17 against defiling the body because it's the temple of the Holy Spirit, Paul explicitly condemns fornication in 1 Corinthians 6:18. He also says that fornication is in direct opposition to the will of God in 1 Thessalonians 4:3. That is our sanctification.

Adultery: Sex outside of marriage. Adultery is clearly condemned in the Bible, so directly that it is an integral part of the Ten Commandments (Exodus 20:14). In the New Testament, Christ took an even more rigid stance against the Pharisees who were limiting sexual sin to just having intimate relations with a married person or with someone other than your spouse. In Matthew 5:27-30, Christ addressed lust that causes a man to fantasize about intimacy with someone other than their spouse as committing adultery in their hearts. In Hebrews 13:4, the author of the book speaks of the dishonor and defilement that adultery brings to the marriage. The warning is so severe that God's judgment is pronounced against the adulterers.

Both fornication and adultery are condemned by the Word of God in both Testaments. That should suffice enough to avoid these sins. However, there is another rationale for avoiding these sins and for understanding why God hates these sins so much. The rationale can only be understood in light of the nature and the purpose of sexuality in marital relationships. As shown in Chapter 3 of this book, the one flesh principle describes not only the intimacy but also the corporal union between a husband and his wife. Paul uses it in that sense in 1

Corinthians 6. The mystery of the one flesh has two significant meanings that has a greater symbolism than just the act of two people coming together to have sex. As husbands and wives demonstrate their oneness in the sexual act, they do so to demonstrate a permanent bond, a total consecration to each other, and an intimacy characterized by the unity of mind, heart, soul, and spirit that is expressed bodily in the sexual act. That one flesh principle in turn translates or gives a visible portrait of Christ's relationship with the church. That's the mystery that Paul talks about in Ephesians 5:32.

Both adultery and fornication destroy that analogy and desecrates that holy mystery between husband and wife and between Christ and the church. When two people have sex before or outside of marriage, they are using the symbol of a reality that does not exist between them. They are, in fact, making a mockery of the act and reducing it to just the animalistic or instinctual practice of sexuality. There is no permanent commitment; there is no covenant; there is no trust; there is no love; there is no emotional interdependence; there is no transparency; there is nothing other than the temporal, selfish fulfillment of one's lusts and desires. That's why both fornication and adultery are so condemned and hated by God. It's only out of his mercy that he does not impose the same swift penalty today as he did in the Old Testament. However, he does not look at those sins any less than before. His grace and mercy should not be interpreted as tolerance. Certainly both adultery and fornication can be forgiven by God where there is genuine repentance and a commitment to *"go, and sin no more"* (John 8:11, KJV).

Sexual Intimacy According the Bible

Sexual intimacy is the exclusive physical act by which a husband and a wife who have become one flesh by virtue of their covenant and their union before God express their love for each other through the reciprocal sharing of bodily and emotional pleasures to the glory of God. Any sexual act that falls outside of the above definition is sinful and does not glorify God.

The Purpose of Sex According to the Bible

Sexuality is not only a gift from God to be enjoyed by husbands and wives within the marital bond, it serves several purposes according to the design of the Creator.

Fruitfulness and multiplication These two terms are used to describe the reproductive capacity that God has given animals and mankind through the enjoyment of sex. If you prefer, the term reproduction or procreation can be used instead. God intended the sexual union to be a means by which the earth can be replenished, not for evolution of the species but for reproduction of the species, each according to its kind (Genesis 1:28). Although reproduction or procreation is not the sole purpose of sexual intimacy, it sure indicates that God intended it to be between one male and one female since only such a mix has the capacity to reproduce. In addition, they are biologically and anatomically built for that purpose. The sexual organ of the female is design to suit the sexual organ of the male. Sodomy was condemned as an abomination because the body part used in such practice was designed exclusively for expulsion of waste, not to receive.

Physical Union as Experience and Expression of Intimacy. The one flesh principle found in Genesis 2:24 expresses the physical union between husband and wife as an experience and expression of intimacy. Sex between husband and wife not only demonstrates their union but serves also to solidify their union through the experience of the physical and emotional closeness. As a husband and wife make love to each other, they not only express closeness, they experience closeness and become closer as a result. There is both a physical and a psychological dynamic in the act that makes it so significant and powerful. That's why many of those who practice sex before and outside of marriage experience feelings of abandonment, guilt, and puzzlement. They create a craving for intimacy that never existed before or was temporary. This is especially true for women who have given themselves to someone whom they thought loved them or would love them if they slept with them. They usually feel empty, betrayed, hurt, and humiliated afterward. Unfortunately, many of them continue trying to fill the void by falling into the same trap again. I was talking to a lady who had been quite promiscuous in her adolescent through early adult years. She admitted that sex was her only way of being loved. She said that it was like an addiction—you keep looking for a high that never satisfies, and so you keep getting more and more because the void is never filled. Unmarried or unfaithful men on the other hand can have sex with a woman out of lust, without looking for intimacy. When lust is gratified and love is absent, they end up resenting the person and start treating them with disdain, like a sex object.

In 2 Samuel 13:14-17, we have the example of how lust when gratified can turn into hatred, leaving the woman feeling like trash. Women who are in such situations are disappointed and hurt because they thought that the more sex they gave, the more love they would get in return. They realize that it's quite the opposite when love was not at the basis of the relationship to begin with. This is different between husbands and wives where love precedes the act. That is why, all things being equal, married couples do get closer to each other by sharing and enjoying more intimate physical and sexual contacts together.

Fun and Pleasure between Husband and Wives. Sex between husband and wife is a lot of fun, especially when they are open with each other to talk about it before, during, and after. There is a lot of joy to share with one's spouse over the act of making love when there's no shame and guilt. When there is transparency in communication and in their attitude toward each other, they feel liberated to express and offer themselves with no reservation to each other. That's a lot of fun. It is clear from Paul's first letter to the Corinthians in Chapter 7 that God also designed marriage to meet the sexual needs of husbands and wives instead of having one's sexual needs met through immoral practices of fornication and adultery, which are clearly condemned by the Word of God.

Proverbs 5:18-19 describes the recreational aspect of the art of making love between husbands and wives. There are some key words and expressions in the passage that speak volumes of the pleasure that is to be shared in the sexual act between spouses: blessed fountain, rejoice, satisfying breasts, and being ravished. That's how a husband and a wife are supposed to feel sexually about each other. Christians can have true fun in their home at no cost. Those who find pleasure in the world through illicit sexual activities often live with terrible consequences in their bodies, in their consciences, and in their families. When fun turns into chagrin and misery, it's not real fun. Those who have contracted sexually transmitted diseases through worldly pleasures either before or outside marriage realize when it is too late that the cost was not worth the fleeting benefit. As one French song expresses it: *"Plaisir d'amour ne dure qu'un moment, chagrin d'amour dure toute la vie."* Translated, it says "The pleasure of love (lust) lasts only a passing moment; but the pain of love lasts for a lifetime." Sometimes the resulting "pleasures" outside the marriage context not only last a lifetime but often shorten one's life. Not so between husbands and wives. They can have as much fun as they want with no guilt, no shame, and no physical, psychological, or spiritual cost. They can enjoy their sexuality while pleasing each other under the watchful eyes and smiling face of God.

Sexual Behavior Between Husbands and Wives.

In light of the above definition, purpose, and design for a couple's sexuality, we can conclude that sex is a natural and vital part of marriage. It should be viewed by both husbands and wives as an important part of their relationship. Just like issues of communication, coping with stress, raising children, managing finances, spiritual or health issues, and sex difficulties at what ever level in the marriage should be dealt with vigilantly, seriously, and consistently when they arise. Couples should be alert to any issues pertaining to their sexual behaviors, attitudes, and feelings about sex in the relationship. Feelings of frustration, resentment, temptations, dissatisfaction, and lack of sexual enjoyment can pose a serious threat to the harmony and the security of the marital relationship. The tendency to ignore or dismiss sexual problems in one partner or the other has caused major marital difficulties and threatened the happiness of the many couples.

The lack of education and inappropriate information about male and female sexuality has caused a lot of damage to the couple's sexual health.

A lot of that information comes from the street, magazines, or other ill-advised sources. As a result, people end up believing a lot of myths about sexuality or using information that may not be applicable in their particular case. There has been a lot of helpful research and tools that are published about sex, such as *Intended for Pleasure* by Ed Wheat and the Masters and Johnson series about human sexuality. However, beyond these sources, you need to know what the Bible teaches about sexuality and be aware of your own sexual health and behavior so as to address any issue that may affect your ability to fulfill spouse's needs in your marital relationship. As mentioned earlier, there is a vicious circle that couples need to avoid in any domain of their relationship, particularly in the domain of sexuality. Unmet needs lead to frustration; frustration leads to resentment; resentment leads to bitterness; and bitterness leads to emotional distance and threatened intimacy between the couple. This leads to more unmet needs and the cycle continues.

There are a lot of myths out there about the sexuality of men and women. The idea that only men are crazy about sex and women do not care about sexual satisfaction is either wrong or does not apply. As we mentioned earlier, the best place to begin about sexuality is in the Word of God. One of the verbs that is used throughout Scriptures for making love or sexuality between husbands and wives is the verb "to know." For example, "And Adam knew Eve his wife: and she conceived . . ." (Genesis 4:1, KJV). I think the verb "to know" here is more than a euphemism for sexual intercourse. It conveys, in my view, something much deeper about sexuality between husbands and wives than just another way of talking about sex. Sexuality involves knowing each other sexually. Much of the confusion and frustration about sex in the marriage is a lack of knowledge of one's own sexuality much less that of the other. A lot of husbands are frustrated because their wives do not know them enough sexually to please them, and a lot of women wish their husbands knew them enough to please them in the act of love making. There are wives who complain of having never had an orgasm, and men who do not know how to delay their own climax to bring satisfaction to their wives. There is a lot to learn about each other's sexual functions, cycles, and responses. Also, knowledge about sexual dysfunction in both men and women may help understand many things that may be going on in a spouse's sexual life and help them address or resolve many of the conflicts that may result from it. The need for knowledge should arise from the fact that sexuality is not only an important part of the relationship, but husbands and wives have a reciprocal duty to please each other sexually as God intended it. However, this is not a legitimate excuse, and may in many cases be a lack of healthy sexuality has been used as a reason for falling into temptations. Especially in a sex-crazed society with so many opportunities for sexual temptations, Christian couples should ensure that they do not give the enemy any opportunity to attack them.

Christ's Teaching about Sexuality

I know what you are thinking: Christ never talked about sex! Yes, he did when he talked about adultery in the Sermon on the Mount. In fact, he introduced a concept that was never understood before—adultery in the heart. Adultery in the heart as defined by the Lord himself is to look on a woman to lust after her (Matthew 5:27, 28). Another form of adultery in the heart that was not available, but certainly anticipated in the times of Christ, is mental adultery that has been created by the pornographic industry. There are many men who would not look at another woman to lust after her, but would look at pornography, dirty magazines, videos, etc. Pornography has been one of the major issues affecting couples' sexual life. I remember a newly married man who came to see me because he was having problems waiting for his wife during the act. Let's just say that he was driving 100 miles per hour while his wife's engine was still warming up or just in first gear. Obviously, the wife was frustrated and let him know it. He was frustrated because he realized that he was not able to please his wife, and that started to affect his manhood. A little background check revealed that before his marriage, he was heavily involved with pornography, and those images were still being played in his mind. He used to view those images for self-stimulation and self-gratification. He was not focusing on his wife. Although his body was there in the act, his mind was elsewhere, as though he was using his wife's body while sleeping with those images in his mind. Since he has married, he cannot just turn them off to enjoy the body of his young wife.

I think adultery in the heart or mental adultery is being fueled by pornography in addition to or as a substitute to lusting after a real woman. It removes the focus on the spouse and places it elsewhere, thus diminishing the sexual appetite and energy that should be devoted to their spouse.

Another problem that men struggle with is the tendency to use pornography to address their sexual dysfunction, especially when they struggle with issues of desire, stimulation, and a "not-marching soldier." They don't take the time to assess the situation and to seek professional help when necessary; they try to solve it on their own, thus creating more problems for themselves. Job's decision to make a covenant with his eyes not to look lustfully after women (Job 31:1) should be our covenant not to view those images that are destroying our healthy sexual life with our spouse.

Another lesson to be learned from the teaching of Christ is that men are more visually stimulated than women. That doesn't mean that women are blind when it comes to looking at men in a lustful way. Research has shown that although pornographic viewing and the search for visual stimulation are disproportionately higher in men than in women, there are women who are also addicted to pornography and are committing adultery in their hearts as much as men. We need to be aware of how those things may compromise our sexual life in the marriage and deal with them appropriately.

Paul's Teaching on Sexuality

In responding to the church at Corinth regarding sexual practices, Paul provides us with some of the best teaching ever given before or since concerning a healthy sexual life between married couples (1

Corinthians 7). In terms of background, the Christians in Corinth were living in the most sexually immoral culture of the Roman Empire. No place on earth was known for more lascivious and licentious sexual practices than Corinth. Those who had converted to Christianity were struggling as to what kind of conduct or practices they should observe in order to honor the Lord. Paul had written to them in Chapters 5 and 6 about the Christians' sexual lifestyle. He warned them severely against incestuous relationships, homosexual practices, fornication, and adultery. Apparently much confusion remained in their minds about what should be the proper Christian conduct with regard to sexuality. They wrote a letter to Paul inquiring about the ascetic teaching that was being promoted in their midst, i.e., total abstinence or refraining from touching a woman. Paul answers back to them and in so doing provides responses to many of our questions.

It is Good for a Man not to Touch a Woman

Sexual abstinence for those who can maintain it is a good thing. This issue was addressed to some extent in Chapter 1 with regard to the gift of celibacy. If you have the gift of celibacy and can remain without touching a woman, bravo! Good for you! God bless your heart! Paul is going to corroborate this statement and modify it: "But if they cannot contain, let them marry: for it is better to marry than to burn" (1 Corinthians 7:9, KJV). In other words, if you are burning with sexual desires, don't impose yourself to an ascetic lifestyle. Paul then proposes the solution to immorality and fornication—marriage. "Let every man have his own wife, and let every woman have her own husband" (1 Corinthians 7:2, KJV). Again, the fact that marriage, though not intended for that, can also fulfill one's sexual needs is clearly taught in the passage.

Sex is a Mutual Obligation

"The husband should fulfill his marital duty to his wife, and likewise the wife to her husband" (I Cor. 7:3). There are several myths that are addressed in Paul's statement to the Corinthians. The first and obvious demystification in the passage is about the passive tendency that is known in many marriages whereby one of the partners becomes a somewhat willing participant or in many cases an observer of the act. The second myth that is blown here is the fact that one partner must always be the initiator, usually the husband, and the other, usually the wife, is just the responder. Many husbands have indicated that if they never took the initiative, it seems that there would be no sex in the marriage. The cultural misunderstanding that women should not appear to be too aggressive or not initiate sexual activities should be replaced with the teaching of the Word of God that indicates that fulfilling each other's sexual needs is not something to be taken lightly. Both husbands and wives should take their responsibility seriously to honor God by meeting each other's needs in the relationship. The third myth that is dealt with here is that the one who initiates the act does so in order to gratify their own needs. The duty here is toward the other. This means that the one who initiates the act does so not for their own sake, but for the sake of the other. Having said that, I know the lines are going to change. It will be more like, "Honey, come here and let me fulfill my biblical duty toward you," to which the response might be, "That's okay, Sweetheart, I am fine, you don't have to, really!" Although this sounds funny, some people do play little games like that, except that these games can be quite hazardous to the health of the relationship.

Besides the demystification of the Word of God in regards to the passive tendency, there are several valuable lessons that the statement is teaching. This obligation that you have is based on your commitment before God to love and cherish each other by doing what is necessary to fulfill each others' needs in the relationship. Also, since it is an obligation, you must be responsible enough to fulfill it well and to ensure that God is pleased and honored with the way you go about it. Furthermore, you have the responsibility to address any issue or obstacle whether in yourself or in the marriage that may stand in the way of the fulfillment of your obligation. Often one partner may refuse the advances of the other because they are not "in the mood." Certainly, mood plays a significant role in sexual responses and attitudes, especially in women. However, it can become an excuse to avoid your obligation.

Just like with any other aspect of the relationship, based on your vows, you are 100% not 50% responsible to fulfill your duty towards each other. There is a significant difference between reciprocity and conditionality. It is normal for a spouse to expect an appropriate and positive response toward the other and vice-versa. However, even in the absence of such responses, you still have an obligation to fulfill. The tendency to use sex in the relationship to manipulate, to bribe, or to punish is not biblical and should not be a Christian practice. In order to fulfill your obligation toward each other before God, you should be educated about how he would want you to fulfill this duty, especially when problems arise in this domain. You cannot choose to ignore them and decide to do nothing about them until they pass. You must address these since they can potentially cause you to be unfaithful in the fulfillment of your duty. These issues might relate to life stress, difficulties in the relationship, your physical health, your spouse's physical health, sexual dysfunction, emotional issues, hormonal changes such as monthly periods or menopause, and even spiritual issues. Some can be addressed through prayer, others via open communication with your spouse, and still others may require the help of qualified professionals who can diagnose the problem and offer appropriate psychological, medical, and biblical solutions to them.

As indicated earlier, whatever may arise as a potential threat to your ability to fulfill your obligation should not be ignored, postponed, or neglected. You need to make sure you address them and not allow them to persist and cause damages to the quality of the relationship. It is your duty, and you must fulfill it.

I will never forget my former Greek professor at Dallas Seminary, the late Dr. Hoehner who, after teaching on this passage, said to the married men in the class, "Listen guys, your assignment for tonight is to go home and fulfill your God-given responsibility to your wives." Although I was single then, I remembered the assignment. Two years later, after I'd gotten married, I made sure I did not disappoint my beloved teacher.

Giving Oneself for the Pleasure of the Partner

The wife's body does not belong to her alone but also to her husband. In the same way, the husband's body does not belong to him alone but also to his wife (I Corinthians 7:4). This, my friends, is the best sexual education you will ever get anywhere. It addresses both the reciprocal activities of the sexual act and the mutual satisfaction that ensues. A wife must give up her body to her husband. There is an implied freedom, ease, security, and comfort in those words that liberates the wife to express herself sexually to her husband and allow him to provide her with maximum pleasure. It removes any feeling of shame, doubt, guilt, fear, or apprehension that often handicap the pleasure that she should experience and express in the act. In your vows, ladies, you have offered yourself to your husband who has taken you to have and to hold, to cherish and to love. That includes your body as well as the sexual intimacy that symbolizes the rest of the relationship. There is no reservation intended here other than that which can bring you and him maximum pleasure. Do not allow faulty teaching, past experiences, or other obstacles to keep you from being the kind of wife God calls you to be. The level of transparency that exists or must exist in the relationship should facilitate this liberation. As we saw in the case of Adam and Eve, they were naked and not ashamed—why should you be!

The same principles apply to the husbands. I have met men, especially those who are in the ministry, who are "too spiritual" to express themselves sexually to their wives with the same liberation. I was told that some pastors don't touch their wives when they are going to preach, others when they are going to serve communion. Brethren and colleagues, you don't know what you are missing! Being intimate with your wife is a sacred act. You can pray before, during (asking God to assist you in fulfilling your duty), and after—thanking God for each other and for the gift. I am not kidding you! You should not let this kind of abstinence affect you. It is not recommended, as we will see later.

When a wife and a husband relinquish their bodies to each other, they allow themselves to know each other sexually. The reason is that sometimes there is so much frustration and dissatisfaction with the sexual intimacy of the marriage. This may be because the couple does not know each other well sexually. The husband does not know what pleases the wife and vice versa. The authority that is released to the husband and to the wife should be used to explore each other's body, to be creative and adventurous. Making love to each other is part of the enjoyable journey. The Song of Songs provides a lot of beautiful figures of such explorations. However, the key statement that I alluded to earlier and is applied to the context of sexuality in the marriage is when the Shulammite bride made the following statement: *"My lover is mine and I am his"* (Song of Songs 2:16). Can you think of a more visible context for this statement than the sexual act? I can't.

Abstinence in the Marriage must be Only by Mutual Consent

"Do not deprive each other except by mutual consent and for a time, so that you may devote yourselves to prayer. Then come together again so that Satan will not tempt you because of your lack of self-control" (I Corinthians 7:5). If you want to use religious or spiritual excuses to avoid fulfilling your sexual obligation to your spouse, you need to make sure that they are as "super-spiritual" as you are. Otherwise, you would be sinning by violating this principle and causing them to be vulnerable to an even graver sin, adultery. The idea here is this: don't play games with your sex life in the marriage. Whatever decision you have to make about your sexuality must be by mutual consent and not by imposition. That would be selfish and not spiritual at all. It should not be for a prolonged period of time. You would be exposing yourself to temptations and making yourself and your spouse vulnerable to sexual sins. Just as in Corinth, sex is everywhere today. The safety of the marital relationship was a shield for Christians to keep them from sexual immorality. The same should be true today.

Of course, there are circumstances that may force you to deprive each other, such as illness, unforeseen trips, and forced temporary separation such as military service and war. However, it is unwise to make voluntary decisions for prolonged separation and deprivation from each other. It is not only unwise it is unbiblical. In those uncontrollable situations, prayer for self-control, self-discipline, and faithfulness to God and each other should help you survive the time. But, inasmuch as you can control it, the admonition is "do not deprive each other, except by mutual consent and for a time."

Marital happiness is what makes the journey enjoyable. Being in the arms of each other and expressing and experiencing the love that binds you is a wonderful gift from the Lord. The choice to be happy in marriage is the choice to enjoy each other emotionally, spiritually, and sexually. The choice to enjoy each other sexually is based on the choice to follow his guidelines for keeping the marriage bed holy, to fulfill our duty to one another by mutual sharing of our body for total pleasure and mutual satisfaction, and by avoiding sexual temptations and deprivation. When we make that choice, the journey becomes more enjoyable, and God is glorified.

❧ IX ❧

ENJOYING THE JOURNEY:
COMMUNICATING WITH ONE ANOTHER

As we travel the marital journey with our companion, one thing that often gets in the way of our enjoyment is the way we communicate to one another. We may be walking in the same direction, but we are not always at the same pace and often not on the same step. At times, we may not even be sure that we are traveling toward the same destination. To ensure that our steps are ordered and our pace adjusted, we have to communicate and do so in a manner that facilitates our interaction instead of impeding it. Many couples often identify their marital difficulties as a communication problem. Others would tell you that they don't communicate at all. The truth is that all couples communicate somehow, about something, and sometimes to one another. The question is not whether we communicate. It is rather how and what we communicate.

There is a little game that I often play with couples in my office on the issues of communication. They would tell me what's wrong in their relationship that brought them to counseling. One of them will start by listing all the negative things that the other had done to mess things up between them. After a while I would stop them and ask the other to paraphrase what they had heard. There are four things that I usually find in their response: 1) a rebuttal or correction of what has been said, 2) a justification of any admission of wrong doing, 3) an erroneous interpretation of what has been said, and 4) their own version of the marital problem that begins in the third person.

It is always a fight to get them to paraphrase or repeat some of the things that has been said. I also discovered most of the time that they were not listening. While hearing some of the things that were being said, their defenses kicked in, and they started preparing their rebuttal before the person finished their part of the communication. The other observation that I make is that even when they were listening, they were hearing the words and some of the facts but missed out on the feelings behind them. For example, a wife was in tears when she was saying that she does not think that her husband loved her because she felt neglected and not valued anymore. She was complaining that he did not spend time with her anymore, and that even when he is home, he is always doing something but never showing any attention to her. My heart was aching as I listened to her words and watched her cry. In the end, I asked the husband to tell me what he thought his wife was saying to him. He paused and then said, "She is saying that I am no good. But, let me tell you . . ." He then proceeded to list all the good things that he was doing and that she did not mention. I could not help it. I stopped him, and rephrased the question a second time, and he finally got it. He took a deep breath and said, "I think she misses me. I did not know she missed me that much."

There were a number of symptoms of poor communications in that simple scenario. First, the wife never took the time to communicate to her husband that she missed him. She was only listing what he was doing or not doing. She failed to list any of the good things he was doing, only the bad ones, so he concluded, "I guess I am no good." On the husband's part, he became so defensive that he could not hear the sadness, and the pain in a wife who wanted to spend more time with her husband. Second, he was not really listening, so only the defenses kicked in. He was already preparing the rebuttal before she could finish her sentence.

I am sure you may be able to identify with one aspect or another of this couples' pattern of communication. Perhaps you can learn a thing or two about communication after reading this chapter.

What Communication Is

Several definitions have been given to the word communication, but there are three that are of particular interest to me. A thinker has defined communication in terms of social and emotional intercourse. Intercourse is used to speak of the give-and-take exchange between a couple toward mutual satisfaction or a shared pleasurable outcome. Judging from this definition, good communication involves reaching an outcome that is pleasant for both parties, and in order for that to happen, there must be a fair exchange. It is social in the sense that it is the interaction between two people. It is also emotional because the two individuals communicate more than words; they communicate feelings, needs, desires, wants, and aspirations.

Another definition that I find interesting was proposed by author of the bestselling book *Games People Play*, Psychiatrist Dr. Eric Berne. He defines communication in terms of a transaction. The word transaction is a commercial term used to speak of selling and buying through bargaining and compromising to conclude a business deal where both parties are satisfied with the outcome. The buyer gets the merchandise he came for, and the seller gets the money he wanted, and everybody is happy. It is likely that these two parties will continue to do business together because their transaction has ended in mutual satisfaction.

Whenever I think of a definition for the term "communication" in marriage, I think of the first two syllables "com-mun." "Commun" is the French word for common. First, the two people must have something in common in order to communicate well to each other; second, they must use a common language to each other, and third, they must envision a common goal. Reaching a common goal is related to the shared outcome that the above definitions already alluded to. When those "common" elements are missing in the transaction or in the exchange, communication is impeded. Communication is facilitated when the parties have something in common. They have a loving relationship and want to be sure that they are on the same step in their journey. They must use the same love language that facilitates good exchange. And they must be proactive to begin the communication with the end in mind. When that end is realized, they will have each other and will be able to continue their journey together—even at a better pace than before.

The bargaining and compromising in the transaction involves the modification of how facts were presented or interpreted as a result of honest exchange, personal clarifications, and offer of apologies or forgiveness when wrong doing was expressed and/or admitted during the exchange. It also involves changing the course of action or the approach as the result of the communication.

What Communication is Not

Often when two people have exchanged words, it does not mean they have communicated. In the example of the husband or the wife who prepares their rebuttal as they wait for the other to finish what they're saying, there is no real communication—two monologues do not make a dialogue! Usually people feel that they are communicating when in actuality all they are doing is waiting to take their turn to give the other person a piece of their mind, and often not the best piece.

Communication is not just using words for the sake of venting. Sometimes, one party does not care what the other is saying. They want to exercise the right to express them self and get things off their chest. Using ambiguous words or terms that only make sense to the speaker may leave the hearer puzzled as to whether to respond and to what.

How do We Communicate?

Verbal Language

Certainly we use language to communicate; we use words; we use a particular vocabulary. Verbal communication is a powerful tool in communicating; however, the kinds of words we use and their meaning within the context may facilitate or hinder our ability to communicate effectively. The use of words must be arranged around a particular content. Some people are very eloquent and use a lot of fancy terms to impress the audience, but when you try to put it all together, the content is bankrupt, and you are left to wonder "what in the world were they talking about?" Sometimes people want to communicate one thing, but their choice of words communicates something totally different from what they had in mind. So while verbal language is important in communication, we need to make sure that we use a vocabulary that does not communicate something other than what we are trying to say. The content must be consistent with the issues that we are trying to address. For instance, if the communication is about money, it may not need to involve a discussion about what would have happened if you had a college degree or not; stick to the finances and deal with the issues of a college degree at another time.

Tone

Besides the vocabulary, the tone we use will determine how much respect, love, fear, suspicion, doubt, or shame we experience or express in our communication. We need to make sure the tone is consistent with what we want to communicate. Sometimes, not only does the tone affect the meaning of the words, but it may also betray some of the feelings we think we are so clever at trying to hide.

Body Language

Sometimes we are saying one thing with our mouth, but our body language communicates something else. However powerful words may be, they are not as powerful as visible demonstration or dramatization. Researchers have shown that we remember three times more of what we see than what we hear. Body language includes rolling our eyes, looking at some body from the corner of our eyes, shaking our heads, grinding our teeth, using our fingers or our fist, hitting or pounding on something, and stomping our feet. Just like tone, body language translates respect, love or the lack thereof, aggression, fear, etc.

Patterns or Styles of Communication

No Communication

Sometimes it's true that people can live together for a period of time without communicating with one another. In reality, there are several types of meaning to no communication. Sometimes, no communication means a lack of interest in any exchange with another person. The lack of interest may be the result of failed attempts to communicate in the past. Why would you waste your time communicating when you know for a fact that it will lead nowhere? Sometimes, no communication suggests fear. This usually happens when the couple has not been able to positively share an outcome. As in the transaction that went sour the last time they tried to communicate, it did not end too well. They felt as if they were taken advantage of; no real compromise was reached. There was a winner, but it was not them. They are afraid of getting their feelings or their hopes crushed one more time, so they avoid communication altogether.

No communication may be a pattern of passive aggressiveness. No communication sometimes sends the message of a lack of care for either party. However inconceivable as that may be, two people can live together as husband and wife, and not even care about what happens to the other person, especially if they feel that the other person does not care to know about them either. They are just cohabitating and not really living together. They are on the same road, but not traveling together. They don't feel the need to communicate. If they do, their communication involves financial arrangements for the bills or some common project, but nothing outside the business they have in common. Sometimes no communication on certain issues may be the way a spouse has of protecting the other party from some harmful, unnecessary information.

When that happens, you need to make sure there are no repercussions and no consequences that may affect them or hurt the relationship.

Aggressive Communication

When either words or gestures or both are used with an angry tone, they convey aggressive communication. Aggressive communication tends to be confrontational, accusatory, or demeaning in tone, gestures, or words. It also involves destructive criticisms and authoritative overtones. It usually provokes defensive or aggressive response, thus creating potentials for a negative outcome. Repeated experiences of aggressive communication in the marriage may result in no communication. Whenever you use your fingers, raise your voice, use insulting words, or hit things, you are communicating aggressively. Aggressive communication tends to exaggerate. It uses words like "you never" or "you always." Sometimes it uses words that dictate rules like "don't" or "you should." When it uses first person pronouns, it often expresses disdain or disappointment. Words like "I hate it when you . . ." or "I can't believe you . . ." Often aggressive communication is perceived as a provocation. If the person is up to it, they might react at the same level. You raise your voice, and they raise their voice higher, refusing to give in or give up. They are ready for a fight, and you will have it if you persist. If the person is not up to a fight, then they just walk away, or if they are more mature, they may use a different kind of communication either to avoid the confrontation or bring you to a level of communicating more appropriately with them.

Passive Communication or Avoidance

This is a form of no communication whereby one person can actually hear what the other has said but chooses not to respond. It's a type of no communication since there is no exchange, no outcome to the conversation. Each one is left with whatever they had in mind to begin with. Also in passive communication, the person seems to agree with the conclusion or sometimes will even communicate a non-committal agreement, when deep inside they disagree. They were just delaying their response or pretending to agree to avoid a fight. One spouse can foster passive communication by being too forceful and too persuasive in their argument. The other can be very emotionally overwhelming. As a spouse said to me once, "Doc, there is no argument to fight the tears. Once they start flowing, I know I have to give up." You have to be a monster not to give up at this point, and I leave it up to you to decide who is most likely to use what approach. That's not being politically correct, that's being smart! Einstein! However, it does not matter who does what in the relationship if it's not constructive or positive for both spouses. If the outcome sabotages the opportunity for more transactions then both parties have lost regardless of what one thinks of the approach that was used. Nobody wants to feel like a loser, but in communication we either both win or we both lose.

It can happen both ways. One spouse tends to be logical, dialectical, syllogistical, and overwhelmingly factual. They present the facts that are to be analyzed and synthesized, and every effort is made to avoid inconsistencies. There is a major premise, a minor premise, and a conclusion, and they are ready to move on. The other spouse uses a different kind of approach: a logical-sentimental approach, with the accent on the latter part. They are very much syllogistical as well. There is a major premise: you never listen to me. There is a minor premise: you are not listening now. There is a conclusion: I don't want to talk to you! This game can be played over and over and nothing gets communicated or resolved until it is sometimes too late. Often those things that are not communicated keep coming back in the wrong place, at the wrong time. Many times the next communication is going to be contaminated with issues that should have been discussed, addressed, and resolved in the previous attempts but were stifled because of the approach that was used.

The worst case scenario is to wait for an avalanche whereby the passive communicator keeps tally of the issues, the hurts, and the losing scores until the cup is full. Some spouses wait until they come to someone's office, or worse, until they are in front of a judge where they feel safe to lash out at the other, expressing things that they have never communicated before. I have seen so many spouses who are shocked to hear some of the things that their wife or their husband is saying in front of strangers. The response is usually, "I never knew that was what I was doing," or "I did not know that is what you think of me!"

Immature Communication

Immature communication occurs when a person reacts in a completely unexpected way, such as acting like a child. Examples of this are when the person's language, gestures, and overall reactions resemble that of the child. The person may be saying things that are completely irrelevant to the subject at hand. For instance, we may be talking about where the family should worship together, and somehow the in-laws or some other issue from the last conversation gets involved in the communication. Sometimes they may say things that just don't make sense and then refuse to give any explanation. They may bring up something that is completely new or strange to the table, but they will fail to elaborate on it or bring any clarification whatsoever, leaving you hanging, guessing, and completely perplexed with a new set of things to challenge or worry about. If pressured, they'll throw a tantrum to avoid taking responsibility for their own communication or action. Often they talk a lot without saying much. They are the worst kind of listeners because they are too much into themselves to listen to anything you have to say.

Immature individuals tend to be extremely sensitive to any kind of confrontation or criticism. They act in a way that makes you feel bad for bringing the issue up. If they throw a temper tantrum, they tend to become moody and totally inexpressive. You perceive that there is something wrong, but when you ask them, they will say "nothing," and you find out later that a few dishes were broken "by accident" or something got spilled or ripped off, still "by accident." In some cases, their knuckles become red, or there is a fist hole in the wall. All of that still occurs "by accident." I have had spouses tell me that they can never get anything resolved with the other party because any kind of communication triggers an immature reaction. It takes a lot of tact to communicate to someone who is immature in their communication style. Sometimes you have to guess what went wrong during the day or the last communication, and what might have triggered it. It's not always easy. It takes a lot of patience. Someone once asked me one of those anonymous questions: "What do you do if your spouse is acting as a child?" My first response was half-jokingly, "Act as a parent." Actually, I meant to say to act as an adult. The last thing you want to do when an adult acts like a child is to either act as a child like they do or act as a parent. In either case, you will foster that kind of interaction for a long time. If you want them to act as an adult, you need to model for them what it means to act as an adult. Acting as an adult is the kind of communication that will be discussed below under the subheading Assertive Communication.

Passive-Aggressive Communication

Avoidance can also be a type of passive-aggressive communication when it is done to communicate disdain, lack of caring, or saying indirectly to the person, "You are not worth it." Passive communication often involves silent treatment, backbiting, and slander. Slander is talking to other people about the person without ever confronting the person. Another form of passive-aggressive communication is the use of sarcasm, saying hurtful things half-jokingly with the intent to hurt the feelings of the person or embarrass them in from of others. Some parents use their children indirectly to attack the other causing emotional destruction in both the spouse and the child. For instance, when a father is talking to a child and says, "You did not get to be that dumb from my side of the family." That says to the child that your mother's side of the family is dumb, and in fact, you inherited your stupidity from her.

Passive aggressive communication often leads to passive-aggressive reactions in order to get back at each other. The argument you might have won in the morning may follow you through the day and through the night. Spouses can do a lot to hurt each other to get back at each other. Passive-aggressive reactions often include forgetting to do some of the nice things you would normally do, neglecting to care as you used to, or just becoming cold in every sense of the word. They can create emotional distance between them by neglecting or ignoring each other's needs and going back to the cycles of frustration, resentment, bitterness, and loss of intimacy. Doing the things that can be detrimental to your spouse and to your relationship will in turn hurt you. It is not the best approach even if you feel justified or are truly right. You need to weigh the cost. It may not be worth it.

When one spouse is engaged in that sort of passive-aggressive pattern, the other might not know how to respond. It is difficult to respond to things that are done indirectly to you. Sometimes, it is even difficult to confront the other person because the excuses may appear legitimate even though they may be used expressly as a way of getting back. How can you blame someone who forgets to pick up something for you? Everybody can forget. You may have forgotten a few things yourself, such as Valentine's Day, or worse, you may have forgotten a birthday. That's a big one! You see my point! If you resort to playing the same game then you are contributing to worsening the problem. The best thing to do is to sit down and confront the issue using an approach that is more constructive and productive, and that leads to a more satisfying outcome.

Delayed Communication

When tensions rise and you feel that responding at this time may make matters worse, you may choose to delay your response. It could be because the person is too angry to discuss the issue calmly. It might be you who are too angry and not prepared to deal with a particular issue. Either one of you or both of you may need to cool off, walking it off before adding more fuel to the fire. Another consideration may be timing. The timing may not be right for any reason, such as fatigue, the presence of a third party who doesn't need to know your business, the place you are in, or other things that need to take priority at the time. On your way to church might not be the time to start a discussion about your preference on where your child should go to school. If either one of you perceives a possible negative impact, any of these factors might play into your communication so that delaying your response might be the wise thing to do.

Delayed communication should never be used as an avoidance tactic thereby never addressing the issue. If the issue comes up, it needs to be addressed. However, if you choose to delay your response, you need to take the responsibility of bringing it up at a more appropriate time. In fact, it might be helpful to give the person who brings the subject up a specific time in which you will address the subject with them. A good response might be something like "Honey, I see this is a very important issue for us to talk about, but I think it might be best for us to talk about it after dinner tonight." Most spouses will agree with you unless the matter is so urgent that it cannot wait, and you do not have the habit of avoiding communication. If the person still persists on talking about it, you might still hear them out, especially if they have the need to get it "off their chest." They may also feel an urgency to communicate something that is important to them, for whatever reason. You may ask for clarification of the urgency concerning the situation, and you may still choose to delay your response if you don't think the timing is right. You can respond by saying something along the line of "I am not ready to discuss it right now; I would appreciate it if you could give me some time to think about what you said and talk to you about it later." But whatever you say, you are bound to it. You need to think about it seriously and make sure you are the one who brings it back.

Again, your delayed response does not leave you off the hook; you might be just dodging the bullet for now, but you need to face it as you have promised. Otherwise it will be perceived as an attempt to avoid dealing with the issue. Nor should it be perceived as a way of shutting the person up. That is why you need to demonstrate a genuine interest in what the person has to say. However, you should not be forced to give a response when you are not ready, especially when that response would only serve to make the situation worse.

Delayed response is based on the wisdom of James 1:19 where we are exhorted to be "swift to hear, slow to speak and slow to wrath" (KJV). The order of these words is important. First, you must always be ready to hear, listening to what the person has to say without cutting them off or ending the conversation by walking out on them, or just saying that you don't want to hear about it or talk about it. That would be quite insulting to the other party. A lady once shared with me a tactic that usually ended the conversation with her husband—she started singing. Usually it is a song that conveys a particular message to the husband to ask him to be quiet. When I asked her how her husband responded to something like that, she said that he usually got angrier and shouted for a while, then he walked out and left her alone. She finally realized that he was building a lot of resentment against her, and she decided to learn how to communicate with him.

No Communication

No communication may convey rejection while ignoring the person's attempt to reach out. Perhaps you feel that your rights were violated, but you don't think you have the right plan of attack yet or a good rebuttal; you choose to just ignore it or move on. Sometimes it may be a sign of stubbornness; you are not saying "Yes," and you are not saying "No," but deep inside, you know what you want. Sometimes it shows a lack of caring. The other person may be dying inside, but since they have not communicated their hurt and pain appropriately enough, you choose to ignore it while they continue to hurt. They knocked at the door, but because they knocked a little too hard, you are not opening it.

Assertive Communication

This category is the opposite of aggressive communication, immature communication, passive communication, passive-aggressive communication, delayed communication or no communication. The only type of communication that may go along with assertive communication is the delayed communication when done appropriately and with the right motives and purpose. Assertive communication is an adult type communication. It is the ability to communicate clearly and factually with balanced emotions. It uses words, gestures, and body language that convey respect and love. It does not attack, criticize, or confront in a way that creates defensiveness on the part of the other party. When a criticism is necessary, it is presented in a very constructive manner that does not embarrass. It begins criticism with an affirmation of the positive. The affirmation must be genuine; otherwise, it will be perceived as manipulation, a way to soften the blow. If the confrontation is about an offense that you might have suffered, you don't begin with an accusation; you present the issues as they were and express your feelings about what was said or done to you, establishing an opportunity for restoration. Assertive communication usually begins with the first person pronoun and a self reference statement and not in the second person pronoun with reference to the other person's wrong doing.

Assertive communication facilitates interaction by offering the opportunity for correction of any misperception or misinterpretation of the fact. It avoids conveying exaggeration, disappointments, and authoritative postures. It tells the truth in love without giving its own meaning. As in the illustration given at the beginning of this chapter, what destroys communication is the tendency to tell the person what we think they meant by what they said instead of what they actually said. Our interpretation or the meaning we give to what was said may be completely off. Sometimes we let the emotions do the interpretation for us instead of the other way around. Many times we find out that our interpretation was wrong and that changes our feelings about what was said. That's why assertive communication offers the opportunity to be corrected by asking for clarification of what they heard before communicating how they feel about it.

The Message in these Patterns of Communication

The patterns of communication imply subtle messages that we communicate to our spouse even when we are not aware of those messages. They often choose to react independently on the message that they receive.

Some people might have already adopted or developed a particular style of responding. So, regardless of our type of communication to them, they will remain consistent with the style unless the circumstances call for otherwise.

In Aggressive Communication

Aggressive Communication communicates an affirmation of our rights while denying their rights. This kind of communication is usually a response to a perceived threat or attack to our rights, our personality, our feelings, or our person and authority. So when we communicate, we do so to reaffirm our rights and in so doing we end up denying the other person's right. What right are we denying them? The right to respect. Since in our mind they have already violated our rights, we react in a way that shows disrespect. We can trigger several reactions based on the other person's style of communication, their past experience, and what they are going through at that particular time. We are still responsible for the type of communication we choose to communicate or to respond to, yet we need to be aware of what's inside of us that might cause or trigger a particular reaction.

Sometimes we are surprised at why our spouse reacts a certain way to our communication. There are several factors that may be involved. First, their previous experiences with authoritative figures from their past. You may be using a tone that reminds them of their father or the police officer or that mean teacher they used to have. Second, whatever their mental or emotional state is at the time. Fatigue, stress, or unresolved issues may cause people to be prone to respond in certain way because they are not processing the information the same way you intended it.

In Passive Communication

This message conveys the same message as no communication except that sometimes we are just postponing our reactions for later on when things have piled up long enough for us to lash out. We are in effect saying,

"I have been hurt; I know I lost the argument, but since I don't have all my ammunition yet, I am letting it go for now; but watch out, you'll get it all at once. You might have scored, but the match is not over." You give this message because the person is aware of the style and will get ready for it and may choose to adjust to it—either to a style of communication that is more constructive or to whatever style they think works well for them.

In Immature Communication

Here we demonstrate a lack of emotional maturity or a lack of ability to tolerate tension or to deal with issues without reacting too emotionally. The emotional fragility keeps people from coming to us with any serious issue to address. The emotional outburst or the temper tantrums are signs that warn people against coming to you lest they should appear too cruel. The message that it gives is "You may be right, but I can't handle it." It tends to make people treat us as children with lack of respect and avoidance to any attempt to resolve serious issues.

In Passive-Aggressive Communication

Passive-aggressive communication acknowledges inwardly that our rights have been violated, but perceive that any rebuttal might be met with consequences for which we are not prepared. We might feel unjustified in our reactions, but we would not openly admit it. We thus resort to covert, indirect, and hypocritical tactics to get back at the person. The message it conveys is a lack of honesty, a retaliatory attitude, and hypocrisy. Pretending that everything was okay, we resort to avenging ourselves indirectly, which will definitely affect the trust that is essential in communication between husbands and wives.

In Assertive Communication

Mutual respect is conveyed here. We feel we have the right to communicate what we think and feel to our spouse. However, we recognize that they have the right for respect, for understanding, and for being given the benefit of the doubt. Even when we feel that our rights were violated, we don't use that as an excuse to violate their rights. We communicate not only respect but love and maturity to the other party who may in turn adjust to our level of communication from whatever level they started off with. When the person is too agitated, we model calmness; when the person is too immature, we demonstrate what a mature conversation looks like; when we feel insulted, we demonstrate what a respectful communication sounds like—even when we are upset. We model honesty, truthfulness, openness, and love.

The Key To Good Communication

Behind every communication are an attitude and a motivation. The attitude should be that of love, respect, trust, and honesty; the motivation should be to communicate feelings and clarify whatever needs to be cleared up, so we can have a better understanding of each other and make the journey more enjoyable for each other.

The attitude of love begins with the thought that our spouse is our friend and has our best interest in mind even if they might have done something to offend us. They are neither your enemy, nor your adversary. You are approaching or hearing your best friend who will continue to be your best friend after this conversation. Your approach is dictated by mutual respect, love, and trust. There is a level of safety that is established for us to communicate openly, directly, and honestly. The communication is not a judgment in a court of law; it is not a football game; it is not about winning; it's about sharing. There is never one true winner or one true loser in the domain of the exchange. It's either a win-win situation whereby both parties experience satisfaction after the transaction, or a lose-lose situation if one of the parties feels they were taken advantage of at the conclusion of the deal.

As most teachers or experts in communication would tell you, the key to good communication is listening. One of the most successful skills that we have as psychotherapists, counselors, pastors, or just as good friends is our ability to listen. People love good listeners because they feel understood, valued, cared for, respected, appreciated, and loved. That's why they'd rather pay money to communicate to a good listener than get rejected for free by a spouse who does not know how to listen. People become frustrated when they don't feel that they are being heard. Women are often criticized for talking too much. Well, it may be because their left brain, the part that controls speech, is more developed than that of men. However, when people feel that they are not being heard, they have a tendency to talk more and to repeat themselves. Unfortunately, once you are known for giving long speeches, people learn at some point to shut their ears even when they pretend to listen to what you have to say. Trust me on this; ask any preacher.

The key to being a good listener is to listen attentively. When you do, you listen not just for words, but for the entire form or means of communication. It includes body language, eye contact, gestures, and the type of vocabulary that is being used. True listeners listen with their ears, eyes, hearts, and body language. Through these media, you communicate ease, safety, acceptance, love, trust, respect, and all that facilitates good communication. If you are not careful, this media can also be used to communicate judgment, disdain, lack of interest, disrespect, suspicion, boredom, fatigue, and lack of love. These things would definitely stifle or ward off good communication.

How you listen is as essential as what you listen to. When you make a total effort to listen, you hear more than words. You listen for needs, feelings, desires, frustrations, and aspirations that are being communicated. This kind of listening puts you at an advantage because it will modify the way you that respond and will prepare you to offer better solutions. The way you listen for those things and show that you are truly listening is through paraphrasing what they are saying and leaving yourself open for correction if you are wrong. For instance, if your husband communicates that he did not appreciate the fact that you spent one hour on the phone with your friend after he had gotten home, you may want to respond by saying, "It looks like you wanted to spend that time with me." He might mumble something back like "kinda, sorta," not wanting to admit it, but deep down you know he is saying that he missed you. What he really is saying is that he wanted to get more attention from you, especially if he is gone for a while. That little exchange can be the beginning of a beautiful evening instead of a reply like "Why can't I talk to my friends? You talk a lot with your friends on the phone, and I never say anything." That kind of response fails to hear the need that your husband was really communicating to you and starts an unnecessary fight.

Another way of showing that you have been listening is when you are able to remind them of what they were talking about when they lose their trend of thought while communicating with you. They know then that you were really paying attention. The other way of doing that is to go back to a previous statement and ask for clarification before you give your response. When you listen in this way, you make it easier for your spouse to come to you with anything at any time knowing that they will be welcomed, taken seriously, valued, loved, and respected. That's good intercourse!

The reverse is also true. By whatever means you reject the communication, the transaction is ended, shortened, or destroyed completely. Rejecting one's feelings or needs is rejecting the person. People take a lot of effort to communicate their feelings, especially men. When they feel rejected, the feeling of rejection and humiliation can be unbearable. Guess what? They learn not to expose themselves again or make themselves so vulnerable.

Good communication is the key to enhancing the intimacy in the relationship. It serves to make the journey enjoyable for both partners. It is the key to building trust, respect, mutual understanding, and knowledge of each other. It also serves to resolve conflicts that will arise in the relationship as we will study in the next chapter.

Imagine traveling a road with someone who does not appreciate you and is constantly cutting you off and rejecting anything you have to say through defensive or judgmental attitude. You would pray for the trip to end soon, or you would avoid any communication with that person.

I'll bet you that the trip will be one of the longest you've ever taken and perhaps the last.

Certainly you know what it feels like to travel with someone who makes you feel at ease, who values your opinions, who cares enough to listen to you, and to whom you can express everything. You would take the initiative to invite this person to come along with you on the trip. Or, just knowing that the person will be on the tour would make you want to go along. It's important for us to be mindful of that and create that kind of context and atmosphere in our marriage.

X

ENJOYING THE JOURNEY: RESOLVING THE INEVITABLE CONFLICTS

This chapter on conflict resolution is closely related to the previous chapter on communication. Sometimes, we may not only be on the same step or pace; we may not even be walking in the same direction. Although deep inside we want the same destination, our preferences, methods, approach, feelings, and attitude may get in the way. Just like communication, at times we may not even be sure that we are traveling toward the same destination. That creates conflict. Conflict is the inevitable part of every relationship. During premarital counseling, I often attempt to assess how much conflict the couple has experienced and what methods they have used to resolve them. While they hold hands and look each other in the eye, the response that I get most of the time is "We don't have conflicts." Well, I make sure they never say that again because I create a conflicting situation just to see how they will fight over it. I then use that to teach them about conflicts.

Besides being unavoidable, conflicts are necessary to the health of the intimacy of the relationship. They are not only a test of the authenticity of the intimacy and of the relationship as a whole, but they challenge us to make the adjustments that are necessary for the growth of the marriage. Certainly, as the relationship grows, we learn not to fight over some things, but there will always be plenty to argue over and to talk about at every stage of the journey.

Just what is the role and purpose of conflicts in the marriage? Conflicts serve as the expression or the manifestation of the differences that make us unique as individuals in terms of our personality, taste, priority, style, interests, opinion, and vision of life, as well as our strengths, weaknesses, and preferences. Conflicts can make or break a relationship depending on how they are managed. Constructive management of conflicts leads to genuine harmony and intimacy. Destructive management of conflicts leads to discord, heartaches, quarrels, and even divorce. We will look at the factors that affect ways of handling conflicts and how to apply the biblical and psychological principles of conflict resolutions in the marriage.

Conflicts and Why They Exist

In addition to being different in gender, we are created as unique individuals. No two people have the same fingerprints. As human beings we are prone to be different from each other just because of the fact that we live in variable time machines where everything changes around us and in us. We don't even remain the same throughout life. We live in a constant state of flux. As Heraclitus, a Greek philosopher of the late 6th century BCE, has said, "You cannot step twice in the same river." It is impossible to step twice in the same river because the river continues to flow; everything has changed, and we change also because, as with the flow, everything about us changes. If we can expect to be different from the person we were before, we also need to expect differences in the other person. We are not only created with biological differences, we are created to fulfill different roles, functions, and expectations. Furthermore, we grow up in different households; we have different upbringing; we have different sets of experiences, and we have different developmental processes. As a result, our personality, temperaments, and character are wired differently. Those differences are not only in our taste, they are part of our core being; they affect our perspective, our value system, our priorities, our goals, our problem-solving strategies, and ultimately our lifestyle. With all these differences, you may wonder how two people can ever get along. Well, that's the beauty of the journey—to be constantly adjusting our step; one is teaching the other to slow down when they are going too fast and vice versa, and one is pointing to the right direction when the other is going the opposite way. That's what marriage is all about—reconciling the differences through adjustments, adaptation, reconciliation, compromises, and concessions. If someone is not ready to go through these processes, they are not fit for marriage.

Conflicts arise when these differences are expressed and manifested in the marriage in the form of decision-making, opinions, problem-solving, coping with life stress, and changes in general. They make the marriage interesting and also contribute to its development and growth. No one is self-sufficient. God created Eve to be a suitable helper to Adam. If Adam could live alone and do it alone with his perspective, his ability, his knowledge, his methods, and his perspective, he would not have needed Eve. Although he was complete, he was finite—not all knowing, all-powerful, or all anything. That would have made him God. We know better than to even think so. Adam needed Eve not only as a helper but a different kind of helper. He needed her to bring a different perspective, to have a different outlook, and to have whatever else she could contribute to the relationship. So the differences are there to enrich the relationship. I always find interesting this quote from Antoine de Saint-Exupéry, in the Citadelle: *"Si tu diffères de moi, mon frère, loin de me léser, tu m'enrichis;"* translated as "My brother, our differences do not hurt me, instead they enrich me." In other words, the differences between the spouses are those things that improve and enrich the relationship.

Conflict exists to reveal the differences that we have so we can adjust to and reconcile the relationship for its betterment and growth. They are a necessary part of the process of becoming one flesh. The more we are able to adjust to each other, the closer we get to each other, and the abler we are to experience true intimacy in the marriage.

People who usually say that they do not experience conflict in the relationship have only experienced intimacy at the superficial level. They have not taken the risks of allowing those differences to emerge, and in reality, do not really know each other. Their love has not been tested since they have not accepted the challenge of deepening their intimacy. Perhaps they are not yet at a point of being able to trust each other to risk being different from each other. There can be no real acceptance of each other if those differences are stifled. There is a level of safety that must exist in the relationship that allows the spouses to reveal their true self without any fear of rejection, retaliation, or separation. It is unfortunate that those who have not allowed the little conflicts to arise and who have not learned to adjust to them would not know what to do when they face significant issues that challenge the security of their relationship. It happens that the first major conflict they experience is a cause for separation. It baffles a lot of people sometimes when they learn that two people who were apparently so much in love could ever consider breaking up at the first major conflict. They apparently were ill-prepared to face the first real crisis of their lives since they have not allowed themselves to learn from minor ones. Whenever something threatened their relationship, they kissed and made up quickly because they have not been able to tolerate any tension between themselves. The tendency to brush things under the rug lest they should reveal who they truly are deprives them of the opportunity to grow and the relationship to grow as well.

The choice we make whether or not to allow conflicts to surface in our relationship will be the choice between true intimacy or superficiality in the relationship. Conflict is the opportunity to know each other and sometimes even to know ourselves. We often surprise ourselves in situations of conflict. It is not uncommon to hear people say, "I can't believe I said this, or I can't believe I said that." I usually respond to them, "Believe it, it's you!" The marital relationship offers us a mirror to look at ourselves and to make the necessary improvement that is needed to become better individuals and better spouses.

Why Couples Avoid Conflicts

There are many reasons that people have expressed over the years of marriage and family therapy. They can be placed under the headings of psychological factors that predispose people to be afraid of conflicts. There are also some religious or spiritual reasons why people avoid conflicts that are often based on faulty teaching and false interpretation of the Word of God. It is often preached that Christians do not get angry. Although prolonged and unresolved anger can be a sign of spiritual immaturity, the experience of anger may not be sinful itself. But what it reveals about ourselves and how we manage anger during its experience and expression may be sinful. Ephesians 4:26 gives the command to be angry and not to sin. It did not equate the two. The force of the imperative and the order of the presentation of the two concepts eliminates the possibility of interpreting anger as a sin in and of itself in that particular text. Just like fever is a symptom of an infection, anger may be an indicator of a sinful pattern or a particular sin in our lives. And just like fever, if left untreated, it can cause a lot of damage. Nevertheless, some people may use their religious interpretation of conflicts to avoid them all together.

Emotional Insecurity

Emotional insecurity can be manifested in two ways. First, there are people who, based on past experiences, have not learned to trust others to love them as they are, and have learned to be careful about offending their love interest lest they should be rejected and unloved. They are afraid of being unloved. They never experienced any consistency in the way they were loved before. If they grew up in a home where love was conditional upon performance or approval, they do not know whether somebody would love them just for love's sake. They always think that they can lose it at any given moment. At times, depending on the relationship, their insecurity is justified by repeated experiences of threats of separation or violent outbursts. Just like in the context of communication, one can judge based on previous experiences within the relationship itself whether it's safe to show any dissent lest they should pay a serious price for it.

Insincerity

Insincerity begins with self-rejection. The person who is familiar with negative feedback may have internalized it to the point of believing that's who they are, and whoever that person is should not be revealed to others. They learn to suppress their emotions or dissensions lest someone else should have the same negative impression of them that they have of themselves. They don't want the truth about themselves to be revealed. Children who grow up in fights fear any sight of argument. Many situations of conflict cause them to panic. It's like having a flash back of a traumatic experience. They'll do anything to keep themselves from re-experiencing the same trauma, even if it means suppressing their feelings, accepting blame, or pretending that everything is okay when it is not.

Saving Face

When there are third parties in the home, especially in-laws, many couples have learned to avoid showing their true colors. They learn to suppress any negativity about their relationship. They want to save face, and so they do not allow themselves to be themselves in front of others. That's why it's important for the couples to have the freedom to express themselves to each other without indirect interferences from others. Where there are direct interferences, people tend to take sides, and it makes it even more difficult.

Wrong Conflict Management

Because they have not learned how to manage conflicts, many couples have had repeated direct and indirect experiences of negative outcomes in conflict management. They prefer to stay clear of conflicts altogether. Because of poor management of conflict, there are still some couples who are living with unresolved conflicts and fear that opening another can of worms may worsen the situation, so they decide that the best thing to do is to drop it and move on. As such, they keep adding to the pile until it cannot build up anymore.

The way we communicate with each other is often a reflection of our methods of conflict resolution. In fact, the patterns and styles of communication identified and discussed in the previous chapter are practiced particularly in conflict situations. They included no communication, aggressive communication, passive-aggressive communication, passive communication, immature communication, delayed communication, and assertive communication. You can review those patterns and see how they apply in the area of conflict resolutions. Conflicts create the opportunity for our style of communication to appear. These styles reveal who we are in terms of our weaknesses and strengths, our sensitivity, and our fragility. It also reveals our perception of ourselves and of each other.

The way we communicate and deal with conflicts in the relationship is a reflection of the spiritual health and maturity of the couple and of the marriage. Conflicts can make or break the relationship based on how they are managed. As indicated earlier, constructive management of conflicts leads to genuine harmony and intimacy. The reverse is also true. Destructive management of conflicts leads to discord, heartaches, quarrels, and even divorce.

In both premarital and marital counseling, teaching couples how to communicate with one another and how to resolve conflicts can save their marriages. It is often sad to note how simple issues can divide and destroy relationships because of poor management.

Nobody likes to have and live with tension. Conflicts create tension, and conflicts are generally unavoidable. The tendency to avoid conflicts is self-defeating. Certainly, some conflicts can be prevented. In fact, as the relationship evolves and matures, we learn not to fight over certain trivial matters. There are issues that by now we learn to accept and cope with in the relationship without fussing over them. Couples have to come to a point of accepting that there are things in each other's temperament and personality that are going to take some time to change or may not change at all. We just have to learn how to live with certain things and continue to love each other. In that case, certain conflicts along the way are prevented and even avoided by learned acceptance.

You remember the couple that I interviewed for one my classes? I wanted to discover their secrets for being able to sustain their love for each other for so long and avoid the place of divorce that is so prevalent in our society. They said something that I have never forgotten. You may be familiar with their words because they are not original as they would quickly admit to you. The words are basically taken from the Serenity Prayer by Reinhold Niebuhr. This is what they said, "We have learned to accept the things that we can in ourselves and to accept the things that we cannot change in each other." What a philosophy! If only more couples would do the same. If only we could have the courage to confront ourselves and ask God to change us and to teach us how to change in ourselves those issues that affect our ability to relate to each other or constitute a source of constant conflict in our relationship. If only we could learn to live with certain things in our spouses and not make a big deal of them! We could then prevent many unnecessary conflicts and experience more peace in our marriage.

However, regardless of how we apply the Serenity Prayer in our relationship, we will experience conflicts at one time or another, at one level or another, or in one area or another. Therefore, we need to expect them. We should not only expect them but welcome them as an opportunity for deeper and more genuine intimacy. When we anticipate conflicts with a disposition to deal with it effectively, we can be more successful at resolving them, and we will learn to create an atmosphere of security, honesty, and comfort for our disagreements and for open expression of differences. For instance, if you have a proposition, regardless of how well thought out it is, you need to leave room for your spouse's input and wisdom and perspective. If you come already with the idea that this is it, it is settled in your mind, then any sign of disagreement will be perceived as an attack to your plan and may cause you to react defensively and use one of those maladaptive patterns of communication that worsens the situation. A proposition is just that and not an already admitted resolution. Your spouse may find something wrong with it and that's okay.

Sometimes it's for your benefit or the benefit of the relationship to have a different perspective and help you to approach things differently. When you anticipate disagreement, you welcome it as a contribution instead of seeing it as a threat to your calculated plan. Creating an atmosphere of trust, security, and acceptance will facilitate the interaction.

The area that may be the most difficult to deal with in the relationship is offenses. While we can anticipate disagreement to our plan, and admit the need for a different perspective on our proposition, we are often ill-prepared to deal with personal offenses in the relationship. If you have a friend, or have been in a relationship for any given period of time, you are going to say or do something that will be offensive to the other person and vice versa. This is not only due to the differences that exist between us but also the weaknesses that exist within us. We are going to disagree; we are going to get angry; we are going to act in anger; and we are going do or say something to one another that we will regret. That's just the fact of life. Because you have offended each other, because you have acted or responded in anger, does not mean you hate each other although you may feel that way at the time.

You husband is not your enemy. Your wife is not your enemy. You are best friends who love one another, but humans often do offend each other. Best friends do fight sometimes but remain friends for life. While writing these lines, I am staying at the home of some friends whom I have known for about thirty-five years, much longer than I have known my own wife of twenty-four years of marriage. They have opened up their home to give me a refuge from my busy schedule in order to finish writing this book. Over the years, I am certain we have said or done something to offend each other. Whatever way we may have offended each other, it did not keep us from continuing to love and to care for each other for that long. You cannot be in any relationship and not expect some offenses to take place.

To think that we are too spiritual to have conflicts is to be holier than the disciples and apostles of Christ. You remember how Paul disagreed with Peter in Galatians 2:11-14, or perhaps Paul's disagreement with John Mark to the point of not willing to do missionary work with him

(Acts 15:36-39), and how Barnabas intervened and saved the day by giving John Mark a second chance (Acts 15:39). But later on that same Paul talks about John Mark as though nothing had happened between them (2 Timothy 4:11). So because your husband offends you or because your wife offends you, it does not mean that they don't love you anymore. In fact, genuine love makes provisions for dealing with offences as it is clear in our relationship with our Heavenly Father.

This is not an excuse to be mean to one another and seek to hurt each other purposely. Offenses taken from those closest to us are hardest to handle at times. When the person who was supposed to be the protector becomes the aggressor, it leaves us disillusioned because this is the last person we expect to harm us in such a way. There are insults that we would easily tolerate if they came from a stranger or someone we don't care about. But, when they come from those who have sworn to have our best interests in mind, those we trust, it's not easy to let go. If a friend turns into an enemy, you have an enemy indeed. That's understandable. There is a level of cruelty and unfairness sometimes in offenses that are done to our spouses. Since we know each other well, we sometimes use that knowledge purposefully to harm them. We use the areas of vulnerability, weaknesses, and needs and turn them into weapons against each other. That's wicked. How can you use that which was entrusted to you in genuine trust, confidence, and love and use it against each other? Hopefully, you did not entangle your life with someone who constantly seeks to hurt you or humiliate you, or seeks in some way, shape, or form to harm you emotionally and physically. If you are in such a predicament, you need a lot of grace and wisdom from above. But most of the time, offenses between people who are in love are a natural part of the process and can be used constructively for the benefit of the relationship. I know a guy who told me that he does not mind his wife offending him because he always looks forward to the reconciliation and the amends that for the most part are sweeter than the offense was painful. I don't know if that is always the case in your situation, but the anticipation of restoration when offenses occur may help to ease the pain and soften the blow a little.

Principles of Conflict Resolution and Management

We need to differentiate between resolution and management. Some conflicts can be resolved by mutual agreement and by reaching a common solution to the problem. Management requires the ability to make concessions and compromise on things that we continue to disagree on for the best interest or the welfare of the relationship. We learn to live with certain things that we cannot change while making peace with one another. Some conflicts can be resolved, others need to be managed. The following principles will help to resolve some conflicts and to manage others while preserving our marital intimacy.

Acknowledge the Conflict and the Issue to be Addressed

The first step in dealing with a conflict is to admit that there is an area of disagreement, or there is an issue that needs to be addressed, discussed, and dealt with before we can move on. Most of the time a problem persists because of denial of the problem. Sometime we rely on the passage of time too much for certain things. Of course, there are things that improve by themselves over time, and all that they require is a little bit of patience and understanding. But there are things that are not so simple. There is a tendency for the disagreement to start because of the perceived weight of the problem. One person minimizes it, and the other sees it as a major issue. The rule of thumb in this regard is if it's serious enough to affect one's spouse, it's serious enough to affect both spouses. Sooner or later it will be enough to have a negative impact on the relationship itself and then both spouses will be concerned. It might seem trivial at first, but it's no longer a trivial matter when it has the potential to affect the health or the welfare of the relationship.

Define the Problem

Any counselor or health care provider worth their salt will tell you that the first need to be established before any intervention is the definition of the problem. In health care circles and in psychotherapy it is called a diagnosis. In determining a diagnosis, information is gathered by listening and by checking for various symptoms to know what to rule out and what may be part of the problem. Well, in dealing with conflict situations, although you may not have to go the same route, you do need to determine what the problem is, what the conflict is, and what the issue is that the couple is fighting about. In so doing, other things can be discarded or ruled out that should not be part of the equation, i.e., what it is versus what it is not. For instance, a couple came to my office and told me that the reason for their visit is that their marriage of fifteen years is not working out at all, and they need to do something about it before they go their separate ways. This sounds alarming. It turned out that they were going through severe financial difficulties and were letting that affect everything in their relationship. They confused the problem and the impact it was having with other aspects of their relationship. Communication, intimacy, and their spiritual life were being affected as a result of having difficulties managing their finances. It was obvious to them that if they could find a way of paying their debts and controlling their expenses, they would not turn so much against each other. They didn't need to see a psychologist or a marriage counselor; they needed to see a financial advisor to work out a solution. Certainly the financial situation raised some questions about how they dealt with other issues, but the other issues were not the main focus at that point.

Many problems could have been solved much more easily if they were not entangled with so many other issues that were not necessary to bring to the table at that time. They may have contributed something to the issues at hand, or they may be impacted by the current situation, but they were not the primary issue of focus. You need to deal with the issue at hand, and if necessary you can address the collateral damages later on, one at a time.

Stick to One Issue at a Time

Sometimes a simple conflict can degenerate into a huge crisis. It can be something as simple as a child bringing a failing grade home. There can be a number of reasons why the child has a failing grade. What happened and what can be done to help the child do better in school should be the focal point. It is wrong to include the fact that you are not spending enough time at home or that your spouse thinks they're stupid and little Cicero might have inherited the Math bad-gene from them. Also to talk about the decision that was made years ago to put the child in that school and to project that the child will never be able to go to a good college because he just flunked a fifth grade Math test is to bring into the conflict a whole can of worms that should not be the current focus. Now imagine how the poor kid is feeling for "creating" the whole mess just because of receiving a bad grade. Worse yet, you may be a parent who resents the child for creating the situation in the first place or who uses the child to displace the anger they cannot express or manifest toward the other parent.

It's good to learn to stick to one issue at a time and not complicate the situation by bringing into it things from the past or making projections for the future. Neither is it helpful to bring individuals or other issues that are not at all relevant to the current crisis. Sometimes we use current situations to try to settle scores from unresolved issues. Sometimes, I have seen couples use things from previous conflicts with specific details on what was said, what the weather was when they said it, and what was currently in the news at that time. Sometimes they remember what they were wearing, what they had for lunch that day, and how they felt then and still feel now. By the time they stop, if they ever do, you don't even know anymore what the issue is you are dealing with. When that happens between the two people, they usually end up being angrier at each other. They have not reached any decision or conclusion, and life goes on until the next crisis. But who is going to help the poor kid?

Settle Matters Quickly

The sooner we deal with an issue the better. When we let things drag, other things pile up on top of it and make it more complicated than it was originally. Just like in the pattern of communication called

"Delayed Communication," there are times when it might be wise to delay addressing a situation. For instance, the timing is not right; the emotions might be flaring; there might be too much anger; or the tension might be at its peak. In those instances, we are not able to hear each other out. It is best to try to restore some calm before we try to deal with a volatile issue. The other consideration is location. Obviously, you don't start a fight with your spouse at a restaurant. The embarrassment might be too costly, or the presence of others might cause you to suppress your true expression and arrive at a solution too quickly just to pacify the moment. There are times that it might be necessary to find a quick compromise for the time being and postpone dealing with the situation in earnest until a later time and in a more appropriate context.

Apart from the case where wisdom dictates that to delay dealing with an issue might be the best course of action, sometimes it is best to put something else on hold in order to address an issue instead of delaying it. Two passages of Scriptures can be used in support of this principle of resolving dispute and conflicts. The first one is Matthew 5:23-26. The second one is Ephesians 4:26 (KJV), which states "Be ye angry, and sin not: let not the sun go down upon your wrath."

The latter passage in particular suggests a very practical approach to resolving conflicts between spouses. For years, my wife and I have practiced this principle, and it has worked for us. We made a commitment to always pray together and kiss each other good night before falling asleep. By applying this passage, we know that we cannot pray if there are matters to settle between us. That forces us to look at any unresolved conflict during the day that needs to be talked about before we pray.

The idea of not letting the sun go down can be applied both literally and figuratively. Literally, as people used to go to bed at crepuscule or twilight, it required them not to go to bed with unresolved issues. They needed to express, resolve and forgive whatever had caused them to be angry. Figuratively, it might simply mean, don't wait till it's too late to deal with an anger-enticing situation. It is that period of time when the anger may cause you to deprive each other of the loving care, attention, and intimacy that you have promised for good times and bad times.

In addition, suppressing your anger for long periods of time not only affects your relationship, it might cause you to have headaches, to become depressed, moody, and bitter. It's not good for your psychological, physical or spiritual health. When you have not dealt with the anger, certainly you have not been able to forgive either. Then your communion with God and your brother and your sister is in jeopardy. The price to holding on to your anger is too much to bear. Anger causes a lot of pain. I have found that love, forgiveness, and resolution are not only healthier in the long run, but they are far less painful than hatred, bitterness, and feelings of revenge. The latter ones will keep you awake at night; the former ones will set you free to do what's constructive, including getting a good night's sleep.

Constructive Confrontation

The word confrontation often carries a negative connotation, suggesting the face-off between two adversaries. It does not have to mean that. It often simply means to go and address an issue face to face with someone. However, admittedly, confrontation is never easy, neither for the offender nor the offended. It can be quite uncomfortable. That's why we tend to avoid it. But Christ taught us a lesson in Matthew 18; if understood correctly, it might help make confrontation easier to approach. In verse 15, he is asking the offended party to take the initiative to go and confront the offender. Then there is the anticipation that the offender may or may not listen to you. Knowing that in advance puts you ahead of the game. It should serve to help you modify your approach to be careful and to use a line of communication that facilitates their hearing what you have to say. In order for that to happen, you will need to be non-aggressive. An assertive approach that is respectful, loving, and that conveys grace would help facilitate the process. We often make it difficult for people to respond appropriately by using the wrong approach and end up blaming them for not listening. Be sure to review the styles or patterns of communication and decide which one might bring you the best results.

The other point of the passage is the concept of winning. That's the whole purpose of the confrontation. It is not about giving someone a piece of our mind because they have dared offend us. It is not about accusing someone of wrong doing and forcing them to fall on their knees and beg for our forgiveness. When was the last time you were able to do that by yourself? The whole point is you want to win your brother and your sister back into fellowship with you and with God. In some cases, you may need to go and settle those matters with them. If you begin with the end in mind of winning then that will determine what kind of approach you use. Before you blame the other party when you fail to win and bring a third party into the situation, make sure that you have used the right approach. If you fail to resolve the issues on a one-to-one basis after you have done your best honestly and spiritually, then you can proceed with the other steps.

Practice Forgiveness

In May 2009, I heard the most unusual and compelling commencement speech. It was during my son's graduation from St. John's University in Queens, N. Y. The speech was delivered by Immaculee Ilibargiza, author of the book *Discovering God in the Midst of the Rwandan Holocaust*. She recounted her ordeal while hiding for ninety-one days during the Rwandan crisis. Her parents and her brother were killed along with hundreds of thousands of the Tutsi minority by Rwanda's Hutu majority. One of the most difficult things she had to do was to forgive those who murdered her family. The line of the speech that I will always remember is *"You cannot move on in life or experience any joy until you experience the will and the freedom to forgive."* As I was sitting there, I thought to myself that if Immaculee could forgive the assassins that killed her parents, not only can we forgive our brothers and sisters who have offended us, but how much more should we forgive our spouse and experience the joy and the freedom to love them and cherish them even when it is hard to do. There is so much joy to experience in marriage. However, lack of forgiveness can prevent us from experiencing the happiness God intends for us. The decision to forgive is the choice of Marital Happiness.

XI

ENJOYING THE JOURNEY: ACCEPTING AND FULFILLING YOUR ROLE AND RESPONSIBILITY

The story is told of a missionary in Africa who publicly rebuked a husband who was walking in the street with his wife. His rebuke included the following questions: "Brother, why do you always have to walk ahead of your wife in the street? Why can't you walk side by side with her as your companion? Does she always have to follow you?" The husband's response left the missionary dumbfounded: "I walk ahead of her in order to protect her. If an enemy or an animal wanted to attack her, they would have to kill me first." What the missionary did not know was the fact that in this man's culture, the husband's leadership means being a protector of his wife. The most loving thing for him to do was to walk in front of her, exposing himself to danger and making himself more vulnerable in order to protect his wife.

As in the case of this missionary, there is a lot of misunderstanding, confusion, and controversy over the role of men and women in the marriage, even in our own culture. As traveling companions in the marital journey, the husband walks side by side with his wife on the road. Walking side by side to the missionary meant to treat her as his equal and his companion. As in the case of that African husband, man is also called to walk ahead of his wife in order to lead, to serve as a provider, and to serve as a protector among other responsibilities.

Our focus here will be to look at the biblical principles that dictate the role of married men and women in the home. This chapter is not about roles of men and women in society or in the church. This is not the purpose of the book. We will provide biblical insight into how biblical fulfillment of the respective roles is essential to the happiness of the spouses in the home. The following issues will be discussed in this chapter:

- The essential equality of man and woman in marriage
- The similar purpose for man and woman in marriage
- The functional difference of man and woman in the marriage
- The basis for man's leadership in the home according to Genesis 2:18-25 and 1 Timothy 2:11-14
- The meaning of "head" in Ephesians 5:23
- The responsibility of the leader in the home: provider, protector, minister, caretaker, etc.
- The responsibility of the woman in the home and the meaning of submission.
- The interdependence of the roles: how a loving husband will facilitate the submission of his wife and how a submissive wife will facilitate the leadership of her husband.

We will conclude by taking a look at the roles of men and women in marriage according to 1 Peter 3:1-7.

The Essential Equality of Man and Woman in Marriage

The controversy and debate over the roles of husbands and wives in the home often center around the meaning of two concepts that have nothing to do with the biblical view of man and woman: superiority and inferiority. According to Webster's Dictionary, inferiority and superiority refer to the quality, worth, value, and ability of a person. Although they also refer to rank, it is in a separate category. Webster did not confuse the two categories—rank never means value or vice versa. Whoever confuses rank with worth would make a categorical mistake. Essence indicates worth or value not rank. The Bible never uses terms like inferiority and superiority to describe the roles of husband and wife in the home. The problem lies in the use of man's understanding and conduct in society and in the home to determine biblical meaning. What we need is the Bible's view of man and not man's view of the Bible. Man's conduct should never be used to dictate the meaning of the Bible; instead the Bible should be used to dictate the meaning of man's conduct.

With regard to worth and value, as discussed in Chapter 2 of this book, the Bible is very clear on the essence of man and woman as being created in the image and the likeness of God with all the rights, privileges, abilities, and capacities that it entails. So the Bible presents man and woman as essentially equal before God and equally responsible to fulfill their God-given roles in the marriage.

The Similar Purpose for Man and Woman in Marriage

Both husbands and wives are assigned specific roles in creation and in the home. As such, they have a similar purpose: to fulfill God's will according to their respective roles for the glory of God. As demonstrated in God's judgment against Adam and Eve following the Fall, they were both accountable to God. The only twist was that Adam as the head bore the greatest burden, spreading his judgment to all humanity while Eve's judgment was only spread to all women.

Both man and woman were given the responsibility to have dominion over the rest of creation and to be fruitful and multiply. It was clear that woman was created as a suitable helper. The word helper does not convey any negative or pejorative connotations since God is called our helper (Psalm 54:4, KJV). The Hebrew meaning of the name "Eliezer" also indicates God as our helper: *Eli from El meaning God and ezer meaning helper.* Both man and woman were given the command to be fruitful and multiply the earth. Whatever assignments were given to both man and woman were expected to be fulfilled responsibly and in collaboration and cooperation with the other. As a helper, woman would fulfill her role in collaboration with man and man would fulfill his role in cooperation with the woman. They were a team designed to work together in fulfilling their assignments. As with any team, it does not matter much who is ahead or behind, the team works in harmony to fulfill the expectations of the coach according to the rules of the game.

The Functional Difference
between Man and Woman in Marriage

Although man and woman were given overall similar responsibility, the part that each one would play was different. There was a functional difference. That functional difference was implicitly described in God's judgment after the Fall. The primary role of the man according to his judgment in Genesis 3:19 was to cultivate the earth and to bring food from it. With sin, this work would be more difficult for him because of the curse placed on the ground. As such, man was assigned the task of being the primary provider—through sweat and toil. That did not mean that woman would not work; she would work in cooperation with man as a helper in that assignment. They would work as a team.

The primary role of Eve according to Genesis 3:16, 20 was that of mother. In fact, she was named Eve because of her role as a mother. Bearing children was made more arduous because of God's judgment. Certainly she would fulfill her role in collaboration with man since she cannot conceive and be a mother without man's cooperation and collaboration. Again, they would work as a team.

Now I am quite aware of the cultural and social debate over the above statements because of how men have interpreted those roles, but we cannot change the Bible to fit the cultural understanding of God's design. We should never change the Word to fit the world; the world needs to adjust itself to the Word and never the other way around.

There is nothing superior about being the one sweating, cultivating the earth to bring forth food, and providing for one's family. There are a lot of guys out there who would give up or have given up that role in a heartbeat and feel quite good about themselves.

Now, I think something is definitely wrong with anybody who would perceive the wonderful role of a mother as inferior to anything or anybody. Can you think of anything humanly more extraordinary than giving life to another human being that you carry inside and that you feed before even seeing them? How can one see something so wonderful as inferior? What can replace the joy of feeling a life moving inside of you, knowing with great anticipation that one day they will be in your arms? Have you ever thought of the joy of a mother nursing a baby, looking at you, and smiling at you while being fed and nurtured by you? As a mother, how do you feel knowing that God has chosen you to play that wonderful role?

I watched my wife throughout the pregnancy of with our boys. The morning sickness, the physical discomfort, and the changes in her body could not come close to the joyful anticipation of becoming a mother. I had the privilege of being at the hospital for the births of both of our boys. I watched and shared with her the labor pains, all fourteen hours of them for our first boy. Once the baby had arrived, the discomfort and the labor pains were all replaced with tears of joy. We were hugging each other and taking turn saying "I love you." Welcoming that baby, the fruit of our love, the baby that she carried for nine months and gave birth to, the baby that she nursed, fed, cared for, and raised in collaboration with her husband, the baby who turned from a boy to a man and all because of her, where is the inferiority in all of this? Do not allow the world's perversion of God's design and ideal for the role of man and woman in the relationship affect your thinking and your feeling about the part that you are called to play in it, either as a wife or a husband or as a father or a mother. The responsibilities in themselves are a compliment to your dignity as a human being. The Creator entrusted you with those tasks because being created in his image and according to his likeness, you were endowed with the ability and the capacity to glorify him by joyfully fulfilling your respective roles. It's so wonderful that even the curse connected to those roles cannot quench the flow of joy that it brings in being able to provide for one's family and to bring forth and raise children together. Any distortion of that is not from the Bible but from a pervert and sinful humanity.

The Basis for Man's Leadership in the Home According to Scripture

There is a rule that is observed by most serious commentators of the Word of God: the Bible is the best interpreter of itself. With that in mind we can turn to 1 Timothy 2:11-14 to find the best interpretation to understanding the basis for man's leadership in the home. Although Paul is addressing another controversial issue of the role of man and woman in the church, in doing so he provides the basis for understanding the leadership role of the home. Again, functional leadership is in view here. The question of superiority and inferiority has already been answered at the beginning of this chapter.

According to 1 Timothy 2:11-14 and referring back to Genesis 2:7-25, the order of creation must be taken into account when considering the rank or the order of the function or the level of responsibility. Paul noted that Adam was created first. It is not the chronology here that is most important. The order reveals to whom the command or responsibility was first given. The creation of woman, as a suitable helper, was to share in that responsibility. As indicated since the beginning of the book, while Genesis 1:26-27 states the creation of male and female in the image of God and according to his likeness, Genesis 2:7-25 provides us with the details and the order of that creation. Paul is saying here that the order is important in terms of understanding the roles of man and woman in the marriage.

Three other observations are worth making here from Genesis 2, 3. First, Adam was given his first responsibilities before Eve was created. In fact, it was during the exercise of his responsibilities that he apparently realized his need for a suitable helper. While naming the animals, he sees that unlike them, he does not have a counterpart. Second, it must be noted that, according to Genesis 2:16, the command not eat of the fruit from the tree of life was given before Eve was created. Obviously, Eve's recitation of that command indicated that Adam had communicated it to her in no uncertain terms. Again that was another aspect of his leadership. The third observation has to do with God's order and scope of man's accountability after the Fall. Although Eve was the one who ate from the tree, when God came to the garden, he called Adam first and questioned him first. He was the leader and the one who had to answer first to God for what went wrong in the garden (home). Also, the scope of Adam's judgment spreading to all humanity (Romans 5:12-17) indicated his overall headship beginning in his household. That is Paul's understanding of the basis of leadership. It's good enough for me.

The Meaning of "Head" in Ephesians 5:23

The word headship or leadership is taken from the Greek word *kephale* that is translated "head" as used in Ephesians 5:23. It is used in the same way that we refer to the head of the company, the head of the state, the head of the school, the one who is in charge or responsible to manage or to lead, etc. In French, the word is translated "chef," the chief. In many other languages or cultures, depending on someone's view or experience with the word "head," it may create a stir. For instance, if one comes from a culture where the head of state is a crook, a dictator, an abuser of power, or simply a wicked individual, calling a husband a chief may convey the wrong idea. It might even convey a very reassuring feeling when the experience and the familiarity suggests otherwise. Sometimes it's not the culture; it's personal experiences that traumatize a person about the meaning of a particular word. Those who come from homes where the "leader" was either an abuser or a loving caretaker might react differently to the meaning of the word. In any case, we should always heed the warning given earlier. We should never let our cultural or personal human experiences dictate the meaning of the Word of God.

We need to have biblical a view of the culture and not a cultural view of the Bible.

Culturally-based experience often causes us to distort the Word of God. If there be any such distortion regarding the meaning of the word "head" or "leader" in Ephesians 5:23, the context and the model that follows should clear that up at once. Unfortunately, the hardening of the hearts of men continues to favor such distortion of the Word. I would venture to say, however, that the exhortations are not addressed to every man and woman in society, nor to every husband or wife. It is addressed to Christian wives and Christian husbands, those who have been transformed by the power of the Holy Spirit and who fills them, so they can live accordingly (Ephesians 5:18). To use this passage to talk to couples who have not experienced such transformation and who are simply the product of their culture and personal experiences is frankly to "cast pearls before swine," if I may use Christ's expression in Matthew 7:6.

Immediately following the exhortation to wives to submit to their own husbands as their leader, Paul gives the model of the kind of headship or leadership he was talking about—the greatest example of leadership that has ever existed. To understand the meaning of the word "head," we need to find out what kind of a leader Christ was. First, judging only from Ephesians 5, we find that he was first and foremost a loving leader. Second, he was a Savior, rescuing leader from danger and from difficulties. Third, he was a self-sacrificing leader. Fourth, he was a sanctifying and purifying leader, setting his love object apart and making it better and better everyday. And finally, he was a glorifying leader who will proudly display the outcome of his love and his work invested in the church.

That's the kind of leader husbands are expected to be. See ladies, no books, no society, and no culture have a higher view of women than the Bible. Nowhere can a husband find a greater responsibility or better rules for the treatment of his wife. Don't you love the Bible, now? Christian husbands, man up, guys. It is a tremendous responsibility and a great privilege for our love and treatment of our wives to be compared to that of Christ. You can't go higher than that. When you understand it this way, you discover not every man is fit to lead and should not have gotten into God's program without adequate preparation or resources. May God grant you the ability to live up to these standards for his glory.

The Role and Responsibility of the Leader in the Home

Leader. First and foremost, a leader leads. He is the one ahead of everyone else to see what's coming and to prepare and to make provisions for it. A leader gives guidance and direction. He has a vision; he knows where he is going before asking anybody to follow him. He is also responsible to lovingly enlist the participation of others, through the use of their resources and their contributions to his leadership. He models what it means to follow. He sees his primary role as doing everything for the interest and the welfare of his family. He would be the first one in line when danger threatens the home. In that sense, he is a protector. He does not inflict harm, but prevents his family from harmful threats. He protects his family from harm in every sense of the word. He is the last one to leave if the boat is sinking. He uses wisdom in managing rebellion against his leadership. He carefully delegates responsibility, knowing that he will be held accountable to God, as in the case of Adam. He is responsible for the physical, emotional, and spiritual welfare of the household.

Provider. As indicated earlier, one of the roles of the husband is to provide for his family. 1 Timothy 5:8 emphasizes this very strongly to the point of comparing a man who fails to do so to be worse than a heathen. This implies that even the heathen understand this particular role. In cases where the wives work and make money, sometimes more money than the husbands, but all things being equal, he still has the responsibility to exercise leadership in ensuring proper management of the funds for the best interests of the household.

Lover. The husband loves his wife as Christ loves his child and would not cause any harm or inflict any injury on them. Just like he would not harm himself or hurt himself without being crazy, he would not harm his wife. As the protector, he can never be the aggressor, knowing that the arms that protect and caress cannot at the same time be the arms that harm, destroy, or God forbid, kill. The self-sacrificing love of Christ is his model, not what some guy in the street says or what the culture portrays in the media.

Minister. As minister, the husband is to wait on and serve his family. As Christ, he does not come home to be served but to serve. If his wife chooses to serve him, it's because he has modeled in other areas what serving is. He appreciates the services that he receives but never imposes them on anyone. The best leadership there is as modeled by Christ is servant-leadership, and it begins in the home. The servant-leadership model was given in John 13 when Christ girded himself with a towel, poured water in a basin, and began to wash the feet of his disciples. Can you imagine the King of kings abasing himself in such a way? When was the last time you washed your wife's feet, husbands?

As a provider, the husband assures the material and financial welfare of his family. As a protector, he assures the physical safety of his family. As a lover, he assures the emotional security and welfare of his family; as a spiritual leader, he assures the spiritual health of his family. As a servant, he humbly ministers to his wife's needs even when it is the hardest thing to do.

What woman would not want to submit to that kind of leadership? Ladies, if you have not married that kind of man, don't make the Bible responsible for the choice that you made. If it is up to the Bible, every woman would be treated as a queen or a princess by their husbands. The man's responsibility in the home is multiple as well as tremendous. While it's an honor to lead, it comes with a price—a rewarding one. For someone to look at your wife today and say that she has become a better person because of your leadership is one of the greatest rewards that a man can aspire to. You will never be more Christ-like than in the manner you treat and live with your wife.

The Meaning of Submission

If everybody leads, there is no leadership. Leadership implies that one leads and one follows or submits. Talking about male leadership in a culture that is justly repulsed by male chauvinism and abuse of power, you need to wear a helmet. Talking about submission in an age where the daughters of the feminist movement are well armed and equipped to fight any tendency to subject women to the mistreatments of ill-intended men is to be perceived as an "outdated obscurantist" as a female colleague well articulated it. That is not what this paragraph is about. In fact, if you have not read the paragraphs before this one, you will not understand any of it. This is not written for every woman in the world. In fact, this is not about women in general. It is for **wives** who are submitted to the authority of the Word of God and the Lordship of Christ. This is for married-women who are indwelt by the Holy Spirit, who understand God's design in creation and in the home, and who voluntarily submit themselves to the leadership of **their own husbands** according to the authority of the Word of God and the Lord Jesus Christ. To be sure, the passage is not asking women everywhere to submit to every man in everything. It is addressed to Christian wives. If you are not a wife or better yet, a Christian wife, this is not for you. You need another book to address the issues regarding your role and responsibilities in the world, in society, and in your given culture.

The word "submit" as found in the Scriptures addresses both man and woman. It has nothing to do with their equality, superiority, or inferiority. The essential equality of man and woman has already been affirmed at the beginning of this chapter; we need not revisit it. Both men and women are called to submit to established leadership whether it's in the government, in the street, at church, or in the park. Once there is an established and recognized authority, everyone is called to submit somehow, to someone, somewhere. It's a fact of life. In fact, we establish conventions, laws, and rules with consequences to ensure that leadership and authorities are followed or submitted to. Why the word "submit" should create so much controversy, I have no idea. Of all the authorities we have to submit to in the world, submitting to the leadership of a husband, especially as described above, should be the most joyful, the easiest, and the most accepted kind of submission.

The submission of wives to their husbands in the context of Ephesians 5 is used as an example of what mutual submission looks like. If you follow the context of Ephesians 5:18-23 in the original language, there is only one imperative that is followed by a series of present participles describing how the imperative is supposed to be demonstrated. The imperative is to be filled with the Holy Spirit and be under his influence as a drunkard is under the influence of alcohol: to act, to speak, and to conduct ourselves in a way that reflects his control. One of the present participles is submitting to one another in the body of Christ. In fact, there is not a verb at the beginning of verse 22. The thought of submission is carried over from verse 21. The word is a pronominal verb. Submission must be voluntary or it is not submission. By marrying this man, you have decided to voluntarily submit yourself to his leadership. If he is not worth your submission then he is not worth your hand in marriage. I know some of you wish you had thought of that before. May the grace of God be sufficient for you, but please do not make the Bible responsible for your decision. I understand you might have been duped into marrying the person that is called your husband thinking that he would be the kind of leader that the Bible talks about. Those of you who are not yet married, you are now well informed as to your ability to avoid making the same mistake.

As a wife, God has blessed you with a lot of resources: intellectual, emotional, financial, and spiritual. These can be great assets in your relationship. As a suitable helper, God has endowed you with talents and abilities that are to be used effectively to benefit your household and your husband. There will be things that you can do better than your husband; you may make more money than he does and be more educated than he is. You don't have to suppress all that in order to submit. You don't have to stifle your expertise in order to submit. Any husband worth his salt will be blessed to have someone as smart, as talented, and as equipped as you are. What submit means is that I am going to bring all that I am and all that I have and place them under his leadership for my benefit and the benefit of the household. I can trust him with my life because as my husband, he has my best interest in mind.

Now, if you realize that you have made a mistake, and the husband you married is not the kind of leader described above, you need to use all the resources available to you to protect yourself against any threats to your protection, personal interests, and above all your personal safety. Having said this, I am well aware of women who abuse the legal and judicial system to their advantage at the expense of their families and sometimes innocent husbands. I am also sure that true Christian wives will not engage in such activities. Just like there are women who have been abused by men, there are innocent men who are being abused legally by vindictive women. Hopefully, these things have no place in the body of Christ.

The Interdependence of the Roles

There is no conditionality in the fulfillment of the roles just as there is no conditional clause in honoring one's vows and covenant in marriage. However, mutual decisions to be faithful in fulfilling one's respective role, each according to their calling, will definitely make the process easier. As such, a loving husband will facilitate the submission of his wife, and a submissive wife will facilitate the leadership of her husband. The call to submit addressed to Christian wives is modeled by the submission of the church to Christ. That submission is voluntarily motivated by love and gratefulness to a Savior who loves the church to death and continues to care for it, making it better everyday. Likewise, the submission of a wife to a loving husband will have the same motivation with the same benefit when she voluntarily yields to the leadership of her husband.

Roles of Men and Women in the Marriage According to 1 Peter 3:1-7

This passage addresses at a different level the kind of relationship model that husbands and wives are to follow in the home. The Apostle Peter had in mind the differences that exist between husbands and wives when he addressed the exhortation about how they should treat each other in the marriage. The context of 1 Peter 3 is a series of exhortations addressed to all Christians, whether as husbands and wives or as brothers and sisters in the Lord. This series of exhortations begins particularly in 1 Peter 2:12 where we are challenged on how to conduct ourselves among pagans. The next series of exhortations concern the submission we have to show to those in authority even if it implies unjust suffering. Then beginning in verses 21-24 of 1 Peter 2, he provides us with the example of Christ who suffered unjustly and yet remained submissive to the end. These are the qualities that the Apostle Peter gives concerning Christ: dependence on God, innocence, selflessness, humility, submissiveness, not vindictive, not retaliatory, nor defensive, and total trust in God in the midst of sacrificial suffering.

In 1 Peter 3:1-7, Peter addresses a series of exhortations to wives and husbands respectively. Each set of exhortations is introduced with the locution "likewise." He is using the virtues of Christ shown above as the model he is setting as the basis for his exhortations. You can find the locution at the beginning of verse 1 as well as in verse 7. In the same way, just like Christ was to the world, so the husband and the wife need to be to each other. Christ is the ultimate model.

The Role of the Wife

In verses 1-6, Peter gives the role of the wife. A wife can win a supposed non-Christian husband without words, just with her chaste conversation or behavior coupled with godly fear. This speaks about the Christian wife being reserved, demonstrating godly fear in her speech and her conduct. She needs to do that in the same manner Christ did. Then Peter added another earthly, human example: Sarah who was a beautiful woman both in the inside and the outside. When women act in a Christ-like manner, they do so as daughters of Sarah. Sarah was a beautiful woman to the point of almost getting Abraham killed. But the beauty that shone in her was the brightness of her inner beauty. The following are some of the characteristics of the daughters of Sarah: a quiet spirit, meekness, submissiveness, and respecting and honoring the husband in a loving way.

The Role of the Husband

In verse 7, Peter gives the role of the husband. In the same manner as Christ displayed his virtues, men are exhorted to dwell or live with their wives according to knowledge. The word knowledge connotes the idea of understanding, wisdom, and consideration. One thing that husbands need to know about their wives is that they are weaker. The word weak here speaks of being more delicate or more fragile, susceptible to being handled with care. Peter is not denigrating women. Women are made biologically weaker and emotionally more sensitive and tender. This is consistent with her role as a nurturing, caring, and tender person. That is not to say that women are always weaker. But, compared to men who are biologically wired to handle more physical pressures, to work in the field, and to handle adversities and fight wars, women are weaker constitutionally. Some women do fight wars and are stronger than some men, but they are the exception, not the rule. The husband needs to know the weaknesses and fragility of his wife and then use that knowledge in the treatment of her. He needs to be considerate, understanding, and wise in his dealing with her.

If anybody thought that Peter was denigrating women and placing her in a lower category than man by calling her weaker, he quickly said something that advocates for the equality of man and woman in the Lord: they are co-heirs with man of the grace of the Lord. The husband is to honor his wife. To honor means to value, estimate, or give weight to her value and respect her as his equal in essence and in grace even if she is physically weaker and different in functions. In other words, he ought to love his wife in a very respectful way. The wife, on the other hand, is to respect her husband in a very loving way.

The Role in General of All Christians

1 Peter 3:8 addresses both husbands and wives and all Christians as shown below.

1. To love your wife in a very respectful and honorable way
2. Respect and honor your husband in a very loving and way
3. The operative word is Loving: both husband and wife love each other but demonstrate it in their own capacity and in their own way according to their needs, and according to their role and according to their capacity.
4. Having one mind, showing compassion and love, being humble and courteous, not rendering evil for evil nor railing for railing.

❧{ XII }❧

ENJOYING THE JOURNEY: REKINDLING
THE FLAME OF YOUR LOVE

"You Don't Bring Me Flowers Anymore." This song, sung by Barbra Streisand and Neil Diamond, brought tears to the eyes of many of the couples at a marriage retreat in Boca Raton, Florida. As they sat listening to the words while the music was playing, many of them could identify with the sadness and the disappointment of a couple whose lives had been altered in the course of their relationship. The song ended with the couple saying "Good-bye" to each other. Many of those couples attending the retreat were afraid that their relationship would end in the same way if they did not do something about it. Fortunately, they were in the right place seeking new ways to rekindle the flame of their love.

Like the couple in the song, many of them were wondering, "What has happened to our love?" The passion, the warmth, and the seduction between husbands and wives were history. They talked about them like the "good old days." No more little love notes underneath the dinner plate, no more phone calls or text messages at work or from work expressing the love and tenderness of the yesteryears. Birthdays are forgotten, special dates become too expensive, no more surprise parties or little niceties that used to make life together very enjoyable. Instead, the conversations are more about the bills than us. The phone calls are more business-like: "Did you take care of this or that;" no games, no laughter, no compliments, and no tender moments. It's more about the bills or the kids or what one of us has done wrong.

I could on and on describing what many couples are experiencing in their relationships. But I have good news: the love gestures or actions may be absent, but the love is not gone. Furthermore, there are practical ways of bringing back the passion that once characterized the relationship. This chapter will address the psychological/emotional issues, the spiritual issues, and the circumstantial and situational issues that are likely to interfere with the marital harmony and how to deal with them effectively lest they should keep the flame from burning as it used to. It will encourage new couples to build long lasting memories that they can fall back to when the flame is no longer burning, and it will encourage experienced couples to do even some of the things they have not attempted previously to regain the flame of their passion for each other.

As a journey, the marital relationship begins with a degree of excitement and emotional energy. There is a sense of optimism and invincibility about the adventure of the trip. We feel confident in the arms of our companion as we embark on the road of love toward happiness. We make sure that we do everything to make the journey enjoyable for each other. We reject any notion of not being able to make it. We are so confident that we listen halfheartedly to the warnings, and most of the time, we inwardly dismiss them as unnecessary. We listen to be polite, but "those things" will never happen to us. But as the journey continues, it gets longer day by day. We discover that joy is needed on the road and not on the destination. The rhythm changes and the pace and the steps are not always in "sync." We discover that the road is filled with little rocks and thorns that cause us to stumble. Yet, we continue to hold hands, but sometimes even that is lacking, and there are other travelers who have joined the trip. They are the product of the relationship and sometimes can be a handful. We are determined, we are marching, but as the road gets more and more arduous, we lack the enthusiasm and the joy that used to characterize the trip. Many lose their energy completely while others continue to travel out of duty and responsibility, but not out of joy. They have forsaken their first love and are in desperate need to regain what they feel has been lost.

Forsaking Your First love

The greatest example of the situations described above concerning the need to rekindle the flame of our love is found in the Revelation 2: 1-7. The church at Ephesus was rebuked for forsaking their first love for God. The rebuke came after the commendation. There are valuable lessons we can learn from both and can apply to our marital situations. I like this arrangement because it shows something that made the situation more hopeful. I also think it's a pattern that couples who are mourning the joys of the early years could learn from. You might have forsaken your first love, things may not be what they used to be, but still you have a lot to be thankful for in your current relationship. Take the time for the commendation before looking at the rebuke.

The Commendation

The first thing that the commendation demonstrates is that those people still had a very good relationship with the Lord. The bond was still strong. They were doing a lot of things right, and they were not discounted. Three close friends were talking about their wives' little misdeeds and sometimes annoying habits. After listening to the first two men complaining about their wives, the third one said, "Everything you said about your wives can be said about mine, but I would not exchange her for anybody in the world." Upon saying that, he started to list all the rare qualities of his wife. The other two were forced to do the same and before they knew it, they concluded their discussion by realizing how blest they were to have such good wives even though there were plenty of annoying things in each one. Once we take the time for commendations, the rebukes are received more easily.

"I know thy works, and thy toil and patience, and that thou canst not bear evil men, and didst try them that call themselves apostles, and they are not, and didst find them false; and thou hast patience and didst bear for my name's sake, and hast not grown weary" (Revelation 2:2).

These are the words that were spoken to the church at Ephesus. The Ephesian church was diligent and zealous in their work and devotion to the Lord. They were known for their patience and their intolerance of evil. They were discerning and did not tolerate liars among them. They were known for their dedication and their capacity to endure hardships and difficulties for God's sake. They were not the kind of people who would give up. They would hold on to the end. They were motivated by love and demonstrated it their sacrificial spirit in the service of the Lord.

In light of the commendation, we understand the hard work of those people. We can also imagine how discouraging it would have been if the letter began with the rebuke and not one word about their hard work. Yet, this is what many spouses experience when their hard work, their diligence, and their sacrifices are overlooked because they fail to do certain things that were expected of them in the relationship. All they hear are the criticisms, their failures, and their weak points in the relationship.

As indicated earlier, the commendation offered a lot of hope for several reasons. They maintained what was essential in the relationship: purity in doctrine, convictions, discernment, and motivation to serve and to endure hardships. These core elements that served to maintain the relationship were preserved. All of that gave them the potential to regain what was forsaken and to do the things that they used to do before. In addition, they were not about to give up, they were going to continue whatever they were doing.

The point of the lessons to be applied in marriage is this, while your spouse might have neglected to do a lot of the nice things they used to do in the relationship, their efforts, motivation, and hard work should not be overlooked and thrown out as if they had done nothing right. Not only do those things need to be taken into account, they need to be expressed as well. Affirming and commending your spouse for what they are doing well is the right thing to do. Keeping track of their hard work in the relationship may also help diminish the frustration that is experienced because certain needs are not being met. I have observed that many spouses tend to focus on one or two things that are not right in the relationship and build their resentment or even bitterness around that one thing they are dissatisfied with in the relationship. Like the third husband with his friends as they conversed about their wives, counting your blessings in the relationship might lead you to praise your husband or your wife more than you complain about them. It might lead you to praise God more often for your spouse than to keep praying that God does something about them.

The Rebuke

The above considerations of commendation are important to keep in mind. They strongly suggest a fair and balanced approach to dealing with unmet needs in the relationship. They were directed at those spouses who tend to look only at the negative aspects of their relationships and who build their resentment over a few unmet and frustrated needs in the relationship while overlooking some key sacrifices that are being made by the other and some essential qualities about their spouse that they are not appreciating.

However, to those spouses who think that because they are doing "all they can," the other spouse should be grateful and satisfied, we recommend the following lessons on the rebuke given to the church. The church was doing a lot, but they missed the point and thus was deserving of the Lord's rebuke. It was not a simple matter. The rebuke indicated a lack of satisfaction with their service. While the Lord was commending them for all the efforts and the sacrifices they were making, he was not at all satisfied with what was lacking. With the recommendation, he was in effect saying, "Good job on all the areas listed; so far so good." But, and this is a huge one, he was not about to grade the church on the curve, he was disappointed in them. Not totally, but there were some key expectations that were not being met. This was no small matter. The tone of the rebuke, the exhortation, and the warning clearly speaks of the severity of the rebuke. The warning about removing their candlestick altogether is definitely a serious threat against their testimony, their opportunity, and their sphere of influence. You can be busy doing a lot of things but fail to show the love that should motivate you to do them. It becomes dry and mechanical and lacks the ingredients that should give flavor to it. It's like eating food that has no taste, no salt, and no flavor. Everything is put together with a lot of effort, but there is nothing inviting about it. You eat it because you're hungry, but there is nothing in the food that attracts you because it lacks flavor. The same is true for doing God's work out of duty and not showing any kind of love motivation behind it.

"Nevertheless I have somewhat against thee, because thou hast left thy first love. Remember therefore from whence thou art fallen, and repent, and do the first works . . ." Revelation 2:4, 5 (KJV). Allow me to point out two positive things about the Ephesian church even in the rebuke. First, they had a first love. That was something that characterized their relationship at the beginning with the Lord. There was a honeymoon; they had souvenirs and a history of some good things that existed between them and the Lord. Second, in the exhortation was an invitation to do their first works. That is a strong indication of a repertoire of behaviors they used to demonstrate toward the Lord. They had something to fall back on in their history with the Lord.

The first stage of any relationship is essential. It's a time to build memories while the energy is at its peak. I always encourage newlyweds to take enough time at that stage to build memories, to establish a good foundation, and to have enough souvenirs that can help them retrace their steps and find something to fall back onto. The flame can be rekindled if it was lit the first time. There was a passion; there was a burning desire inside to please each other and to avoid hurting each other. You remember the honeymoon, when there was an offense it was dealt with swiftly lest it should get in your way to express love and affection to each other. You focused on the other person. There was a need to do little things to please the other person. Those things that were significant and important to the relationship at the beginning are still important today. As the relationship matures, there are other things that are done that may not be exactly the same as in the beginning, but the motivation, the manifestation, and the open expression of love is still present.

They did not stop working for the Lord, but they had forsaken their first love. As most commentators have pointed out, they have not lost their love, but the warmth, the demonstrative aspect of their love, their burning desire was diminished, and their first affections were no longer evident. Judging from the candlestick metaphor used in the rebuke, it appeared as though their light had become dim. You know the kinds of light that you can turn brighter or dimmer depending on what's going on, such as in the theater or in the dining room. The light is always there, but it can become dim or bright. It appeared that was the case for the Ephesians. Deep down, the light was still there, but it was not shining as brightly as in the beginning because they had grown cold; they ran the risk of losing the opportunity to shine altogether.

In marriage, when spouses grow cold toward each other, they may still love each other deep down, but they let other things get in the way, and their passion for each other has become dim over time. The longer the coldness lasts, the more frustration and resentment are built in and the greater the risk is of losing the opportunity to rekindle the flame of their love. With the passage of time, unless an effort is made to "do your first works," the opportunities become less and less in the marriage. The exhortation is to repent. They needed a change of heart and attitude about their relationship. This involved taking responsibility for the failure in the relationship and admitting their fault or negligence in not doing anymore that which used to characterize the relationship. True repentance always begins with admission of guilt. Unless someone is conscious of his fault and takes responsibility for it, they will not repent. The same is true in the marriage. No spouse will change because of nagging, finger pointing, or the blaming game. Change begins with repentance and repentance begins with the agony of taking responsibility for wrong doing.

Repentance is also accompanied with a clear understanding of the areas of failure in your life. To know from whence you have fallen is to make an assessment of where you are now in your current relationship and where you used to be. It may be at the level of attitude, affectionate gestures, communication, etc. This is the place you need to go and pick up where you left off in order to regain what has been forsaken.

The best news in all this is the opportunity to start over before it's too late. Although I'd like to believe that it's never too late to begin again in marriage, I am afraid that there are opportunities that you have that if you wait too long and miss out on them, you may never have another chance. As you read this, I hope you take the opportunity to go back and see where you can pick up. You may have lost some opportunities, but there is still time for others, take advantage of them.

I am painfully aware of the fact that some opportunities may be lost completely. If you have a chance to find new ones, you need to take full advantage of them. I helped a friend of mine who was in deep pain and agony over the eventual departure of his loving wife for eternity. He was begging the Lord to give him at least another year with her. He wanted to undo certain things and have the opportunity to do a few that he had missed out on. He was extremely ravaged by chagrin and remorse over the fact that he had let the light grow dim in the relationship. By the time he realized that, the wife had suffered a stroke, and she never recovered. We said "Good-bye" to her just a few months after my conversation with him. He was devastated. He remembered well from whence he had fallen in his relationship; he was remorseful, and I believe he did repent. He wanted to date her again, let her know how he loved her, take a vacation together, or a little stroll in the park, but he never again had the chance. It was too late! His grief was mixed with sadness, regrets, and anger turned inward. It was a painful situation all around.

I hope you don't wait until it's too late. If the light has grown dim in your relationship, take this opportunity to do what my friend did not have a chance to do. Some opportunities are lost through illness, death, or availability of means. Others are lost through separation or divorce. In either case, the pain is unbearable. You can avoid it by taking advantage of the time and the opportunity you have right now. Do not delay any longer.

The observation that I have made with some couples is the fact that there is no death, no separation, and no divorce, but they have grown so cold toward each other that it seems as though it's too late to do anything about the relationship. They literally don't know where to start. Those yesteryears are so far gone that it seems that they have lost any hope of recuperation. They are still living together, well, I should say that they live under the same roof, but there is no love, no commitment to change, no movement toward the other. I have couples sitting in my office whose hearts have grown so cold and so hardened toward each other that I am tempted to ask them not to ride together nor go back and live under the same roof. The bitterness that has set in is so thick you could almost touch it.

To those who are still living together in that kind of situation, I think there is still hope if you care enough to let go of some of the bitterness and make an attempt to start treating each other as human beings since you are not even treating each other as friends. It often happens that spouses treated their neighbor, a stranger, or even their animals much better than each other. They look at each other with disdain and are repulsed by each other's words and attitude. I've never seen someone more miserable than a bitter person whose heart has grown completely cold or hardened.

The Bible describes bitterness as a poison that can defile many (Hebrews 12:15; Deuteronomy 29:18). It is like an infectious disease; it infects one part, but if untreated, it can be easily spread to other parts. It takes one bitter person in the home to make everybody else miserable and to destroy the home. Ecclesiastes 7:26 said that a bitter woman can be worse than death. And we know too well in our society that some men who are bitter cause the death of their wives. Your spouse is not something to play with. If you feel that your heart is growing cold toward each other, it's time to do something about it before bitterness sets in and destroys both of you in the relationship.

Rekindling the flame of your love begins with repentance. With genuine repentance comes forgiveness from God and from each other. Forgiveness is the cure to bitterness. With forgiveness, the hardened heart can be made soft again. For those of us who are children of God, we believe in the Gospel and the power of the Holy Spirit to change lives. In fact, the beauty of the Gospel is seen in the transformation of lives, turning bitter men and women into lovers of God and of each other. We all have witnessed it. At the time you are reading this, there are men and women all over the world whose hearts were hardened and who now are being transformed by the power of the Holy Spirit. Some of them were murderers, adulterers, fornicators, and persecutors of the Gospel as in the case of Paul.

With the transformation of your heart, you may learn to retrain it to being loving, tender, and affectionate toward your spouse. All that you need to do is to start treating each other in a loving way even if the feeling does not yet match the action. Often we spend a lot of time waiting for the right feeling to come in order to act, ignoring the fact that actions can produce feelings just like feelings lead to actions. It takes a decision and a commitment to treat each other in a loving way. The feeling will follow. Trust me on that. You can fall in love with a rock or any object for that matter by making it an object of affection and treating it as such. That's how people become idolaters. It should be a little easier with your spouse.

Couples so often fall out of love because they stop acting lovingly toward each other. I had a client who admitted not having any feeling for his wife. The wife was devastated when he told her that. It is one of the most painful things to hear the words "I don't love you anymore." It hurts even when they are said jokingly. You can imagine how this woman felt. She managed to have him come to the clinic. The man was tough. He had survived the Vietnam War but continued to carry the emotional scars of the trauma he experienced there. He was willing to live with his wife and fulfill his duty as a husband provided that he did not have to be romantic, nor show any touching-loving feelings about the whole thing.

After a couple of individual sessions with him, I discovered several promising things about this man. The first thing that I appreciated about this man was his commitment to stay with his wife. After assessing that he was not going anywhere, I realized that I had something to work with. Second, he was willing to get help; that means there was deep inside a willingness to please his wife, even though he did not know how to go about it yet. You can't drag a man to a psychological clinic or office against his will if he is not willing at least to try something new.

I asked him to list some of his wife's complaints about him. He gave me a long list, and we joked about some of them a little, but emphasized along the way that if it's important to his wife, it probably should be important to him since it is not about what pleases him but what pleases his wife. He should let his wife worry about what pleases him. His job was to find out what pleases her. I asked him to rule out some of the things that might be too difficult for him to do, at least for now, and pick out the ones he felt most comfortable about. He surprised me; he picked out more than I had anticipated. We were both feeling good about it so far. The last thing I asked him was to pick out three of the things that he could start working on right away. By the way, I am not telling you what they were on purpose—I don't want to destroy your creativity in finding out what you could do to please your wife in the relationship and vice versa. I enlisted him to commit to doing those things that he had picked out. We discussed a few ways to go about doing them. I knew that we had a winner because, being a former military man, this man was disciplined. His word was his bond. I told him that I would see him in three weeks.

On the day of the appointment, he came early and he looked at me funny with a nice grin on his face. After greeting him, he said to me, "Doc, you tricked me!" I said, "What do you mean, I tricked you?" He answered, "You tricked me into falling in love with my wife!" The truth of the matter is I did not trick the man; I helped him discover the love that was dormant in his heart for his wife. All I helped him do was to activate it. He realized that doing those loving things for his wife was bringing so much joy to his wife that he himself started to enjoy doing them more and more. The wife's response to him was extremely appreciative and encouraging, thus giving him more reasons to do them. Even his own need for affection that was suppressed was now being met because of what he himself was doing in the relationship. His needs were met by meeting his wife's needs. There is a nice ring to that, don't you think. The man let me in on a secret that I can't help but share with the ladies. He said the most encouraging part of it all was when he overheard his wife bragging to a friend about how sweet he had been lately. Got it? It can happen to you, too. Get with the program!

Overcoming the Barriers
to Rekindling the Flame of Your Love

We have already identified indirectly many of the barriers to regaining what was forsaken in the relationship. They include feelings of resentment and bitterness, failing to take advantage of opportunities, waiting until it's too late, waiting for the right feelings before doing the right thing, and lacking of forgiveness. However, as with the above illustrations, many couples realize that there is something missing in their relationship, but they can't pinpoint what it is. They know that they are frustrated with each other, and there is a feeling of general dissatisfaction in their marriage but are unaware of the specific starting point. They wish they had a restart button that they could just push and everything would go back to the beginning as things were on their first day. Others have giving up completely. Another case scenario that I have observed in counseling is the fact that one or both of the spouses know there is something that needs to be done, but they are waiting for the other party to take the first step or make the first move either toward communicating to each other or taking the initiative to turn things around. There are many other barriers to rekindling the flame of your love. Some of them will be discussed in the following paragraphs.

Failure to Pay Attention to the Needs
that are not Being Met

As indicated above, we may be doing a lot of things and miss the mark because we are not attentive to the needs that are not being met. We think because we are providing for the family financially, we are regular on the bills, we keep the house in shape, and we fulfill the general duties such as finances, meals, sex, and the general care of the household, we have done our job and everybody should be satisfied unless they are ungrateful. But there are a lot of other needs that may be neglected, such as the quality of time that is spent together, the need to listen to each other, or to laugh together.

The Various Levels of Intimacy

We tend to ignore or neglect the various levels of intimacy in the marriage. There are several levels of intimacy that we need to cultivate in the relationship. They are the physical level, the social level, the affective/emotive level, and the spiritual level. They are all part of the intimacy that must be cultivated in the marriage.

The Physical Level

The physical level ranges from non-sexual physical touch, such as holding on to each other just to keep each other warm or to feel close to the act itself. Physical touch should not be limited to the sexual act nor even progress to the sexual act. But once in awhile during the day, your wife may just need a hug, or a kiss on the cheek, or a rub on the shoulder or just want to sit on your lap. I am giving you too many cues already!

The Social Level

The social level may consist of playing board or card games together, or sharing a few jokes with your spouses. Sometimes we forget to act as friends, and it is good just to treat each other as friends for a change.

The Affective Level

This level involves sharing from your heart to each other, sharing that which pleases you about each other, as if talking to a confidant: your needs, your desires, your worries, and your aches.

The Spiritual Level

This level includes praying together, doing a study together, reading the Bible together, or sharing spiritual insights with one another. It may include commenting on a sermon or lessons learned together, etc.

These are only some general ideas. What may be pleasing for one spouse may not be pleasing to the other. If you care enough about their real needs, you need to pay attention to them. Some of the needs can be communicated by the other partner, especially after times of waiting to get some attention. This was evidenced in a woman who, with tears in her eyes, told her husband, "It looks like you only consider me as the mother of your children. I hope I am more than that to you; I am your friend. I don't expect you to give me flowers every day, but some affectionate gestures from time to time would go a long way." Come on, guys, do you really have to wait to hear that? Some needs can be perceived by an attentive spouse, while still others can be learned through responses and feedback and little gestures and surprises. If you pay attention, you will find plenty of things you can do. You don't have to copy what someone else does for their spouse. You can invent and create your own repertoire. All you need is to be a little more creative.

Lack of Creativity

I have called 1 Corinthians 13 the operational definition of love. The key is in the word "operation." Love-work—it is neither passive nor stagnant; it is active, so active, in fact, that it can be measured. Each of the constructs in the chapter can be broken down into specific activities that love does and does not do. Yes, love is in the heart but is shown through the hands and lips (I don't mean just kissing); it communicates, and it acts in very demonstrative and visible ways. The relationship does not have to be boring. Often we hear people say, "I don't know how to be creative." That's a lie; we are creative people when it comes to things that we care about. All you need is love to care enough to want to do things to please your spouse. There are great ideas that you can get from various sources, including the Bible. For instance, the book of Song of Songs is filled with imagery of creative activities, even to the kind of perfumes the king was wearing. You can expand on some of those things and put them in the context of your own relationship with the taste and the preference of your spouse. Shame on you if by now you don't know what would please your wife or your husband. You need not only to pay attention; you need to pay close and constant attention. Taste, preferences, and likes change over time. Don't use a routine that is predictable. You need to be creative and mix it up a little bit. You don't enjoy eating the same meal everyday, do you? So don't expect your spouse to enjoy the same thing over and over for the next decade—if they live that long. From the looks of things, they might die of boredom before then! Caring love is creative!

Taking Each Other for Granted

One of the greatest mistakes that people often make is to assume that their spouse is happy just the same way they are. Because they do not complain or say anything does not mean that they are happy. Some people often suffer in silence. Like French novelist and poet, Victor Hugo said it, *"Il y a des douleurs muettes d'une eloquence despotique"* translated as "There is a silent eloquence in despotic pain." Many spouses often realize when it is too late that their wife or husband had been suffering in silence for a long time. Don't take happiness for granted; it is something you experience or produce through a lot of effort, endeavor, and disposition. A lack of mature communication patterns in the relationship often prevents a lot of needs or frustration from being known. In these cases, they are suppressed only to be manifested later on either directly or indirectly or when you are least prepared to handle them. A volcano takes time to form, but when it erupts, the damage is devastating and in most cases irreparable.

Another thing we take for granted is that our spouses will always be around regardless of how we treat them. Not true. People change. The most docile person can turn into a monster after years of abuse, mistreatment, and suppression of negative feelings. You have observed it over and over even in politics and in society as a whole. When people who have been oppressed for so long find an opportunity to vindicate, the avalanche is usually uncontrollable. We are in no means encouraging this. It's only a fact of life that has also been observed in marriages. After a while, when the person says, "Enough is enough!" it's like—It's Enough! I have seen husbands and wives literally on their knees for a second chance after the spouse has reached a point of no return. Before you reach that point in your relationship, you need to find ways to rekindle the flame of your life.

Life is short and the road can be arduous. You can make the journey more enjoyable by making the right choices. One choice is to rekindle the flame that once characterized the relationship. If you are reading this and still married, but the flame is out, it's not too late. With repentance and forgiveness, healing can take place. If you have failed before, you don't have to fail again. There is hope for restoration for starting over if you are willing. You can retrace your steps and regain what has been forsaken along the way in the relationship. Find out at what level you need to start (from whence you have fallen) and do the works you did before. It takes effort, commitment, and resolution to regain the first love. Beginning again is not easy, but it's worth it. Don't be discouraged; you still have time to experience the joy you have always wanted. However, it will not happen by accident or by chance. It happens by choice. The choice to rekindle the flame of your love is the choice of marital happiness.

ENJOYING THE JOURNEY: ADJUSTING TO THE STAGES OF MARRIAGE

As with any journey, marriage involves various stages or points of interest that the couple has to adjust to along the way. In addition, as they travel together, there are various stages of development in the relationship. There are two factors that are involved in any process: the passage of time and the experiences or events. Passage of time alone is not sufficient for growth; adjusting to the various events of the stages will determine the growth of the relationship. Whenever you talk about stages, phases, and events, you must be prepared for changes. Changes are always stressful and require adaptation and coping skills. The process varies from one couple to the next. It depends on the nature of those events, the personal resources of the couple, their style of coping, their ability to manage the stress of the relationship, and the stresses of life itself. Those life events may pose serious hurdles for the couple. Many marriages fail because of inadequate resources to deal with the pressures experienced during the journey. Sometimes events such as an unplanned pregnancy, the death of a child, the loss of jobs and careers, child rearing difficulties, and the loss of health may pose serious threats to the enjoyment of the journey. Let's look at the stages and understand the various events that may come into play in adjusting to them.

Stage One: Illusion of Passion or Foundational Phase

The first stage of marriage is usually the most optimistic one. The couple is finally together; their dreams have come true; they are husband and wife; their parents are not around; and they finally have each other for themselves. They feel invincible; their love will conquer all and overcome every obstacle. They aim at pleasing each other. Conflicts are quickly resolved and brushed away. Nobody wants to be the first one to bring up an issue; nobody wants to disappoint the other. There is a sense that they are going to prove the others wrong and that all those warnings and advices are good, but they don't really need them because they have each other. They walk holding hands; they wink at each other and kiss in front of others; they give little messages; they smile at each other every time their eyes make contact. That's beautiful. I call it the Memory Bank Phase, when the couple has the opportunity to have the great souvenirs of those days, months and years that they had to themselves. It is the foundational phase of healthy habits and patterns that they can fall back to later on when they are at a different stage in their relationship. The first stage is the honeymoon stage, the phase of romantic love. The questions are, "How long is this going to last? Will it remain the same? Does the honeymoon have to end?" Before addressing these questions, let's look at some other aspects of the honeymoon phase.

While it is the phase of optimism, it can also be the phase of denial. During the first stage of marriage if anything negative in their personality surfaces, it is dismissed as "no big deal." If it is not dismissed, it is expected to change or improve overtime. There is a level of patience or even tolerance that exists during the first stage. They are not easily offended, and they learn to quickly forgive.

How long does it last? At one of the marriage retreats, a young couple who had just been married for about six months said to the group as they were introduced, "We are still in our honeymoon." To which another couple asked, "How long will it last?" "Never!" They responded in unison, as though they had rehearsed it.

I agree with this couple. Although they were extremely optimistic, they were right to some extent; the honeymoon does not have to end. It takes a different dimension in the relationship, and it adjusts to the realities of life, but does not have to end. What couples do not often realize is that those things that they are doing at this early stage of their marriages are foundational to the relationship. The patterns they establish for themselves during those early days of their marriage are important disciplines to be practiced along the way to make the journey enjoyable for each other. This is the stage of "first love"

As we studied earlier in Chapter 10, the first deeds of the relationship, the first love phase was so crucial that the Ephesian Church was not only rebuked for forsaking it, but was also asked to repent and go back to those first deeds. So when that young couple said that their honeymoon would never stop, they were on to something. However, we have observed in many cases that not only does the honeymoon not last, but it has become interrupted before even taking roots. The couple may not be prepared to adapt to too many changes in their lives during the honeymoon phase. Learning to adjust to each other should be enough at that stage. However, there are other things and events that become part of the equation, and they have to attend to them.

The honeymoon period is not always without its challenges. However optimistic and tolerant the couple might be, they still have to learn to share for the first time their life with someone else. Little habits such as leaving the toilet seat up have to be changed and replaced with others. Sleeping with someone who snores is something new for most couples. Besides these minor adjustments, there are more serious ones that might not have been anticipated. Sometimes there are unpleasant surprises that are not revealed until after marriage. Some of those things might serve to interrupt the phase, depending on their severity and the resources of the couple.

An unplanned pregnancy could bring a lot of stress into the marriage during the first stage of the journey. Some of those issues could be prevented through open communication and planning during premarital counseling or discussions. Whether to have children right away should have been addressed during premarital sessions. Depending on their age or life situation, I often encourage young couples to wait at least until their second year of marriage before having children. They often are not prepared to handle a difficult pregnancy and to make the necessary arrangements to welcome a baby before they have a chance to establish a good foundation for their relationship.

A man found out that his company was going to close just a few weeks after coming home from his honeymoon. It was devastating. His income was the major part of their budget. Instead of focusing on themselves, now they had to focus on what they were going to do to pay for all the bills and debts that ensued because of the wedding expenses.

Another difficult situation that a couple had to encounter in their very first years of marriage was the husband's diagnosis of cancer.

In both of these cases, the couples were able to survive. Surprisingly, there are couples who have been married for years and who have not been able to handle major changes in their situations or their relationship. Both of the above couples had three key elements to help them overcome the obstacles: spiritual and emotional maturity, mutual support, and commitment to love in good times and bad times. Without these elements, they as well as many other couples would have forsaken the journey before it started. Although they had a difficult start, their resolve, their determination, and their courage inspired by those key elements helped them make it through. There are a number of spouses who would have just walked away, leaving the other to cope with the crisis by themselves. Although the relationship did not have time to mature, their own personal maturity at the spiritual and emotional level was able to sustain them and their spouse. They were able to offer support to each other because their commitment to love each other in those difficult situations was very strong.

Too many couples are ill-prepared to face crisis in their marriage, much less in the honeymoon phase. Yet crisis situations are part of the deal. When the vows are tested early, it gives the couple an opportunity to establish a foundation based on those elements that would serve them well later on when other crises arise.

Stage Two: Disillusion Versus Adjustment

After the optimism and the denial phase of Stage One, reality begins to set it. Some of those character traits, some of those "little mistakes" have persisted and become bigger; the perfect little husband or the perfect little wife is not that perfect after all. The frustration tolerance level is becoming lower and lower. Welcome to reality! You are discovering that they are a human being after all, just like you.

Some people refuse to accept reality. They become rather disappointed and start expressing or demonstrating their disappointments both directly and indirectly in the relationship, sometimes without saying a word to each other. When reality starts to set in, it removes the illusion that sometimes characterized the dating and engagement period. There is a fictional mask that people wear prior to marriage and often carry during the first phases of their marriage. However, sooner or later and sometimes sooner than anticipated, the real person starts to show, sometimes gradually, other times all of a sudden. Sometimes it's a crisis or a conflict that causes the mask to drop. It is often in times of crisis that you know who you truly are and who you are married to. The couple starts to discover who they truly are. They can use this stage as an opportunity to grow and to allow the other party to grow as well. However, too often, they are not prepared to deal with the disappointments they experience.

Resolving the conflicts of Stage Two is not always easy. There are several steps or aspects that can be considered in this process. It is a time for rejection or acceptance based on several considerations that will be discussed in the following paragraphs.

Self-Awareness

The major problem in adjusting to each other in marriage is the fact that we don't even know ourselves very well. We are not aware of our strengths and weaknesses, and we tend to ignore or minimize our frailties. The first person that we need to look at in this phase is not the other person, but the person behind the mask—the person that we really are.

Someone may ask, "How come we don't really know ourselves much less the other person?" It is a reality that we must be aware of. Without the conviction of the Holy Spirit, we tend to see ourselves in the best light possible. We don't often see ourselves the way we are, but the way we like others to see us. We look at and present ourselves in a socially desirable manner. We practice pleasing the other person so that they don't think we are a monster, and we suppress any tendency to the contrary.

We are not always acting consciously to deceive the other person, but the more we knowingly or unknowingly deceive others, we end up deceiving ourselves into believing we are what others take us to be. We need to become real with ourselves. Growth begins with self-awareness and a commitment to change. Sometimes it takes the ministry of the Word of God, and at other times, the feedback of a friend, a colleague, or a professional to help us realize that we are not who we think we are.

A "vis-à-vis" or face-to-face relationship gives us the opportunity to grow. A spouse can be the mirror that reflects who we truly are. When feedback comes from a trusted friend and in a constructive, loving manner, it helps us to be aware of some of those things we tend to ignore in ourselves. Sometimes we are not even aware of how we come across to the other person. Sometimes they discover us long before we discover ourselves.

It is human to want to see and present ourselves in the best way possible. We think we are our best friends and would do anything to protect ourselves from appearing as mean, deceiving, self-centered, or even angry. In so doing, we stifle our needs and opportunities for growth and are usually the last to know how annoying we can be. Before we can begin to accept others for who they truly are, we need to learn to accept ourselves just like we are. Self-acceptance begins with self-awareness.

It is important to clarify what we mean by self-acceptance. It is not self-tolerance; it is rather an honest assessment of who we truly are and admit to being the person behind the mask in order to do something about it. James 1:23 urges us not to walk away after looking in the mirror of the Word of God without doing something about what we see. Self-acceptance is not used here as an excuse to remain the way we are. The reason we look into a mirror is to see what needs to be fixed. Otherwise, what would be the point? Self-acceptance means to admit to ourselves that this is, in reality, who we really are. Accepting the fact that this is indeed you, however uncomfortable, painful, or embarrassing it might be, should lead to the decision and commitment to grow and change. This lack of awareness, this lack of admission as to who we truly are was addressed by Christ in Matthew 7. While we are prone to see the mote in our brother's eyes, we need to be aware of and willing to admit that there is a beam in ours.

When we drop the mask, we begin by admitting that we are a sinner saved by grace or in need of salvation and who needs to grow and hopefully is growing into the likeness of Christ. We have all the resources available to us through the ministry of the Holy Spirit and through the church to continue to grow. We do have some good qualities about us; otherwise, we would not be in a relationship at all, but we are not yet what we are to become. There is hope.

The honest evaluation of ourselves and our level of honesty help us to extend the same consideration to our spouse who, hopefully, is doing the same thing as we continue to help each other grow. The reality, my friends, is that when two individuals are married, especially Christians, they do not get married because they are all they're cut out to be. Marriage is a great opportunity to become together what God has designed us to be together.

Growing Together

Stage Two offers us the opportunity of growing together that will continue throughout life. Unfortunately, some couples have not had the courage or the patience either with themselves or with their partner to allow growth to take place. Instead of mutual acceptance, they experience mutual rejection. Some couples, instead of taking advantage of the opportunity to grow, run away. Others choose to remain in the relationship but end up resenting each other for being deceived.

Disappointment with Ourselves

Another fact that needs to be admitted is when we are not really deceived by the other person, but disappointed by our own unrealistic perceptions and expectations of the person. The person never pretended or promised to be an angel. It is we, for whatever reasons, who have cultivated those false ideas and expectations about the other person. Sometimes they try to live up to those expectations for a time until it becomes unbearable, and they cannot keep up with those standards. Sometimes the expectations are created by the way we talk about them, what we say to them, and how we act when they give the slight hint of failure to meet them. When the reality sets in, they will appear to be just like us, a human being who has the capacity for growth but who is imperfect with all the human frailties that we have.

I received a phone call from a wife who had been married for about two years and who had discovered some of her husband's vices. Her disappointment was so great that you could hear it in her voice and in her choice of words. "You mean my husband could be doing this?" "I did not marry that kind of man!" I responded, "Yes, that's your husband," and I added, "f you don't allow him any room to fail, you will not allow him any room for growth either." Something else I could have added is, "If you don't allow him any room to fail, you will not allow yourself any room for forgiveness either." Unfortunately, this hypothesis became the sad reality of that marriage. It ended up in divorce. Lack of forgiveness and resentment made it impossible for them to use the stage as an opportunity for growth. They could have gone to counseling together with a willingness to change, so the marriage could have survived. Sadly, it was not the case.

Stage Three: Commitment Versus Resignation

Depending on how the couple copes with the issues of stage two, they may enter stage three of their relationship with various attitudes and dispositions. If their relationship does not end up in divorce, they enter the next stage with either a sense of resignation or commitment. Resignation is when someone has come to the realization that regardless of what they do, things will not change or improve. They come to realize that they have no control over whether their spouse changes or grows. In fact, the balance for better or for worse seems to tip more on the latter side. For worse may not always mean circumstances or situations; it may be the person who is becoming worse. All the little things, the little hints that something might be wrong, all the things that we overlooked because we thought they would get better over time have now become a big deal and are worsening. Yet, they decide to stay in the marriage, not accepting but resigning themselves to their situation.

Resignation was illustrated best by Seligman's dog that learned to be helpless and hopeless through conditioned behavior. The problem with learned helplessness in human beings is that it results in resentment and bitterness. It's like accepting to be miserable for the rest of your life since there is nothing you can do about the situation. I have seen couples so bitter and so hopeless that they come to a point of refusing to do anything about their situation. They are tired of trying, tired of fighting, and tired of hoping. Their hopes have been crushed so many times that they don't want to set themselves up for another disappointment. The bitterness that they carry in their hearts is so heavy that it weighs them down emotionally, spiritually, and sometimes even physically. They have no joy and no zest for life, and everything in their lives is affected by it. Sometimes they try to find joy outside of the relationship, making themselves vulnerable to sin and temptation. Many try to find joy in their work or ministry, but deep down, there is a nagging sense of dissatisfaction that makes any experience of joy outside of the relationship frivolous, trivial, and temporary. It does not take long to realize how bitter they are. Even when they do their best to hide it, their resentment is forever present in their conversation, mannerism, and gestures so that they often betray themselves unknowingly, leaving others to wonder what's going on in their relationship.

One of the things that motivated me to consider a career in the field of psychology, marriage, and family counseling was an experience I had when I was only in my early twenties. I had a daily radio program for youth and young adults. I talked about a lot of things, including dating, relationships, and marriage. Most of the time, I would just read books and come to share various authors' insights with my listeners. One day a man who used to listen to the program walked into the radio station and requested to speak to the host of the program. He wanted to discuss some of the issues that he was dealing with in his marriage. When I was introduced to him, he could not believe it. He thought that I was an old married man who had so much good advice to give. He was surprised to know that I was not even dating anyone at that time. However, he was desperate enough to sit down and talk to me. He was a very successful engineer; he had a very good salary; he was well respected at work by his colleagues, and he was being considered to head the firm for which he was working. He said something to me that I remember to this day! "I would give anything to experience a part of the joy I experience away from home." He said, "I could have a good day at work where I feel good about myself and where I feel valued and appreciated. But all that vanishes when I put the key in the door and enter my house. There begins my misery until I leave the next day to go back to work."

The children in such a home live with the tension; they sense it; they live it; they are hurt by it; and there is nothing they can say or do about it. At a Catholic school, a child was asked to define hell as part of a catechism class exam. The teacher was shocked when one of the students, instead of giving the answer that was taught in that class, answered the question in this way, "Hell is a place where love is completely absent." When questioned about it, his response was "I could not think of a place worse to be than where there is no love." Further inquiry revealed that he was describing his household where the bitterness of the parents toward each other filled the whole house, and the children were contaminated by it. It was only then the teacher understood why this ten-year-old boy was always irritated and easily angered or provoked.

Resignation may last for a long time. Sometimes a couple stay together because they find reasons to justify it, accepting to remain in the situation that they would normally avoid or abandon. Sometimes it's their religious convictions against divorce and remarriage. Other times it is socio-cultural or familial pressures to stay together, no matter what. In many instances, it's because the financial situations do not allow them to consider separation. The burdens and losses because of finances would be too much to bear by either or both spouses. In other instances, it's the kids. They feel bad for them and are not willing to expose them to the pain of divorce. Sometimes one must wonder if they would not have been better off coping with the separation than living a constant experience of "hell" in the home. In fact, research has demonstrated that children of divorce are better adjusted than those who live in dysfunctional families with constant friction and expression of bitterness and resentment between the husband and wife.

There are several choices that couples who find themselves in such predicament can make. Although the reasons that they give themselves to justify staying in the relationship may not always be healthy, the fact that they stay together suggests that there is some hope if only they decide to make the right choices.

Making Use of or Refusing Available Resources

If it's worth staying in the relationship, you might want to try to do something about it. Some couples would refuse help even if they were drowning, especially on the part of the husband. They are either too proud or too embarrassed to admit that they need help. They'd rather let the situation worsen than do what they have to in order to save it. Some couples have become too angry at each other to even consider sitting together with someone to discuss their issues. There are resources that you might have attempted that have failed for whatever reasons. Counseling might have failed you. Before you throw in the towel, what have you not tried? Maybe the changes that need to occur are not about the marriage or your spouse. It might be you who needs to change. Have you considered working on yourself? Could it be your personality? Your lack of forgiveness? Has the resentment become so deep that you need some personal healing before considering your spouse or the health of the marriage? You may need to consider giving a closer look at the person in the mirror and use whatever resources that are at your disposal to improve the condition of your life and the situation you are in.

Commitment to God Versus Commitment to a Conviction

It's sometimes painfully ironic to hear people say that the only reason they continue to stay in the marriage is because they don't believe in divorce. A husband said this to me after describing the pain and the misery that he was enduring in the marriage. I anticipated his answer when I purposely asked him why he did not believe in divorce. His reply was because "God hates divorce," referring to Malachi 2:14. Listening to this man, you hear the bitterness that filled his heart against his wife. He had come to see me about his marriage because of pressure from a family member who constantly nagged him to seek help. He was committed to a conviction against divorce, knowing that his church would never remarry him, but he was not really committed to God. Being committed to God is demonstrated by obedience to his Word—not just in matters of abuse, of mistreatment of his wife, of divorce, but also in forgiveness and reconciliation.

It is not unusual for people to be committed to a principle at the expense of a real relationship with the Lord characterized by faith, love, and obedience. What this man did not realize was that God hates divorce as much as he hates dealing treacherously and acting violently against your spouse in the marriage.

I applauded my friend's conviction. It is good to hold on to God's principle against divorce. However, it is even better to obey his principles for marriage. The God who gave you the conviction against divorce has given you a lot of resources to use to improve your marriage. Obedience to his Word is better than the sacrifice of enduring the pain and the misery of the relationship.

Commitment to Each Other Versus Commitment to the Marriage

The above observation has another aspect to it. Just like some people are committed to a conviction versus being committed to God and being obedient to his Word, there are couples who are committed to the marriage, but not committed to each other. In many cultures or religious circles, being divorced is seen as shameful. They remain in the marriage to save face before their family, friends, society, and church. I would think that the effort that one has to make to remain in a loveless marriage would be harder than trying to make it work if there is a commitment to God and to each other. It is good to be committed to the marriage for all the right reasons. It is even better to be committed to each other and to make every effort to improve the marital relationship so that we can bring a level of joy and happiness to the person we are living with instead of making their lives miserable. I don't think saving face or financial arrangement should be worth more than the honoring of our vows to love and cherish each other in good times and in bad times.

Happiness Versus Consented Misery

If in the above situations people can find reasons to stay in a miserable marriage, they definitely have more than what it takes to make their marriage work. The truth of the matter is we deceive ourselves into thinking that it's easier to live with our pride than to humble ourselves and seek forgiveness and reconciliation. Although it is not easy to overcome pride because of our carnal nature, it really takes much more pain to maintain it than to lose it. Imagine being angry at your spouse and refusing to forgive. You have to continue to ruminate over the offences; you have to keep avoiding each other; you have to make a lot of efforts to convince yourself that they are not in your best interest.

The emotional energy that you have to spend to maintain your pride through the day and the difficulties sleeping and concentrating are a big price your heart and your brains have to pay to maintain that. Admitting that you are wrong and asking for forgiveness and being able to forgive and let go might take you less than five minutes, and you can move on with your life with all the hugs and kisses that come with making up. The hardest work is making the decision and mustering up the courage to take the first step, but once you do it, you discover it was not that big a deal after all. It's like taking a shot, especially like a child taking a shot. They think of it and start crying; they see the needle and think it's a sword; the doctor looks like an executioner to them, and they can't believe that their parents can be accomplices to this crime that is about to be committed on them. However, not counting the time to pin them down and hold them still, it only take a few seconds for the shot to be administered and it's over. They can now enjoy life feeling protected against those viruses. The same is true in marriage. The choice to make peace with your spouse may be hard at first, but once you make it, you discover that not only it was the simplest thing to do but the best thing to do for them and for you. Be smart. If you count the cost of hatred versus the benefits of love, there is really no comparison.

Stage Four: Resolution Versus Dejection

As you take an honest inventory of yourself and your marital situation, you will discover that on one hand, there is much room for improvement both in yourself and in how you treat your spouse. And certainly, when you've evaluated the way you have been treated in the relationship, there would also be plenty of room for improvement in that as well. We all think we deserve better even though sometimes we get exactly what we deserve and most of the time, more than we deserve in the relationship. There may be feelings of remorse, regrets, and plenty of guilt to go around between the two of you.

On the other hand, you might also discover that there have been many more blessings to enjoy along the way. Perhaps you have even taken them for granted and not really appreciated them enough. What are you going to do? You can dwell over the remorse, regrets, and the guilt feelings and feel dejected while concluding that your life together has been miserable and curse the day of your wedding. Or you might want to look at the areas of blessings and thank God for your spouse. What choice are you going to make? Even if you were to look at the negative side alone and become dejected, you still have an opportunity to turn things around. The feelings of remorse and regrets do not have to lead to feelings of despair. You have within you the capacity to enjoy the company of your spouse and enjoy the rest of your life with them. The efforts that you have made over the years to remain in that relationship can be channeled toward a more positive approach and outcome. You may just have to let go of your pride and learn to forgive. You also have let go of a few things that have held you back and prevented you from releasing the potential that God has given you to be the kind of spouse you were created to be and that God expects you to be.

It's not too late. You may think that you have treated each other so badly that there is no hope. All you have to do is try one more time. You can cancel the appointment with the lawyer and ask him to annul the court date. You can turn the car around, make a phone call, and say, "Let's talk!" I know what your pride is dictating to you, but I also know the pain and misery that you will have for the rest of your life if you listen to it.

The part that I hate about my job in working with couples is the pain of pity and compassion that I feel from being with some of them. Two people that once were in love with each other and that are still hungry for love and affection from each other are now at each other's throats. You look at them; you know deep down there is nothing that they want more than being in the arms of a loving husband and caring wife. Yet the hurt, the bitterness, the resentment, and the pride constitute a big wall or a big pile of trash that keeps them away from each other. If only they knew what they were doing to each other or missing out on!

A man whose wife had left the house and moved back with some family members because of the way things were going at home was filled with rage over her departure. He decided that he would have nothing to do with her and that he would change the locks. The wife left a note with the address and phone number of where she could be reached. He did not even look at it. After a couple of sleepless nights, still filled with anger, he realized that he had to make a decision. He had to make a choice between continuing to go to bed with his pride and feeling miserable or talking things over with his wife and obtaining her forgiveness while forgiving her in return. He wrestled with the idea for a while and then concluded: "I gain nothing with my pride other than misery, pain, remorse and guilt. I will swallow my pride and do whatever I have to do, including some begging, to have my wife back." He did. He has been able to sleep ever since. The choice to swallow his pride, to make amends, and to smooch with his wife was a choice for marital happiness.

ENJOYING THE JOURNEY: COPING WITH THE STRESSES OF LIFE

The marital journey is part of the journey of life in general, and the journey of life can be quite difficult at times. Whatever means of traveling it you may choose, and whatever your station in life, whether married or single, you are sure to face obstacles, threats, tribulations, and challenges that often make the trip very arduous at times. Those who travel by air will face the wind and the turbulences of the air. Those who use ground transportation will face bumps, holes, mountains, slippery slopes, curves, and gravels. Those who travel on water must be prepared to face the waves and the storms that often threaten to sink the boat. In fact, the storms of life is the most common metaphor used in the Bible to speak of trials, difficulties, tribulations, and calamities. Marriages will not be exempt of such experiences.

In addition to be affected by the storms of life, the marriage itself will have its own share of difficulties. Some have discontinued, many have collapsed, others have hung in there grinding their teeth, and still others have survived while still finding a way to enjoy the journey together. Sometimes the greatest storms are the ones raging inside threatening to drown us while sinking in depression, resentment, and bitterness.

The journey is not always smooth, and the road is not always paved. The road can be bumpy at times with just the normal life circumstances, stress, trials, and suffering. These life events may pose serious hurdles for the couple. Many marriages fail because of inadequate resources to deal with the pressures experienced during the journey. Included here are various ideas on how to go through these hurdles while still enjoying the journey.

The most common word that has been used to summarize all the adversities or challenges that we face along the way is stress. It is a very comprehensive word because it encompasses everything that we have in order to maintain the balance we need in our journey. It can be any circumstance (real or perceived) that threatens a person's well-being and equilibrium. It can affect us at any level or any dimension of our lives. Some other words that have been used interchangeably to express the same idea are the demands of life, pressures, trials, tribulations, and others.

The word "stress" is taken from the medical/biological model that describes the activity of the organism to deal with any change that affects the system. Whenever there is change, there is stress because a response must be given to adapt, fight, run, or collapse. Of course, there are minor and major changes. The more significant the change, the greater the stress, such as changes in relationships, health, finances, or life in general. It can occur just from having to take a different road to your destination in the local area where you live because of a major catastrophic event, such as the loss of a loved one.

When stress is anticipated, some preparation can be made to soften the blow a little. However, more often than not, we are ill-prepared to face the sudden onset of some situations, and we have to respond—not just respond—but do so in such a way to limit the damages to ourselves and our surroundings. While we may not anticipate every stress that will come our way, we need to expect life's challenges to be part of our journey, so that we are not completely cut off guard. If anybody tells you that you should not have stress, and that if you have enough faith, you will be exempt of life's storms, not only are they deceiving you, but they are doing you a disservice by causing you to be even more disappointed and ill-prepared to face them. In John 16:33, Christ told his disciples to anticipate tribulation in this world. Nowhere does the Bible promise the children of God that they will be spared from the common trials of life. Both James 1:2 and 1 Peter 1:6 speak of the trials of life in a very matter-of-fact way for Christians. Lastly, our Lord Jesus can identify with all of our difficulties in this life because he himself was exposed to all kinds of stress, trials, pressures, and temptations (Hebrews 4:15). So, if you going through some difficulties in your marriage or in your journey of life in general, all I can say to you is "Welcome to life!" But I will also offer you some ways of responding to them, so they don't destroy you but rather make you stronger and more capable of enjoying the company of your spouse as you navigate together over the troubled waters of life.

Some of the most common life stressors that we often have to deal with are financial difficulties, major illnesses, unemployment, job-related difficulties or changes, moving from one place to another, health difficulties, and the death of a loved one. In addition to those life circumstances that befall everybody, there are specific stresses related to the marriage itself. They include pregnancy, birth of a child, caring for sick children, children leaving to start school, children moving away to go to college, changes in sexual activity due to illnesses or other issues, and adjusting to the various stages of the relationship with all the changes and adaptations that they entail.

Since we must face some or all of these at one time or another and at one level or the other, the best thing to do is to learn appropriate ways to respond. Responding to the pressures of life is a balancing act. It requires facing life's demands while maintaining our equilibrium.

Personal and Marital Equilibrium

You do need to cultivate some personal resources to help you in the storms. Before you can even support one another, you need to learn for yourself how to deal with some situations, whether internal or external. Personal resources are important for each spouse to develop and cultivate. I always find it interesting when I travel by plane to hear the flight attendant say to the passengers, "In case of loss of cabin pressure, the oxygen mask will drop; make sure you put yours on first before assisting somebody else." Each spouse needs to have their own "oxygen mask" in place before they can help the other one. Married couples are better equipped to face stress because they have each other, provided that each one has developed some effective way to deal with the stress of life.

The word that is often used to describe our response to life's demands or pressures is the word "coping." Various definitions have been proposed for this word. The one that I like the most is the following given by psychologists Dr. Richard Lazarus and Dr. Susan Folkman: "The process of <u>managing</u> demands (internal or external) that are <u>appraised</u> as taxing or exceeding the resources of the person." I have taken the liberty to underline a couple of words that I want to emphasize in their definition. First, it is a process of managing, not eliminating or mastering. More often than not, we have no control over the stress; all we can do is manage it. Management involves allocating appropriate resources to address a particular problem, need, or situation. Sometimes the management has to do more with our emotions than the situation. The first person to manage may be ourselves with regard to the situation as we will explain later. The second word is "appraised." Appraisal, as in the case of appraising a house that's for sale, is to estimate the value of or to put a price tag on that house. We all evaluate circumstances of life differently, and depending on our appraisal, the situation may be above or within the range of our internal or external resources. By the way, external resources may relate to seeking outside help, material resources, help from our environment, or help from a professional in order for us to deal with the problem. The internal resources include our capacity to evaluate the problem appropriately, our level of emotional or spiritual maturity, our capacity to maintain equilibrium, and our faith.

There are various styles of coping that one may adopt to deal with a given situation. Some are adaptive and others are maladaptive. Borrowing from the medical model, we are wired in such a way as to produce a response to either fight or flee when there is a threat to our safety or well-being. This is how the body reacts to a foreign body. It incorporates it into our system and activates its defenses to fight it. Although all of us experience the same "general adaptation syndrome," we often choose to respond differently to life stress.

Styles of Coping

Freezing Panic

Most of us face situations that sometimes catch us off guard, and we don't know at first what to do. At times it is the appraisal of the situation that causes us to be in such panic that we don't respond at all or respond the wrong way. To avoid freezing panic, we need to practice some first-aid tip to help us when those things happen. After the initial shock, people tend to call up a friend, a church leader, a colleague, or someone whom they trust to help them sort things out. If able, your spouse might be such a person if the crisis does not involve them, and it is not about them. Some people like to be by themselves and pray about it. Others like to withdraw temporarily from the situation and take time out to better assess the situation before figuring out what they need to do by way of responding to it.

Procrastination

Although a precipitous decision may not be the best response to the crisis, a prolonged delayed response may also be counterproductive. A delayed response may be wise in order to gather your resources, so you can better appraise the demands. This can be quite healthy. Procrastination, which consists of being irresponsible, waiting for time to pass, and hoping that the problem will go away, is not healthy. This may cause a simple crisis that will generate into a bigger mess, and that will require greater intervention. For instance, if you are diagnosed with a major illness, although getting a second opinion may be appropriate, buying time as a delay tactic may sabotage early intervention that might have alleviated or reduced some of the damages.

Prayer

Prayer is a good resource that we have as Christians whenever we face trials, tests, or tribulations. 1 Peter 5:7 encourages us to cast our burden upon Christ because he cares for us. To know that whatever it is we can take to the Lord in prayer is already reassuring enough to help us begin to cope with the problem. Nevertheless, praying does not exclude our responsibility to act diligently and responsibly and to seek available and appropriate ways to deal with the situation. God is sovereign in his will and in his power to deliver us or to help us manage the situation. We can pray as the Bible encourages to do. However, God has entrusted us with some resources (both internal and external) that we can use to help ourselves through the storms. We should be responsible enough to use them.

Problem-Solving Strategies and Planning

Sitting down with a piece of paper or talking to someone about it may help us come up with some creative ways of approaching the problem, such as breaking the problem down or looking at it from different angles. That's all part of managing the demands. A problem that is well defined is at least solved by one-fourth. Having a plan is like having a road map to follow. You are being active, wise, and vigilant about the problem; you are being responsible.

Worrying /Complaining

Some people are professional worriers. They have a problem, and they are not doing anything about it. They are not even looking for solutions or problem-solving strategies; all they do is complain and complain and keep worrying about the problem. In their complaining, they keep adding meaning to the problem instead of looking at it for what it's worth and seeking an appropriate solution. Worry does not help in stressful situations; it creates even more stress for the other spouse who is trying to figure things out. Although it is human to complain and worry, it is Christian to have faith and to act responsibly when we face life's difficulties.

Being Irritable

One of the signs of being stressed out is being constantly irritable and oversensitive to anything that seems to add to the pile that we are already building. Often marital communication is the first thing that is affected when people are stressed out. They are not in the mood for anything, and everything gets on their nerves. That's the time to withdraw temporarily from what is going on, to make a reassessment of the problem and of themselves with regard to the problem, and to better prepare ways to deal with it. Being irritable may mean that they are angry at God, at themselves, their spouse, or at their life in general. They are sabotaging both their internal and external resources in the process. It will definitely get in the way of managing the situation. They might need a new appraisal.

Things That Husbands and Wives Need to Avoid in Coping with Life Stress

Confusing Life Stress with Marital Stress

As mentioned previously, there is life stress and there is marital stress. Stress is stress, of course. But the differentiation may be necessary to avoid confusion that may be counterproductive. Often stress can be a good test of the health of the marital relationship. The way the couple manages stress may reveal their strengths and weaknesses as part of the symptoms of a dysfunctional relationship, communication patterns, and conflict resolution issues that often come into play in the management of the stress. However, life stresses like financial difficulties, job-related difficulties, and even health issues in the family are not necessarily marital problems. Granted they will impact the marriage depending on how they are handled or cause a pre-existing marital problem to worsen. But we need to avoid confusing the two. The best way to make this distinction is to ask that whether this problem is solved or not, do we still maintain our intimacy in the marriage?

Blaming Each Other/Being Critical of Each Other

It may happen sometimes that the problem might be the result of a mistake or the negligence of one spouse. Now it becomes "our problem," and we have to deal with it. Blaming each other, pointing the finger, and turning against each other will only serve to sabotage your resources and create a bigger problem. Now we are turning a life stress into a marital stress. Yes, there may be plenty of lessons to learn from our mistakes in order to avoid repeating the same experience, but that can be done after we've crossed the river, not while we are in the middle of it. We might drown together in it if we are not careful.

Ignoring/Neglecting Each Other's Needs

One of the surest ways of turning our life stresses into marital issues is while in the middle of them we forget our needs and responsibilities toward each other. Granted there are times we need to show support and understanding with regard to the fact that some of our needs may not be met for various reasons in a crisis or a difficult situation. However, stress should not be an excuse for neglecting one another.

Displacing Negative Feelings

Displacement is a defense mechanism used to transfer our feelings or irritation to a less threatening target. Often men who feel humiliated at work or elsewhere start demanding more respect at home. The most classic example is to be angry at your boss, but since yelling at him might not be the wisest thing to do if you want to keep your job, you yell instead at your wife for some insignificant reason.

Getting the Wrong People Involved

There is a difference between intervention and interference. You would be wise to know which one may be going on, and whether it is the wise thing to do when you are experiencing stress either in your marriage or in life in general. Going to other people may not be a good asset at all and may cause major interferences in your marriage. If you want to have other people involved, make sure it is by mutual consent. Also, make sure that the person is qualified to intervene in order to help you in addressing the issues, and they are not just interfering in your marital harmony thereby causing more discord instead of reconciliation.

Resentment and Passive—Aggressiveness

Sometimes, if one spouse is to blame for the problem or the stress, you may not want to directly blame them or rub their nose in it. You are too clever for that—you just build resentment inside and make them pay for it indirectly either by withdrawing from them or depriving them of your attention and/or your affection during that time.

Disrespecting and/or Embarrassing Each Other

Disrespect and/or embarrassment can happen when we solicit help from others, especially the in-laws without consulting the other spouse. Sometimes it involves even a more dangerous practice that consists of getting a member of the opposite sex to do something for you that your spouse might not be able to do for you at the time or is against their expressed or unexpressed consent.

Making Personal Decisions that will Likely Affect Both of You

A lot of reasons have been given by well-meaning spouses acting as a lone ranger in the relationship. Among them is the fact that they may not be able to handle it, or it is none of their business, or they are protecting their spouse from getting involved in a difficult situation. However plausible those excuses might be, they reveal an imbalance in the relationship that must be addressed and discussed to avoid that this particular issue does not turn out to be a disaster. It happens more often than not in financial decisions. If there is a problem at that level, it must be discussed and resolved so that the pattern does not continue. When things go wrong as they often do and will, issues of trust come into play. Even if you were well-intentioned, they can ruin the relationship.

Effective Methods of Coping

Experts in the area of stress, especially those who subscribe to a cognitive behavioral approach, such as Psychologist Richard Lazarus (1922-2002), have proposed two primary methods of coping. First, there is the problem-oriented approach, which focuses on the problem itself. This approach raises the question "What can I do about this problem?" It diligently and actively seeks ways of managing the problem by tapping on external resources available to deal with the problem. Second, there is the person or emotion-oriented approach. This approach focuses on the self with regard to the problem. The question that is raised is "What can I do or need to change about myself with regard to the problem?" In this approach, the person activates their internal resources; they challenge their ability to process and interpret the problem, and they challenge their feelings about the situation. Let's take a closer look at these two approaches.

The Problem-Oriented Approach

Define/Redefine the Problem. The first step in solving a problem is to define it. In doing so, we figure out what exactly we are dealing with and rule out what we are not. First, as in the example given above, a financial problem may not need to be a marital problem although it may be the result of a marital problem and has all the potential of becoming one. But if it's a question of how we manage the money, or what we need to do to pay the bills or get out of debt, it's not a relational problem since there is nothing fundamentally wrong with the relationship per se. We may need financial advice in terms of being wiser in managing the funds, but not necessarily marital counseling unless the problem is a symptom of some deeper issues in the marriage. Second, referring back to the definition of coping, this approach makes a realistic appraisal of the problem. Sometimes a catastrophic event may need to be redefined with regard to the real impact it has or will have on the family. There are times that we tend to exaggerate certain situations causing us to panic for no reason. Granted, a tragedy is a tragedy regardless of how we define it or redefine it, but breaking it down to its real meaning and impact may maximize our resources to deal with it.

Make specific plans. There is a couple that will still talk about the time they came to my office some nineteen years ago. I gave them each a piece of paper and asked them to make a list of things that they could do to solve this problem. They told me that they had tried everything, and I responded by asking them to write down all the things they had already attempted and failed and to add the things that they had not attempted. They may have considered them but for some reason had decided not to go that route. They were amazed to discover the solutions to some of their problems on their own. All I had to do was to coach them a little bit and to challenge them as to what may have handicapped their plans.

Prioritize Issues. In prioritizing issues, a couple needs to make a list of things. The next step is to relist them in the order of what can be done right away and what can be delayed. Resources are then looked at that are currently available or that need to be sought or developed with regard to managing the problem. The issues are also ranked by order of importance. There are things that can wait; there are others that need to be addressed right away depending on their urgency. There are discussions that can be postponed for a later time. For instance, discussion of how we are going to pay the mortgage this month should take precedence over worrying about where our 5th grader is going to attend college.

Be creative. Sometimes people get stuck and can't move past a particular problem or issue that blocks every avenue to the solution. That's when the "what if" questions can come in handy. Raising possibilities forces people to creatively think of ways of handling the situation. Sometimes I ask people to make a typical grocery list. They are to write down the things they normally buy, and then I ask them to modify it. They often find that they are buying things that are unnecessary or not even good for their diet, and that there is a brand that is cheaper and has the exact same nutrients. Issues of taste and preferences are discussed. Then they realize that it's not really about groceries, it's about being creative in ways of dealing with the issues by challenging their thinking and coming up with other possibilities concerning those issues.

Seek Outside Help. There are times when we have exhausted our personal resources and need to seek the help of someone else. It might be an expert in a particular field, or it might be the advice of a local pastor, a colleague, or just a friend. It's a sign of maturity when we can decide that a particular problem is beyond our capacity to handle, and we need to humbly seek the help of others, especially those in the body of Christ. The Bible tells us in Proverbs 24:6 that there is safety in the multitude of counselors. Sometimes, there are available solutions that we are not seeking because of pride, secrecy, and ignorance. God has blessed many in the body of Christ with gifts, talents, and expertise in various domains, such as finances, health/mental health, child-rearing and development, marriage and family, computer repair, and mechanics. You name it, and you can find it. The problem is we often think that we have to come up with our own solution. There are times, instead of using God's wisdom in seeking appropriate help to our difficulties, we impose our faith on God and expect him to deliver us in the way we want, not the way he has already ordained. It is not a lack of faith to see a dentist if you have a toothache. Certainly, God can make the pain go away, but he may want you to be humble enough in your faith to pay the dentist a visit and ask him to extract the tooth. When the dentist helps you, you can still thank God for giving him the expertise to extract your tooth. There are other experts, depending on what you are going through, that God can use to help you in your dilemma. Trust God and use them. He wants you to. His name will be glorified if you do.

Emotion or Person-Oriented Approach

Define/Redefine the Person. Take a look at yourself with regard to the problem and the kind of things you are saying to and about yourself in the midst of the problem. The first defeating statement you can make is that you should not have to deal with this, or you don't deserve this. Christians often ask, "Lord, why me?" Reverse the question, and ask "Why not me?" What makes you think everybody can have problems except you? What makes you so special, or an exception, all of a sudden? Is it because you are too good or better than others or more faithful than everyone else? There is a lot to say about the messages we give ourselves with regard to our problems. The worst that I have heard is "What will people say?" Once you start asking questions like that, you set yourself up for a lot of emotional problems. Isn't it enough that you have a problem? Why should you now have to worry about what people say? The solution then will be more about saving face than anything else. If you keep that up, people will drive you crazy!

Define/Redefine the Needs, Desires and Wants. Many of the problems we face have nothing to do with our needs. They are things that we can live without. However, we have emotional voids that we want to fill with things. So we covet; we want more; we become greedy and discontent, thus creating a lot of mess that is hard to get out of. A car or a house becomes a statement about who you are and what you are worth. My friend, if you want to make a statement, get a microphone; a car is just a car that's taking you from point A to point B. If it speaks and makes a statement about you, return it; there is a devil in it. Cars are not supposed to speak.

Re-adjust priorities. Readjusting priorities may be hard to do because it may involve putting certain things on hold that you consider to be very important. Some things you may have to forgo altogether.

Change of Lifestyle. That's a big one especially if your lifestyle was a statement about you and helped you answer the question as to what people will say. Again, what you have does not determine who you are. The more inferior you feel, the more you will feel you need to get attached to certain things to feel secure and display who you are to others. At what cost? The people you worry about will not help you pay a dime when you get entangled in debt. In fact, you may need to change your lifestyle to get out of your financial predicament.

Find Contentment in All Things. Paul gave us a great example to follow in Philippians 4:11-13. Our contentment should not come from outward circumstances or whether we have an abundance of things or a lack thereof. We can find peace and joy regardless of the situation. After all, happiness is a choice not based on our circumstances. We <u>can</u> do all things through Christ who strengthens us.

Choose to be Happy Together. Never let your problem put a wedge between the two of you, especially if the problem has nothing to do with the relationship. You <u>can</u> choose to be happy together. As long as the two of you are together, that's what counts the most. Don't let things sabotage what you have. You are the most important asset that you have in the house. What's the point of having expensive furniture and accessories when you cannot enjoy them in the company of each other? What's a grandpa's nice horologe going to do for you when you are filled with bitterness in an unhappy home? It might tell you it's time you did something about yourself, and then it would be worth having, but things, such as timepieces, will never make you happy. They may give you passing pleasure, but not happiness. However, there is nothing like coming home to a smiling friend in whose arms you can't wait to fall. That's happiness!

Remember Your Vows. You have promised to be a friend, a lover, a supporter, some one who loves and who cherishes the other. You need to live up to those vows in the midst of the stress that you face in life and in your marriage.

Trust-Pray-Obey. This trilogy may not work for everyone, but it will do wonders for those who have a personal relationship with God through Jesus Christ. We need to trust God in the midst of the storms. He is in control. We can take our problems to the Lord in prayer. We need to learn to practice obedience to his Word, his will, and his principles in the midst of our difficulties. His will for us is to use the resources he has already given us—both internal and external. We can use those resources to deal with the problems while seeking to honor and glorify God during and after the passing of the calamities. These additional tips will help you as a couple to deal with stress while maintaining harmony and experiencing the joy of being married even in the midst of the worst crisis or the most stressful situation.

1. Committing to being a team—he or she is not the enemy (Ecclesiastes 4:9-12)
2. Cultivating love and intimacy—do not neglect each other's need
3. Holding each other accountable—challenge each other to act responsibly
4. Being vigilant and alert to areas of conflicts—settle matters quickly
5. Supporting each other—never turn against each other
6. Forgiving one another—don't keep score, avoid building resentment
7. Committing to growth individually and as a couple—trials build character
8. Seeking outside help—with mutual consent use available resources.
9. Fellowshipping with other couples—you are not alone, be part of the body
10. Praying and worshipping together—commitment to God and each other
11. Cherishing each other's company—don't wait until it's too late to show how much you love each other.
12. Appreciating each other—let your spouse know how much of an indispensable blessing they are to you.

"In this world ye shall have tribulation" (John 16:33, KJV). These words from the Lord put us ahead of the game. Some situations will surprise us, but as far as having and experiencing difficulties in our lives, we should not be surprised. That's just a part of being human. Because we are imperfect people, living in an imperfect world, filled with other imperfect people, something will go wrong sometime, somewhere in our lives—be it in our marriage or in our lives in general. The stress can bring us closer, or it can destroy us depending on the resources we use when we face them. There will be various changes that we will go through in life. They will bring stresses or circumstances that we will have to adjust to. Being together as a couple gives us an advantage as expressed in Ecclesiastes 4:9: "Two are better than one." That is particularly true in times of crisis and difficulties. Having someone to help share the burden, to cry with, or plan with is an underrated blessing.

As indicated at the beginning of this chapter, one of the common metaphors used to describe stress, trials, and the difficulties of life is a storm. As we travel together, we will encounter life's storms along the way. There will challenges that will threaten to sink our boat. Sometimes we may come so close to drowning that our boat may seem to have broken into pieces. Such was the case literally for Paul in Acts as he was on his way to Rome. Although Paul had warned the sailors of the eventual difficulties on the trip, they did not listen to him. After all, he was just a prisoner. But as his prediction came true and the storms arose, he emerged as a leader in their midst. God used his faith and wisdom to guide the rest of the crew and passengers to safety. The account of this storm from the life of the Apostle Paul is filled with lessons that will help us during the times of crisis situations and stress.

Biblical Principles in Dealing with Life Storms and Pressures Taken from Acts 27

1. Do not confuse faith with presumption. And do not tempt God by making foolish decisions on the pretext of faith, especially when there is clear warning of the danger ahead.
2. Faith does not preclude wisdom, prudence, and intelligent decision-making. Therefore, listen to the sound advice from the Word of God and from trusted men of God.

3. Being in the will of God does not exclude obstacles, difficulties, and setbacks. They are all part of the process. But you can be sure of his presence. We are never alone.

4. We can trust God for the ultimate outcome, but the process may still be very difficult.

5. Just like Paul, we sometimes suffer because of others' lack of responsibility or stubbornness. That's also part of life, but we can still learn and grow out of it.

6. Even if you have failed before, you can still learn from your mistakes and not worsen the situation by lack of wisdom and obedience

7. Never cross your arms and wait while doing nothing. Often God acts supremely through human efforts. Use all your knowledge, all your experiences, and all your resources in the middle of crisis while praying and trusting God to deliver you.

8. Christians do get depressed at times. The weight of the experience may be heavy physically, emotionally, and even spiritually. It's okay to cry, but never to despair. It's good to pray, but never grumble out of bitterness. Never lose hope. Remember 2 Corinthians 4:8, 9: "We are hard pressed on every side, but not crushed; perplexed, but not in despair; persecuted, but not abandoned; struck down, but not destroyed."

9. Take care of your body. It is the temple of the Holy Spirit (1 Corinthians 6:19, 20). Don't let one crisis cause you to lose your health by lack of sleep, lack of eating, overeating, or lack of generally caring for yourself.

10. The child of God must always maintain their communion with God through his Word, prayer, obedience, and worship.

11. Trials and tribulations are opportunities to witness for God before others.

12. Trials and tribulations are opportunities to reaffirm our relationship with God and to strengthen our faith and convictions.

13. Use your faith to encourage those who are weaker even when we are in the same boat.

14. In as much as you are able, set an example of endurance and courage and faith in the midst of the trial.
15. Always take time to be thankful and to worship. God is still good; he is good all the time, in spite of what you are going through.
16. Do not jump ship or try to escape. Assume your responsibility and God will see you through.
17. Some losses may be necessary for survival. So, get rid of the non-essentials in order to preserve the essentials. Some of the non-essentials may be related to your personality, your priorities, your values and even your perception of the problem.
18. Your presence in the boat, house, job, etc, might save the lives of others. Do not compromise or miss the opportunity to be God's instrument as a life preserver and as an influence in the lives of others.
19. Use your resources wisely, each one according to their own abilities. We are in this together and must support one another.
20. Know that after the darkness light will come. The sun will rise, and it will be a new day.
21. Know that God controls the outcome; he is Sovereign over the waves and the sea, and he is faithful. He always keeps his Word.

EPILOGUE OF

MARITAL HAPPINESS IS A CHOICE

To the Reader

I wrote this book with you in mind. Yes, you who are sitting and looking at the statistics on divorce and broken marriages and wonder or not you should ever take a chance and become part of that mess. You know that you don't have the gift of celibacy, you feel lonely, yet you are afraid, you are not sure if you will find Ms. Right or whether Mr. Right will come along and find you. I also mean you who are in a bad marriage where all you hopes and dreams for happiness have been crushed and it has come to point where you feel you wish you were never married and at times were never even born. This has become so bad that you would welcome death in a heartbeat. I also wrote this book for you who are currently married and enjoying the company of your spouse but face some challenges that threaten the stability of your marriage. You start to feel insecure and you are deeply concerned that things may take a turn for the worse. I wrote this book even for you who might have already failed and are ravaged by, remorse, sorrows and guilt and wondering there is any hope for restoration.

I hope by now you realize what I meant in *Marital Happiness is a Choice*. It's a wonderful journey filled with adventure and experiences. It was designed to be enjoyable and pleasant, not by my own definition by the definition, the plan and the blueprint of the Designer Himself. Misery comes when we depart from His plan, ideal and purpose. As we go and venture in this pursuit, leaving His principles behind or ignoring them along the way, taking matters into our own hands, only to discover that apart from Him we can do nothing.

As you read those pages I hope you realize that you have the potentials to experience the joy and the happiness that some are enjoying and others are vainly pursuing through the wrong means and approaches. In fact, we have, hopefully, demonstrated, happiness is not something to be pursuit like reaching a goal at the end of an endeavor, it is something to experience in the process of traveling the journey as the result of following God's established principles for the marital relationship. The pursuit is usually in vain when the motives are selfish and deprived of the true purpose of God for our lives that is to glorify Him in all that we are in all that we do. Happiness is experience when we seek to honor God by focusing our emotional energy toward making life better for the person whom we married. The mutual investment in each other produces a boomerang effect that makes the investment more and more worthwhile and enjoyable. In other words, achievement is experienced through the mutual commitment to each other's happiness. So instead of looking for someone to make you happy, you may start looking for someone whom you think deserve a measure of happiness in his and her life and you are the right person to provide that.

It is my hope that you have discovered by chance or experience through passively crossing your arm and waiting for something good to happen to you depending on the caprice, the mood, the attitude or behavior toward you. First, nobody can make you happy no matter how hard they try, unless you, yourself, make the choice and sometimes the hard choice to experience happiness. It's always risky to make someone else responsible for your happiness; your life may then a roller coaster ride, depending on that person. Second, the choice of happiness may not be easy since you are more often than you care to admit the one standing in your way to experiencing real happiness. There are certain things in you and around you that have to be let go in order for you to experience the joy of being in the company of your spouse. In case you wonder, here are some final tips that I will leave you with until the next book on spirituality and human relations!

Personal Tips to Create and Maintain Marital Happiness

Faithfulness and Obedience to God—Don't ignore or bypass His blueprint. You can't do it on your own. Even those who do not have a personal relationship with Him can, and have been able to, under common grace, follow His principles for a happy marriage. How much more should you, who are saved, be able to experience His intended joy for you by following His blueprint and principles for the marriage?

Maximize or Accentuate the Positive Qualities Of Your Spouse.—Just like you, your spouse is not perfect. She does have some positive qualities about him and about her that might have forgotten or overlooked. Learn to accentuate those by cherishing them more and by encouraging them more. Sometime you are more blessed than you think.

Learn to Accept and Pray for Your Spouse.—An honest evaluation of yourself should lead you to accept your spouse the way she/she is. Sometimes you might even be grateful that she is not perfect. If he/she were, you would not deserve each other and living with a perfect person while being imperfect would cause you so much misery. As we travel the road together, we can grow together. The Holy Spirit is still working in us producing Christlikeness in us. We will become what He design us to be, we just have to be more patient with one another while accepting each other and praying for each other.

Don't Try to Change Your Spouse.—You are not the Holy Spirit. Nagging, rejecting, embarrassing and constantly criticizing your spouse will make them more resistant to change. Remember the secret of the old couple married for 55 years: it is based on the serenity prayer. "Lord, I want to change me, give me the courage to change in me the things that I can and the patience to accept the things that will not change in my spouse and the wisdom to know the difference."

Revisit Your Expectations.—Often we begin the journey not only with a set of false notions and expectations that we gather from magazines, books, friends, and TV shows. Then we impose those expectations on our spouse and anticipate them to perform accordingly. We set ourselves up for disappointments and for resentment on our part as well as on the part of our spouse

Engage Constantly in Behaviors toward Marital Happiness.—Since marital happiness is a continual choice we must have the discipline to engage in constant activities that will bring happiness to our spouse. The process in doing so will be enjoyable and that will be our own happiness

Ultimately, Glorifying God is the Key to All Happiness.—The choice to follow God's blueprint and to obey His principles is the choice to marital happiness. It is at your disposal. When you do so, the honeymoon will take different phases but will never end and His name will be glorified. That's what it's all about!

CPSIA information can be obtained at www.ICGtesting.com
Printed in the USA
BVOW030108180613

323579BV00002B/2/P